# Bertolt Brecht
# Plays : One

### Baal
### The Threepenny Opera
### The Mother

The first volume in this three-volume selection of Brecht's best-known work for the theatre contains three plays from quite different genres written before Brecht was exiled from Germany by the Nazis. *Baal*, his first play dating from his student years, uses a heady mix of expression, symbolism and lyricism to portray the unheroic progress of an ugly, dissolute poet and his fatal attractiveness to women. *The Threepenny Opera*, immortalised by Kurt Weill's music, was Brecht's first commercial success; based on the 18th-century *Beggar's Opera*, it makes Macheath into a gentleman crook, an incarnation of the bourgeois values Brecht so distrusted. Drawing on a novel by Gorky, *The Mother* remains Brecht's best didactic play, charting a working-class woman's dawning awareness that the unjust social system she takes for granted can be overthrown by revolutionary activity.

Each volume is introduced, with a chronology of Brecht's life and work, by Hugh Rorrison.

The other two volumes contain *Fear and Misery of the Third Reich*, *Mother Courage and her Children* and *The Good Person of Szechwan* (*Plays: Two*) and *Life of Galileo*, *The Resistible Rise of Arturo Ui* and *The Caucasian Chalk Circle* (*Plays: Three*).

**BERTOLT BRECHT** was born in Augsburg on 10 February 1898 and died in Berlin on 14 August 1956. He grew to maturity as a playwright in the frenetic years of the twenties and early thirties, with such plays as *Man Equals Man*, *The Threepenny Opera* and *The Mother*. He left Germany when Hitler came to power in 1933, eventually reaching the United States in 1941, where he remained until 1947. It was during this period of exile that such masterpieces as *Life of Galileo*, *Mother Courage* and *The Caucasian Chalk Circle* were written. Shortly after his return to Europe in 1947 he founded the Berliner Ensemble, and from then until his death was mainly occupied in producing his own plays.

The front cover shows a detail from Netherlandish Proverbs by Pieter Bruegel reproduced by courtesy of Bildarchiv Preussischer Kulturbesitz. The back cover photo of Bertolt Brecht is by Gerda Goedhart.

*in the same series*

Aeschylus (two volumes)
Jean Anouilh
John Arden
Arden & D'Arcy
Peter Barnes
Brendan Behan
Aphra Behn
Edward Bond (four volumes)
Bertolt Brecht (three volumes)
Howard Brenton (two volumes)
Büchner
Bulgakov
Calderón
Anton Chekhov
Caryl Churchill (two volumes)
Noël Coward (five volumes)
Sarah Daniels
Eduardo De Filippo
David Edgar (three volumes)
Euripides (three volumes)
Dario Fo
Michael Frayn (two volumes)
Max Frisch
Gorky
Henrik Ibsen (six volumes)
Lorca (three volumes)
Marivaux
Mustapha Matura
David Mercer
Arthur Miller (three volumes)
Anthony Minghella
Molière
Tom Murphy
Peter Nichols (two volumes)
Clifford Odets
Joe Orton
Louise Page
A. W. Pinero
Luigi Pirandello
Stephen Poliakoff
Terence Rattigan (two volumes)
Sophocles (two volumes)
Wole Soyinka
August Strindberg (three volumes)
J. M. Synge
Oscar Wilde

# BERTOLT BRECHT
# Plays : One

### Baal
*translated by Peter Tegel*

### The Threepenny Opera
*translated by Ralph Manheim and John Willett*

### The Mother
*translated by Steve Gooch*

## Introduction by Hugh Rorrison

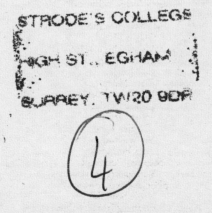
Methuen Drama

**METHUEN'S WORLD DRAMATISTS SERIES**
This collection first published in Great Britain as a paperback original
in 1987 by Methuen London Ltd
by arrangement with Suhrkamp Verlag, Frankfurt am Main.

Reprinted 1992 by Methuen Drama
an imprint of Reed Consumer Books Ltd
Michelin House, 81 Fulham Road, London SW3 6RB
and Auckland, Melbourne, Singapore and Toronto

Printed in Great Britain by
Cox & Wyman Ltd, Reading, Berkshire

*Baal* first published in this translation in 1970 by Methuen & Co Ltd.
Original work entitled *Baal*. Copyright 1953 by Suhrkamp Verlag, Berlin.
Translation copyright © 1970 by Stefan S. Brecht

*The Threepenny Opera* first published in this translation in 1979
by Eyre Methuen Ltd. Original work entitled *Songs of der Dreigroschenoper*.
Copyright 1928 by Gustav Kiepenheuer Verlag, renewed 1968 by
Helene Brecht-Weigel. Translation copyright © 1979 by Stefan S. Brecht.

*The Mother* first published in this translation in 1978
by Eyre Methuen Ltd. Original work entitled *Die Mutter*.
Copyright 1957 by Suhrkamp Verlag, Berlin.
Translation copyright © 1978 by Stefan S. Brecht.

Introductory material copyright © 1987 by Methuen London Ltd

British Library Cataloguing in Publication Data

Brecht, Bertolt
    Plays : 1. – (A Methuen paperback) –
    (Methuen's world dramatist series)
    I. Title II. Brecht, Bertolt. [Baal. *English*].
    Baal III. Brecht, Bertolt. [Songs of der
    Dreigroschenoper. *English*]. The threepenny
    opera IV. Brecht, Bertolt. [Die Mutter.
    *English*]. The mother
    832'.912            PT2603.R397

    ISBN 0–413–15140–9

# Contents

Chronology of life and work      vii

Introduction      xv

BAAL      1

THE THREEPENNY OPERA      63

THE MOTHER      143

# Bertolt Brecht
## Chronology of life and work

Brecht's life falls into three distinct phases demarcated by his forced exile from his native Germany during the Hitler years. From 1898-1933 he is in Germany; from 1933-1947 he is in exile in various parts of the world; in 1947 he returns to Europe, first to Switzerland then to Berlin.

**Germany**

1898    Eugen Berthold Friedrich Brecht born on 10 February at Augsburg where his father was an employee and later director of the Haindl paper mill.

1908    Brecht goes to Augsburg Grammar School (Real-gymnasium) where he is an indifferent pupil and a rebel in his quiet way, numbering among his friends Caspar Neher, later his designer. Brecht was almost expelled for taking a dismissive, anti-patriotic line when set an essay with the title 'It is a sweet and honourable thing to die for one's country'.

1917    Brecht enrols as a medical student at Munich University, where he also attends Arthur Kutscher's theatre seminar. He samples the bohemian literary life of the city.

1918    Brecht is conscripted and serves as a medical orderly, though he still lives at home. He writes *Baal*, a rumbustious, even outrageous dramatic tribute to natural drives and anarchic sexuality, and writes articles for the local newspaper, *Augsburger Neueste Nachrichten*.

1919    Brecht writes *Drums in the Night*. His Augsburg girlfriend, Paula Banholzer, bears him a son, Frank.

He meets the comedian Karl Valentin, the theatre director Erich Engel, and actresses Elisabeth Bergner, Blandine Ebinger, Carola Neher and the opera singer, Marianne Zoff. He writes theatre reviews for *Volkswillen*, a local Independent Socialist daily.

1920    Brecht visits Berlin.

1921    Brecht's registration at Munich University is cancelled. An attempt to make himself known in literary circles in Berlin ends with him in hospital suffering from malnutrition. His new friendship with Arnolt Bronnen, the playwright, leads him to change the spelling of his name to Bertolt, or Bert.

1922    Brecht marries Marianne Zoff. He writes *In the Jungle of Cities*.

1923    Brecht's daughter Hanne is born. The activities of Hitler's National Socialists are hotly discussed in Brecht's Munich circle. The first productions of *In the Jungle of Cities* and *Baal* take place in Munich and Leipzig respectively.

1924    Brecht directs Christopher Marlowe's *Edward II* which he and Lion Feuchtwanger had adapted. He was already using certain devices (plot summaries before scenes, white face make-up to indicate fear) to induce critical detachment in actors and audience. He finally settles in Berlin and is taken on as dramaturg (literary adviser) at Max Reinhardt's Deutsches Theater. Elisabeth Hauptmann becomes his secretary/assistant. The actress Helene Weigel bears him a son, Stefan.

1925    Klabund's *The Chalk Circle*, premiered at Frankfurt and Hanover in January, is directed in Berlin in October by Max Reinhardt with Elisabeth Bergner in the female lead.

1926    *Man Equals Man* premiered at Darmstadt and Düsseldorf. Brecht's work on a play (which he never finished) called *Joe Fleischhacker*, which was to deal with the Chicago Grain Exchange, leads him to the study of

Marx as the only adequate method of analysing the workings of capitalism.

1927   Brecht divorces Marianne Zoff. He works with Erwin Piscator, the pioneer of communist political theatre in Germany, on a dramatisation of Hasek's novel *The Good Soldier Schweik*. He publishes a volume of poems, the *Hauspostille* (Domestic Breviary).

1928   *The Threepenny Opera*, music by Kurt Weill, words by Brecht (based on a translation of John Gay's *Beggar's Opera* by Brecht's friend and collaborator Elisabeth Hauptmann) opens at the Theater am Schiffbauer-damm and becomes the hit of the season. Brecht had provocatively transferred bourgeois manners to a Soho criminal setting.

1929   Brecht works with Elisabeth Hauptmann and Weill on *Happy End*. He marries Helene Weigel. Elisabeth Hauptmann attempts suicide. *The Baden-Baden Cantata* is staged at the Baden-Baden Music Festival, music by Hindemith.

1930   Brecht's daughter Barbara born. His Lehrstück or didactic play, *The Measures Taken*, is given its first performance in Berlin. The communist didactic plays for amateur performance were intended to clarify the ideas of the performers as much as the audience. The first performance of *The Rise and Fall of the City of Mahagonny*, an opera with words by Brecht and music by Kurt Weill, causes a riot as the Nazis voice their criticism at Leipzig. In his notes on the opera Brecht tabulates the difference between the traditional *dramatic* (or Aristotelian) and the new *epic* (or non-Aristotelian) theatre at which he is aiming. Brecht objects to the *Threepenny Film*, sues Nero Films and loses, but accepts an ex gratia payment to refrain from an appeal.

1931   Brecht completes *St Joan of the Stockyards* (first performed in 1959).

1932   Brecht's only film, *Kuhle Wampe*, is held up by the censor. He visits Moscow when it opens there in May. His dramatisation of Maxim Gorky's novel *The Mother* is performed by a left-wing collective in Berlin, music by Hanns Eisler. It demonstrates the development of a worker's mother towards proletarian class-consciousness. Beginning of Brecht's relationship with Margarete Steffin. Brecht studies Marxism under the dissident communist Karl Korsch.

## Exile

1933   The Nazis come to power. The night after the German parliament building (the Reichstag) is burnt down, Brecht flees with his family to Prague. He moves to Vienna, then Zurich, finally settling on the island of Fyn in Denmark. His relationship with Ruth Berlau begins. He visits Paris for the opening of *The Seven Deadly Sins*.

1934   Brecht visits London. The themes of flight and exile enter his poetry.

1935   Brecht is stripped of his German citizenship. He visits Moscow where he talks to the Soviet dramatist Sergei Tretiakov about the 'alienation effect'. He attends the International Writers' Conference in Paris. He visits New York to look in on a production of *The Mother*, which does not meet with his approval.

1936   Brecht attends the International Writers' Conference in London. He writes anti-fascist poetry.

1937   Brecht attends the International Writers' Conference in Paris with Ruth Berlau. *Senora Carrar's Rifles* is premiered in Paris.

1938   Franco's right-wing Falangists emerge as the likely victors in the Spanish Civil War and Chamberlain signs away the Sudetenland in the Munich Treaty in an effort to appease Hitler. *Fear and Misery of the Third Reich* is given its first performance in Paris. Brecht writes *The*

*Earth Moves* in three weeks ending on 23 November. He revises it with the assistance of Margarete Steffin, adds a fourteenth scene and retitles it *Life of Galileo*.

1939   In a radio interview with scientists of the Niels Bohr Institute he hears of the discovery of a great new source of energy, nuclear fission. His first response is positive. In April he moves to Stockholm with his family. He finishes writing *Mother Courage and her Children*.

1940   German forces march into Denmark. In Lidingo Brecht completes *The Augsburg Chalk Circle*, a short story set in the Thirty Years War. Brecht's household moves to Helsinki in Finland where his friendship with the writer Hella Wuolijoki begins.

1941   Brecht completes *Mr Puntila and his Man Matti*, *The Good Person of Szechwan* and *The Resistible Rise of Arturo Ui*. He writes war poetry and 'Finnish Epigrams'. Leaving Finland Brecht travels through the Soviet Union via Leningrad and Moscow (where Margarete Steffin dies) to Vladivostock and sails to the U.S.A. He arrives in Los Angeles in July and settles with his family in Santa Monica. He makes contact with other exiles (Heinrich Mann, Lion Feuchtwanger and Fritz Lang, the film director) and with the natives (Orson Welles). First performance of *Mother Courage and her Children* in neutral Switzerland.

1942   Brecht prepares his *Poems in Exile* for publication. He works on the screenplay for Fritz Lang's film, *Hangmen also Die*. He participates in the anti-war, anti-fascist activities of exile groups. He meets Charles Laughton.

1943   The first performances of *The Good Person of Szechwan* and of *Life of Galileo* take place in Zurich.

1944   Brecht becomes a member of the newly formed Council for a Democratic Germany. In April Jed Harris, an American producer and director, enquires about *Galileo*, and Brecht looks afresh at its 'moral'. He writes the first version of *The Caucasian Chalk Circle*, and almost immediately starts reworking it. He studies Arthur Waley's translations of Chinese poetry. In September he begins to revise *Galileo* with Charles Laughton. Ruth Berlau bears him a son who does not survive.

1945 *Fear and Misery of the Third Reich* is performed in New York under the title *The Private Life of the Master Race*. Brecht and Laughton complete the English version of *Galileo* but the dropping of the atomic bombs on Hiroshima and Nagasaki in August gives rise to another revision which stresses the social responsibility of the scientist.

1946 The first performance of Brecht's adaptation of Webster's *The Duchess of Malfi* takes place in Boston.

1947 Charles Laughton appears in the title role of *Life of Galileo* in Beverly Hills and New York. Brecht appears before the *House Committee on Unamerican Activities* and proves himself a master of ambiguity when cross-examined about his communist activities.

**Return**

Brecht and Helene Weigel go to Zurich, leaving their son Stefan, who is an American citizen, in the U.S.A. Brecht meets Max Frisch, his old friend and designer Caspar Neher, and the playwright Carl Zuckmayer.

1948 Brecht's adaptation of *Antigone of Sophocles* is performed in Chur, Switzerland, and *Mr Puntila and his Man Matti* is given its first performance in Zurich. He publishes the *Little Organum for the Theatre*. Brecht travels to Berlin and starts rehearsals of *Mother Courage* at the Deutsches Theater in the Soviet sector of the city. *The Caucasian Chalk Circle* is first performed in Eric and Maja Bentley's English translation by students at Northfield, Minnesota.

1949 *Mother Courage* opens at the Deutsches Theater with Helene Weigel in the title role. Brecht visits Zurich again before settling in Berlin. The Berliner Ensemble, Brecht and Helene Weigel's own state-subsidised company, is formed and opens with *Puntila*. Brecht adapts J.M.R. Lenz's *The Tutor*. At Gottfried von Einem's suggestion Brecht applies for an Austrian passport (H. Weigel is Austrian) as Caspar Neher had already done. He works with Neher on a play for the Salzburg Festival, which is to be an international showcase for his work.

1951 *The Mother* is performed by the Berliner Ensemble. Brecht finishes the first version of his adaptation of Shakespeare's *Coriolanus*. His opera with music by Paul Dessau, *The Trial of Lucullus*, is tried out and meets with official disfavour.

1953 Brecht writes *Turandot*, and the *Buckow Elegies*. Ethel and Julius Rosenberg are executed in the U.S.A. for betraying atomic secrets to the Russians. Brecht is elected President of the German section of the PEN Club, the international writers' association. On 17 June there are strikes and demonstrations protesting about working conditions in the German Democratic Republic. Brecht writes a letter to the Secretary of the Socialist Unity Party which is released to the press in a doctored form.

1954 The trial of atomic physicist Robert J. Oppenheimer begins in the U.S.A., and Albert Einstein writes an article inveighing against this modern 'inquisition', but the idea that science is subordinate to state security gains currency. Brecht is awarded the Stalin Peace Prize. The Berliner Ensemble moves into its own home, the Theater am Schiffbauerdamm (where he had triumphed with *The Threepenny Opera* in 1928), and performs *The Caucasian Chalk Circle*. The prologue, *The Struggle for the Valley*, is now designated as Act I. Brecht makes public his objections to the Paris Treaty (which incorporated the Federal Republic of Germany into NATO) and to re-armament in general. The Berliner Ensemble's productions of *Mother Courage* and Kleist's *The Broken Pitcher* are enthusiastically received as the highlights of the Paris Théâtre des Nations festival. *Mother Courage* is awarded the prizes for best play and best production.

1955    Brecht adapts Farquhar's *The Recruiting Officer* as *Drums and Trumpets*. He goes to Moscow to receive the Lenin Peace Prize. In December Brecht begins rehearsals of *Life of Galileo* using the third version of the play, a modified retranslation into German of Laughton's English version. Ernst Busch takes the title role. Harry Buckwitz, directing the West German premiere of *The Caucasian Chalk Circle* at Frankfurt, omits *The Struggle for the Valley* as politically inopportune.

1956    Brecht's health prevents him from carrying on with *Galileo* and he hands over the direction to Erich Engel. He visits Milan for Giorgio Strehler's production of *The Threepenny Opera* at the Piccolo Teatro. Brecht is preparing the Berliner Ensemble, which by this time has become generally recognised as the foremost progressive theatre in Europe, for a visit to London when he dies of a heart attack on 14 August. The visit goes ahead and *Mother Courage*, *The Caucasian Circle*, and *Trumpets and Drums* are presented at the Palace Theatre at the end of August for a short season – a landmark in Brecht's reception in the United Kingdom.

# Introduction

**Bertolt Brecht: 1898–1956**

Brecht is an elusive figure, part Baal, part Schweyk, part Galileo – the list could go on. He could use people and yet command absolute loyalty, not least from the many women in his life. He was a dedicated survivor who learnt to co-exist with many masters. A Communist from the late twenties, he never joined the Party. Aware of the excesses of Stalinism (which devoured some of his friends), he never took a public stand against the Soviet Union, yet in 1941 he ended up in California rather than Moscow. Arraigned by McCarthy's House Committee on Unamerican Activities, he convinced his interrogators that he was not a Communist without prejudicing his long-held convictions. When he returned to Europe he chose to have an East German theatre, a West German publisher and an Austrian passport, all for the best of reasons.

His work can be as ambiguous as his behaviour. Try as he might to make plays like *Mother Courage and her Children* and *Life of Galileo* say one thing, they always ended up saying something else behind his back, and they are the better for it. The pragmatic British on first acquaintance took an overdose of Brecht's theories and made him seem dull. Brecht himself was too pragmatic to take his own theorising seriously when he had a stage in front of him; since the days in Berlin when, unathletic as he was, he consorted with boxers and racing cyclists and pointed to their fans as the kind of connoisseurs and enthusiasts he would like to see watching his plays, his aim had always been to entertain as well as inform.

Brecht was born in 1898 in the sleepy Bavarian provincial town of Augsburg, where his father managed a paper mill. He grew up in comfortable circumstances with an avenue of

chestnut trees outside the door and a moat full of swans not
far away. His mother was Protestant and his father Catholic
but this seems to have caused no tension; indeed, being
brought up in his mother's church produced the bonus of
early familiarity with Luther's German Bible, which remained
a fertile source of vocabulary and incident all his writing life.
His schooling was also free from pressure, and he later
claimed that if he had learned anything, it was in spite of his
teachers. He certainly pitted his wits against the system: one
anecdote tells how the young Brecht watched one of his
friends erase some red pencil and claim, unsuccessfully, that
his homework was undermarked. Brecht then added a few
underlinings and asked for an explanation of the 'errors',
forcing his embarrassed French teacher to raise his mark.
Brecht was not very good at French.

Out of school he pursued his own cultural interests,
admiring, at one time or another, Napoleon, Nietzsche and
Hauptmann, and developing a taste for literary outsiders.
The bohemian lives of the French poets Villon, Rimbaud and
Verlaine fascinated him, and in German he was drawn to the
anti-classical tradition of Büchner and Wedekind and often
sang the latter's saucy little songs to his friends, accompanying himself on the guitar.

Brecht was already gregarious and his circle included
Caspar Neher, who would later be his designer, Georg Pfanzelt
(nickname: Orge), Otto Müller (nickname: Müllereisert).
Their adolescent discussions on life and art in Brecht's attic
den or on the river bank were the germ of his later production
teams. According to Brecht he had his first experience of sex at
seventeen, and from then on he seems to have been something
of a stud – an Americanism that would have appealed to him.

In 1917 Brecht enrolled as a medical student at Munich
University, possibly to stave off conscription to the Great
War, since he certainly was never committed to medicine.
One course which interested him was Artur Kutscher's drama
seminar. Professor Kutscher was a friend of Wedekind and

his biographer, and he enjoyed a reputation as a theatrical pundit. But Brecht was unimpressed and did not hesitate to criticise one of Kutscher's favourites, the minor expressionist Hanns Johst, who later became a prominent Nazi. Johst's *The Lonely One*, a stage biography of the nineteenth-century dramatist, boor and misfit, C.D. Grabbe, was deemed by Brecht to be sentimental and nauseating, and he volunteered to write a better play on the subject himself. *Baal* was the result, and it was the professor's turn to be nauseated. They parted in mutual contempt.

Brecht sampled what Schwabing, Munich's artistic quarter, had to offer. He saw Wedekind play *The Marquis of Keith* and was impressed with the way, as the immoralist hero of his own play, he controlled his audience, despite his shortcomings as an actor. He met the eccentric popular comedian Karl Valentin, and his one-acter *Respectable Wedding* is his homage to Valentin's zany Bavarian sketches.

In 1919 Brecht wrote his second play, *Drums in the Night*, a cynical response to the post-war months. Its hero, Kragler returns late from the war to find his fiancée Anna pregnant and engaged to an 'upwardly mobile' war-profiteer of whom her family approves. Snubbed by her, Kragler repairs to a pub and mobilises support for a Communist rising in the newspaper quarter. It is 1919 and the 'German Revolution' is in progress. Then Anna comes after him and he cops out with the line, 'I am a swine, and swine go home'. Kragler's abandonment of the revolutionaries in favour of 'a big, broad, white bed' later embarrassed Brecht, and he tried to argue that Kragler was a negative, comic figure. His next play too, *In the Jungle of Cities*, is cynical: it is set in Chicago and shows an unmotivated rivalry between Schlink, a Malayan timber merchant, and Garga, an assistant librarian. Brecht wanted the audience to forget about meaning and sit back and admire the technique of the combatants. He was already trying to sharpen audience responses: for *Drums in the Night* he had festooned the auditorium with banners which instructed the audience to take an unromantic view of the proceedings.

The first of Brecht's plays to be performed was *Drums in the Night*, with which Otto Falckenberg opened the 1922/23 season at the Munich Kammerspiele. It received a rave notice from Herbert Ihering, one of the top two Berlin critics, who praised the imagery and power of the writing and claimed that Brecht had altered the literary landscape at a stroke. Ihering then gave Brecht's career a further boost by awarding him the Kleist Prize, Germany's premier dramatic award. 1923 saw productions of *The Jungle of Cities* at Munich and *Baal* at Leipzig, and in 1924 Brecht, whom Falckenberg had taken on as dramaturg, or literary advisor, directed an adaptation of Marlowe's *Edward II* on which he had collaborated with Lion Feuchtwanger, an established novelist who later became famous for *Jew Süss*. It was a strikingly unusual production. The story goes that Brecht asked Karl Valentin what soldiers going into battle looked like. 'They get the willies, go white' was the answer, so he put the soldiers in white-face, one of the first shock effects of the type later invested with ideological significance and canonized as 'alienation effects'. He was a rising star, and he was sedulously cultivating his career.

Berlin was the mecca of the German theatre in the Twenties, and Brecht visited it in 1920 and 1921 when the idealistic phase of Expressionism was giving way to Black Expressionism, which invested the new loose forms with a harsh and brutal pessimism. Brecht became friendly with one of the most combative of the new shockers, Arnolt Bronnen, and changed Bertold to the snappier Bertolt, just as his new friend had done. He persuaded Bronnen to let him direct his play *Parricide* but the matter ended in shambles when the two stars, Heinrich George and Agnes Straub, walked out quivering with rage and shock respectively at Brecht's requirements. It was only in 1924, when he had two plays accepted in Berlin, *The Jungle of Cities* at Max Reinhardt's Deutsches Theater and *Edward II* at the Prussian State Theatre, that he moved there permanently. He was put on a salary as dramaturg at the Deutsches Theater, but according to Carl Zuckmayer, another aspiring playwright Reinhardt had on the payroll, Brecht only went into the office to pinch coal in his briefcase. Germany was just recovering from the hyper-inflation of 1923.

In Berlin Brecht met Elisabeth Hauptmann and persuaded his publisher that manuscripts would come in faster if he could have her as his secretary. More and more he was taking to discussing work in progress with his friends and trying out new pieces on anybody who dropped in, so frequent rewrites became necessary. Elisabeth Hauptmann was always around to make unobtrusive notes and prepare new drafts at all hours for the next day's work. She had a hand in all of his plays between 1924 and 1933, and it is from her records that we know of Brecht's awakening interest in Marxism in 1926.

From 1924 one of the leading directors in Germany was Erwin Piscator, who had returned from service on the Western Front as a Communist and begun politicizing the German theatre with agitprop plays in 1920. By 1926 he was using film, documentation and constructivist sets to bring out the political and economic context of the plays he staged. Brecht knew him and tried to write a play called *Wheat* when Piscator set up his own company, the Piscatorbühne, in 1927. He abandoned the project when he realised that capitalist commodity trading – the action was set in the Chicago Grain Exchange – made no sense, except for a few speculators. Marxism seemed to offer a means of coming to grips with social processes which otherwise defied dramatic analysis.

Brecht also met Kurt Weill in Berlin. Weill had set plays by Georg Kaiser and Yvan Goll to music, and he was interested in working with Brecht. Elisabeth Hauptmann had begun to translate John Gay's *The Beggar's Opera*, which had been successfully revived in London. Then E.J. Aufricht chanced on Brecht in a café one day when he was looking for a piece with which to open a theatre he had just leased, and Brecht offered to update Gay's ballad opera with Weill for him. His offer was accepted and he and Weill put the opera together in the South of France that summer. The rehearsals were chaotic and dogged by accidents and it came as a surprise to all concerned when *The Threepenny Opera* became the hit of the season and a considerable money-spinner for its authors. With its underworld setting, its police corruption, its rapacious characters and its risqué songs the piece cocked a snook at respectable society, and respectable society loved it. Only later, when he was preparing a film version, did Brecht seriously try to put political teeth into *The Threepenny Opera*, for by that time his political views had hardened, not least after seeing the police opening fire on a peaceful May Day parade in 1929.

Brecht and Weill and Elisabeth Hauptmann tried unsuccessfully to repeat the formula with *Happy End*, but the real sequel was in a sense *The Rise and Fall of the City of Mahagonny* which took Brecht's unlovely modern subject matter and Weill's jazzy, popular, unmistakably contemporary music into the genteel confines of Germany's opera houses.

At the time of his biggest popular hit Brecht's attention was however more and more turning to politics. He devised, for amateur performance, a number of short *Lehrstücke*, or teaching plays, as demonstration models of political commitment in action. In the most radical and controversial of these, *The Measures Taken*, a Soviet agitator in China has been liquidated for sympathising openly, against orders, with the coolies. The play reconstructs the events leading to his death and makes it clear that the individual must submit absolutely to Party directives. In *The Exception and the Rule* a bearer travelling through the desert is shot by his master when he reaches for his water bottle to share the last drops with him. A court acquits the master on the grounds that masters can normally assume that servants want to kill them. In deciding where the original mistake lay in such an instance, audience and actors would raise their political consciousness. The biggest of these directly political pieces was *The Mother*, an adaptation of Maxim Gorky's novel, which showed the title figure's progress from maternal quietism to socialist activism in pre-revolutionary Russia. Helene Weigel played the lead and Margarete Steffin, who was to be Brecht's next close collaborator, had a bit part. That was in 1932 and the political situation was tense when the play opened. The police eventually banned performances in working-class districts on the pretext that some of the venues were not licensed for theatrical performances, and the play was given as a reading, in which 'alienated' form Brecht found it even more effective.

He had by this time codified his ideas on the epic theatre that was to replace the traditional dramatic or Aristotelian theatre which he regarded as a dream factory that turned out comforting illusions. Epic theatre would be a stimulant rather than a narcotic, and would help change the world. It would tell stories, but in such a way that audiences would be forced to weigh up and judge the events they saw. Smooth, seamless plots would give way to strings of independent incidents moving in jumps and curves, and these 'montages' would keep the audience alert and critical of the way things developed. Brecht believed that characters could be dismantled and reconstructed – he had demonstrated this in *Man Equals Man* – so the classical fixed hero was to give way to figures conditioned by their social situation who changed when that situation changed. At the same time he saw the individual as the agent of social change, so there was to be a constant dialectic or process of reciprocal influence and change. Brecht modified and developed these ideas in later years, but the basic notion remained intact: that theatre had a part to play in bringing about a better, socialist world.

Hitler came to power on 30 January 1933, the Reichstag burnt down on 27 February, and Brecht went into exile the next day. He eventually bought a house in Skovbostrand on the Danish island of Fyn. For the next fourteen years he had neither a theatre nor a public that understood his language. After Hitler's annexation of Austria, only Switzerland,

notably the Zurich Schauspielhaus, offered politically
unfettered professional facilities for German-language plays.

Brecht now turned to the anti-fascist cause, attending
conferences in Paris and London and co-editing a journal that
was published in Moscow. He subscribed to the Party line that
fascism was the final stage of capitalism, a conspiracy of the
rich against the poor which would collapse of its own accord,
and his writing in this phase is uninspired, with the happy
exception of his poetry. That more private art seemed to
prosper in those dark days. He and Kurt Weill wrote an off-
beat ballet, *The Seven Deadly Sins*, for Weill's wife, Lotte Lenya.
He turned to straight realism, first with *Fear and Misery of the
Third Reich*, a string of scenes from life under Hitler, and then
with *Senora Carrar's Rifles*, a morale-booster for the Spanish
Civil War.

He was however gradually finding his feet in Denmark with
his wife and family and Margarete Steffin at his side, eventually joined by Ruth Berlau, a Danish actress who took on the
task of promoting his work in Denmark. He was out of
Germany, and the working-class voters who were the target
of the *Lehrstücke* were out of range, so the political message in
his plays became more general and oblique. In 1938 he wrote
*Life of Galileo*, the first of a series of masterpieces, which used
historical and exotic subjects to deal with contemporary
issues. Galileo's cunning, in the first version at least, offered
intellectuals in Germany a seventeenth-century recipe for
survival in an authoritarian state. *Mother Courage and her
Children*, still in the seventeenth century, was a warning
against war, which was directed in the first instance at the
Danes, lest they should think they could fraternise with the
Nazis and come off unscathed. *The Caucasian Chalk Circle*
offered a parable on the equitable use of resources from
ancient China as a model for what should happen in Europe
after Hitler's defeat. The pared-down economy and the
schematic figures of the *Lehrstücke* gave way in these plays
to a wealth of colour and incident and a parade of some of

the most memorable figures in modern theatre, Galileo, Courage, Grusha and Azdak.

Brecht moved to Stockholm in 1939 and to Finland in 1940 where he wrote *The Good Person of Szechwan*, as well as a comedy, *Mr Puntila and his Man Matti*, and a satire, *The Resistible Rise of Arturo Ui*. The last two were aimed at the U.S.A., but were too unconventional to stand much chance on the American commercial stage. In 1941, with Finland threatened by the Germans, he travelled to Moscow. Margarete Steffin had to stay behind there and died of tuberculosis, while the Brecht ménage moved on via Vladivostock to the United States.

In the United States Brecht settled in Santa Monica, close to Hollywood. It was his intention to break into films, but he found working conditions and the prevalent ethos uncongenial. Friends like Fritz Lang and Peter Lorre (whom Brecht had discovered) tried to help, but he could not adapt to the American scene which had been such a fertile source of inspiration in Berlin. His memories of the Theatre Union's efforts to produce *The Mother* in New York in 1935 made him cautious of small-time theatre, but he dreamed of success on Broadway. *The Caucasian Chalk Circle* was conceived as a Broadway vehicle for Luise Rainer, an Austrian who had won two Academy Awards for film roles, and when he revised *Life of Galileo* with Charles Laughton his hope was that Laughton would sweep New York off its feet. Nothing much came of these things, because the American theatre was geared to entertainment, and laughter and tears were not part of the Brecht formula: there, as in Britain, it was to take another ten years before the techniques and something of the spirit of Brecht's theatre began to be assimilated.

Besides being a devastated country, Germany was under military occupation when the war ended and Brecht did not leave the U.S.A. until 1947. By that time McCarthyism was at its height and he appeared before the Committee on Unamerican Activities. He outwitted his investigators with ironic half-truths and skilful innuendo. The Committee thanked him for being an exemplary witness.

Brecht went to Switzerland in 1947, and then, because of visa problems – he had been stateless since 1938 – he returned to Berlin, as he had escaped in 1933, via Prague. He arrived in the Eastern Sector on 22 October 1948 to a warm welcome from the Communist cultural establishment. Brecht needed a German audience and his decision to settle in East Berlin was a natural one, given his unswerving conviction that Communism was the future, its warts necessary but temporary. He was no sycophant though, and observed, when the government announced that the people had let it down in 1953, that perhaps the government should elect another people.

East Berlin treated Brecht lavishly. He was given facilities to direct *Mother Courage* at the Deutsches Theater in 1948, then his own company, the Berliner Ensemble in 1949, and finally his own theatre, the Theater am Schiffbauerdamm in 1954. Brecht was now mainly a director, and it was in these years that he directed the meticulously rehearsed model productions of *Puntila*, *The Mother*, *The Caucasian Chalk Circle* among others, introducing techniques and effects that have since become standard – revealed lighting, uncluttered, spartan sets with a few solid, workmanlike props, well-worn costumes, visible scene-changes, demonstrative, unhistrionic acting, banner captions between scenes, songs – all of which in his hands added up to productions of startling freshness and conviction. Some of these were known as alienation effects designed to make the familiar seem odd and thus stimulate critical appraisal. Stepping out of the action to sing a song could do this in the fifties when plays mainly tried to sustain a consistent illusion, but in the theatre today's innovations are standard practice tomorrow, so new ways constantly have to be found of keeping Brecht's plays sharp and fresh. His reputation has suffered, not least in Britain, from leaden productions which tried so hard to be Brechtian that they forgot the wily old pragmatist's favourite English proverb, the proof of the pudding is in the eating. He spiced his plays to suit the audience's palate, and foreign directors should do so too, with discretion.

In Berlin with Helene Weigel managing the Ensemble, with the assistance of Elisabeth Hauptmann (scripts) and Ruth Berlau (photographic records), and with a bevy of young actresses around him, Brecht should have been happy, but he was under constant strain – from work, conflicting relationships and political irritation (the German Democratic Republic was not quite his kind of Communism). By 1954 his work in Berlin was internationally acclaimed, even in England where Kenneth Tynan was campaigning vigorously for him in the *Observer*. He was preparing the company for a visit to London when he died of a heart attack on 14 August 1956. The visit went ahead and left an unmistakeable mark on the British theatre which, with the Royal Court and the Royal Shakespeare Company in the vanguard, was to change radically under Brecht's posthumous influence.

### Baal

*Baal* is Brecht's first play. He wrote it as a student to work off his dislike of Hanns Johst's *The Lonely One*, an expressionist piece in which C.D. Grabbe, an interesting but unsuccessful nineteenth-century dramatist, is presented as an unrecognised genius driven to drink and worse by outrageous fortune, yet recanting in the last scene to die in decent, if maudlin, Christian humility. Brecht's Baal by contrast is close in conception to the hero of a Chicago number Frank Sinatra once sang, 'Bad, bad, Leroy Brown, the baddest guy in the whole damned town'. Baal was a pagan deity associated with a fertility cult who came into conflict with Jehovah and lost. In using his name Brecht signals that his hero, like Wedekind's equally primitive-sounding Lulu, is bound by no conventions and will breach taboos without compunction. The world will not be his oyster but his orange, to be squeezed dry and discarded in an uncompromising quest for self-realisation.

In this he is a latter day exponent of the Nietzschean cult of vitality.

Baal's nature is set out in the 'Hymn of Baal the Great', which traces his progress from his mother's white, protective womb to death in the dark womb of earth. While sinners huddle in shame Baal sleeps in untroubled nakedness, he is a match for the thrusting thighs of Dame World of whom he takes his pleasure in the passing, he even dines on the incautious vultures that await his death. Baal has intimations of the sky above even in the womb, and it forms a permanent canopy over his life, a symbol of infinity and eternity to which he constantly refers, not for solace but to confirm his conviction that his brief, finite existence can only be expanded qualitatively, by experiencing it with the utmost intensity. The changing sky above him runs through the Expressionist palette, violet for his drunken nights, pale apricot as he repents in the dawn, at other times green, orange, purple, yellow, but always a visible reminder of the impassive infinity which encloses all human life. Baal is aware of death, but that awareness is the spur to experience life to the full in the time allotted, and he perishes with sky in his eye to spare, a hero of hedonism who in losing has won. That the sky is once more large and pale, the world young, naked and endlessly marvellous after his death seems in the hymn to vindicate the way he has lived. Whether the play leads to the same conclusion will be considered later.

Like most of Brecht's plays *Baal* underwent several revisions: the first version was provisionally called *Baal eats! Baal dances!! Baal is transfigured!!! What's Baal up to?* and had 29 scenes. This was cut, its naturalism and its links with Johst's play were toned down and Baal's depravity was provocatively heightened in a revised version which was published in 1922 and forms the basis of the present text.

As the play now stands Baal is seen in society only in the first scene. The poet has been discovered as a clerk in Mech's firm and is being lionised by the local literary set. Mech offers to print his poems, but Baal is more concerned with gorging himself, fingering Mech's wife and cadging a few white shirts. Baal senses that this grotesque coterie, especially Mech, who serves his guests 'dead eels' and deals in 'butchered forests', would be death to him and insults his hosts until he is shown the door. Baal smells of the jungle; he is an incarnation of sexual drives, not for reproduction (he fears babies), but to merge with nature. This explains his contempt for Mech the exploiter, whose despoiled cinnamon trees symbolize nature at its most exotic, fragrant and desirable.

In the scenes that follow Brecht tilts at taboos in a series of erotic exchanges. Mech's wife becomes his mistress and has to submit to a mauling in a truckers' café. Baal explains to the uncomprehending Johannes that embracing virginal loins makes a man a god, then seduces Johannes' girlfriend, who drowns herself. Two under-age sisters squabble in his attic about who will go first this time. Baal accosts Sophie in the street and she too capitulates. How is his success to be explained? He is direct in his approach, but his victims all surrender willingly. Sophie Barger can't understand what is happening to her and Baal explains: 'It's April. It's growing dark and you smell me. That's how it is with animals . . . Now you belong to the wind, white cloud.' He is crude and poetic in turn and in Brecht's macho dream of conquest the women love him for it.

Baal's gross ugliness is repeatedly stressed, yet he has an erotic aura to which women succumb. He is a heroic fornicator drawn with Rabelaisian gusto, whose animal attraction is devoid of aesthetic appeal. In a sense Brecht, in youth a puny figure, projects himself into this fantasy of sexual prowess in which he combines elements of *Beauty and the Beast* and *Don Juan*, stripped of any moral framework, into a myth of his own. The white bodies of innocence long for the black mud of experience. Sophie decides she loves Baal precisely when she hears that bodies have poured through his room like water: later when she is pregnant she refuses to go

with Ekart, only for Baal to abandon her instantly to the
terrors of the forest at night. Only Ekart resists Baal's
magnetism. It is he who first suggests escape into the wider
world of bars, cathedrals, cowsheds and forests, those
symbolic stations in life's progress which in this early play are
closer to the world of expressionism and Brecht's French
sources, Villon and Rimbaud, than to the mythical America
and concrete jungles of his other work in the twenties. Ekart
too is an artist but he does not share Baal's absolute
immoralism. Baal can take away his girls, he can even have sex
with him, but he cannot possess him exclusively, so when
Ekart flirts with a waitress Baal kills him in a paroxysm of
rage. They have been on the road eight years.

Behind Baal's destructive egotism lies a deep sense of
isolation. It makes him sneer 'None of you would lift a finger
for me' to the seventeen-year-old Joanna, whom he has just
seduced. It makes him snarl perversely at Sophie, 'Why can't
a man make love to a plant?' It makes him moralize cynically,
'A man's a man and in this respect most of them are equal', as
he drags the unwilling Young Woman into a thicket. And
after the death of Ekart Baal, in decline though still a
predator, finds himself in a hard world of policemen and
woodcutters who are as tough and callous as he is, and who
have no compunction in leaving him alone to crawl out under
the stars to die, defiant to the last.

He started as an outsider and he ends isolated, a corpse to
be unwillingly buried, full of stolen eggs as the hungry
woodcutter discovers to his chagrin. Eggs in a corpse, birth
and death, a final grotesque image in a play that constantly
goes over the top but is always saved by the controlled
exuberance of Brecht's language.

Brecht later came to see his plays as experiments in social
behaviour. What might his first be intended to demonstrate?
That a one-man male chauvinist sexual revolution leads
nowhere? Baal is certainly an experimental animal, best
perhaps viewed with the detachment of the Third Woodcutter

who repeats with disbelief that all that was in his mind as he died was listening to the rain. The Viennese writer Hugo von Hofmannsthal construed *Baal* as a blow against individualism. Brecht himself later in East Berlin found the play lacking in wisdom and Baal anti-social, though he did suggest this was forced on him by an anti-social world.

The first of Brecht's plays to be staged was not *Baal* but *Drums in the Night*. Brecht invited Herbert Ihering, the leading Berlin critic, to the première at the Munich Kammerspiele, and Ihering gave him an enthusiastic notice in the *Berliner Börsen-Courier* which could equally well apply to *Baal*:

> Brecht is impregnated with the horror of this age in his nerves, in his blood . . . Brecht physically feels the chaos and putrid decay of the times. Hence the unparalleled force of his images. This language can be felt on the tongue, in the ears, in the spine . . . It is brutally sensuous and melancholically tender. It contains malice and bottom-less sadness, grim with plaintive lyricism.

## The Threepenny Opera

By the time Brecht wrote *The Threepenny Opera* he was an established figure in the Berlin theatre world. He had been awarded the prestigious Kleist Prize in 1922 for *Drums in the Night*, the first of his plays to be staged, and he had followed this up with *Edward II*, *In the Jungle of Cities* and *Man Equals Man*, all in the same abrasive, anarchic, anti-bourgeois vein. He moved to Berlin in 1924 where he was for a time nominally on the literary staff as a dramaturg for Max Reinhardt's theatres and avidly watched rehearsals all over the city. His own plays were being performed occasionally, and he acquired a large car by writing advertising copy for the manufacturer, but he still had to work hard to make a living. *The Threepenny Opera* changed that.

It was a hastily commissioned work that owed its existence

to an encounter with Ernst Josef Aufricht, a budding
impresario who had leased the Theater am Schiffbauerdamm
with money from his father and who needed a play to open
with. Brecht had just seen the Piscatorbühne, Berlin's first
large-scale exercise in political theatre, go into bankruptcy in
April 1928. He had worked for Erwin Piscator on the scripts
of *The Adventures of the Good Soldier Schwejk* (after Hasek) and
*Boom* (a comedy about the oil industry by Leo Lania) and was
trying to write a play for him about the Chicago Grain
Exchange, *Joe Fleischhacker*. It was not what Aufricht was
looking for, so Brecht mooted another possibility, a German
version of *The Beggar's Opera*. Nigel Playfair had mounted a
long-running revival of John Gay's 1728 ballad opera in
London in 1920 and Elisabeth Hauptmann, a young language
graduate who was Brecht's secretary and close collaborator
during the Weimar years, had been working on a translation
for several months. In 1927 Brecht had put together a little
'Songspiel' called *Mahagonny* for the Baden-Baden Music
Festival with Kurt Weill and he wanted to work with the
composer again, so he suggested that he and Weill should
update *The Beggar's Opera* on the basis of Hauptmann's
translation. Aufricht took up the offer and Brecht and Weill
spent the summer working on an adaptation at Le Lavandou
in the south of France.

Rehearsals started in Berlin on 1 August and went badly.
Carola Neher (Polly) walked out when her lines were cut,
Helene Weigel developed appendicitis and her part was
removed altogether, Rosa Valetti (Mrs Peachum) refused to
sing 'The Ballad of Sexual Obsession' and that was cut as well.
Erich Engel, the director, left with the observation that every
show Brecht touched was a shambles. Harald Paulsen, a
musical comedy star, insisted on playing Macheath in a
snappy suit with a pale blue tie and spats, and Brecht was
forced, inspiredly as it happened, to write in a new opening
number, 'The Ballad of Mac the Knife', to make Macheath's
incongruous appearance work to the plot's advantage.

The dress rehearsal lasted until 6.00 a.m. and even then 45 minutes still had to be cut from the running time. All of this was common knowledge in theatrical circles and a spectacular flop was expected. On the night however after a cool start the audience rose to Macheath and Tiger Brown's 'Cannon Song', and the evening ended in triumph. *The Threepenny Opera*, as it was called at the suggestion of Lion Feuchtwanger, became the hit of the season. Brecht began to enjoy large royalties for the first time in his career.

*The Beggar's Opera* was partly a parody of Italian opera, partly contemporary satire (Peachum the fence and Macheath the womaniser were read as allusions to the Prime Minister, Robert Walpole) but mainly it was an entertainment. Brecht went about updating it without any concern for historical verisimilitude. It seemed to be set in Edwardian Soho because that was the period of the costumes that happened to be available, but Macheath's furniture arrived in lorries and a Queen was about to be crowned; Peachum, turned from an old-fashioned fence into a racketeer taking percentages from organised begging, brought in echoes of gangsterdom; and beggars themselves had been a fixture on Berlin's streets since the war. Through all the anachronisms, the play seems set in a 1920s 'Brechtland' of his own devising.

Macheath too was modernised: the rakish highwayman became an arsonist, murderer and rapist in white kid gloves. He is head of a gang of crooks and Peachum sees him as a threat to his business empire. In the farcical wedding scene, Brecht's only original addition to Gay's plot, Macheath's pretensions to style ('Fancy not knowing the difference between Chippendale and Louis Quatorze') are as important for the comic effect as the incongruity of rigging up a stable as a bridal suite. Macheath is a predator, but unlike the rustic Baal, he is an urban predator whose immoralism and womanising are accompanied by notions of material success which lead him to put on style and to think in terms of moving into the cleaner world of banking. In the last scene he laments that middle-class artisans like himself are being 'swallowed up by big corporations backed by the banks', but in fact his fate is sealed by the treachery and self-interest of all around him, including his girls. His occasional social aperçus like

> What's a jemmy compared with a share certificate? What's breaking into a bank compared with founding a bank? What's murdering a man compared to employing a man?

are swamped by the pessimistic view of man which is built up by the songs in the opera, like the cynical 'Song of the Insufficiency of Human Endeavour' or the 'First Three-penny Finale' with its refrain,

> So that is all there is to it.
> The world is poor and man's a shit.

Brecht had still to discover Marxist man, who was a product of a society which he could change and with which he would himself change in turn.

1928 audiences enjoyed *The Threepenny Opera* as a pastiche of operetta and an outrageous contemporary satire. Georg Kaiser had already discovered Weimar society's propensity to laugh happily at its own excesses when *Side by Side* (*Nebeinander*) became his biggest hit, largely because audiences recognised the meteoric rise of its hero Neumann from pawnshop customer to film magnate as typical of the new ruthlessness that was everywhere. Weill's music made *The Threepenny Opera* even more palatable. He had found a haunting idiom which was tough and melancholy, hard and sexy and combined the rhythms and instrumental sounds of jazz – the saxophone is prominent – with an unmistakeable tinge of bittersweet Central European depravity. Where he was romantic, as in the duet 'The Ballad of Immoral Earnings', the content (the good old days when Macheath was Jenny's pimp) and the situation (Jenny has just fetched

Constable Smith to arrest him) undercut any tendency to schmalz. The hard edge of the songs was an astringent antidote to any intrusive sentimentality. America, not least jazz, was fashionable and had already influenced one highly successful opera, Ernst Krenek's *Johnny Strikes Up*. Weill's melodic inventions have a timeless appeal, as frequent revivals of *The Threepenny Opera* all over the world testify. In exile he was to write successful Broadway musicals.

As Brecht's political views hardened he revised his ideas on *The Threepenny Opera*. In 1931 he wrote notes for future productions in which he stressed Macheath's class affiliation,

> The bandit Macheath must be played as a bourgeois phenomenon. The bourgeoisie's fascination with bandits rests on a misconception: that a bourgeois is not a bandit.

Brecht then goes on to analyse Macheath as an archetypal, habit-ridden petit bourgeois. When *The Threepenny Opera* was filmed in 1931 Brecht tried to stiffen it with a dose of ideology, and he eventually aired the subject's political implications fully in *The Threepenny Novel*. Modern directors and theatregoers have to make up their minds which of Brecht's perspectives to adopt. There is an unbroken evolution in his style. The shifts of gear – for example when Polly steps out of the knockabout wedding parody to sing the vengeful chambermaid's ballad, 'Pirate Jenny' – the captions to the scenes and songs, the three lights that are lowered in on a bar and the yellow filters for the 'song lighting' were all to be invested with a political function and become 'alienation effects' in the framework of epic theatre.

Brecht's original finale reflected Gay's which ended with Macheath on the gallows and the author and the manager arguing about how to get out of the tragic impasse the plot had ended in. Tiger Brown, Macheath's old Indian Army pal, then dashed on in his gala uniform with a reprieve from the Queen. The present happy ending heightens the satirical effect by bringing on Brown on horseback as the traditional mounted messenger, and he not only pardons Macheath but also announces he is to be raised to the peerage with an estate for life. It seems that the old boy network has triumphed yet again, so Peachum's swift conversion to the view that Macheath is a victim of injustice is ironic, and the final enigmatic quatrain is an expression more of hope than Marxist expectation.

> Injustice should be spared from persecution:
> Soon it will freeze to death, for it is cold.
> Think of the blizzards and the black confusion
> Which in this vale of tears we must behold.

## The Mother

Brecht began to explore Marxism in 1926 when the *Joe Fleischhacker* project came to a halt because commodity trading proved to be not only resistant to dramatisation but also unintelligible. Marxism seemed to offer a means of analysing it. In 1927 he met a Marxist sociologist, Fritz Sternberg, and they discussed the implications of Marxism for the drama. By 1929 Brecht was publicly committed to Marxist–Leninism, though he never joined the Party: it is often said that witnessing the police shooting into an unarmed demonstration on May Day in Berlin that year finally decided him, but it was a decision that had been maturing for several years, and he never went back on it. 1929 was the year of the Wall Street crash and the beginning of mass unemployment; Germany seemed to Brecht ripe for revolution. The workers' movement was strong, if split, and with the growth of National Socialism capitalism appeared to be moving into its final fascist phase, which in Marxist theory heralded its imminent collapse.

In 1929 Brecht also began to apply Marxist principles

systematically to his work, and in the last years of the Weimar Republic he wrote his most directly political pieces, the *Lehrstücke*, or 'teaching plays'. The first of these was *The Lindbergh Flight*, an operatic sketch for which Weill and Paul Hindemith composed the music for alternate scenes. It was staged at the Baden-Baden New Music Festival in 1929. These *Lehrstücke* were designed for amateur performance, and they were as much learning as teaching plays, their aim being to raise the class consciousness of Communist youth groups, school classes and workers' clubs who performed them. *The Measures Taken* is a good example. Four Soviet agitators despatched to China have recruited an enthusiastic young Communist as guide at the Chinese border, and in the course of their mission the man has repeatedly proved unable to obey orders and has finally blown his cover in an outburst of sympathy for the coolies. This endangers the whole mission and he must die. He accepts this. The play consists of the debriefing of the agitators in Moscow. It is performed by a Control Chorus; the agitators report what has happened and it is then re-enacted by the Chorus, different actors taking the role of The Young Comrade in each scene to avoid individualisation. The characters have no names. The Chorus's collective verdict is that the agitators have fulfilled the mission of disseminating the classics of Marxism and that their handling of the situation was exemplary. The episode has highlighted the difficulty some individuals have in reconciling their insights with those of the collective. Brecht's uncompromising view of the need for total aquiescence displeased the Party and seemed to non-Communists to prove that Marxist–Leninism was inhuman; the play has remained one of Brecht's most indigestible pieces. Brecht withdrew it from performance for fear of misrepresentation. It is however typical of the *Lehrstücke* in that it takes an extreme situation, pares it to the essentials, peoples it with non-individualised figures and sets it up as a model. In coming to terms with the situation in the play the performers clarify their responses and acquire criteria for real life situations.

*The Mother* is a *Lehrstück* of a less radical kind. It has characters rather than ciphers, it presents a complex sequence of historical events, and it is intended to be performed for an audience rather than as a group exercise in political awareness, but it still has the economy and the unmistakeable message of the genre. It is based on a novel written by Maxim Gorky in 1906, a classic of socialist realism. It had already been turned into a historical play for the Berlin Volksbühne in 1931 by Günter Weisenborn when Brecht entered the project with his collective (Slatan Dudow, Emil Burri, Hanns Eisler). They decided to retain the pattern of Pelagea Vlasova's development but to structure the action so as to highlight direct parallels between conditions in pre-revolutionary Russia and the mass unemployment, the pauperisation of the workers and the endemic government crises that racked Germany during the Depression. The novel was set in 1905 but the play takes Vlasova's career up to the October Revolution of 1917. It was intended as an incitement to revolution as the appropriate response to the situation in Germany in 1932. To take one example: the 'Report on the 1st May, 1905', where 'orderly people who'd worked their whole lives' were mowed down by the soldiers, was an unmistakeable allusion to Bloody May in Berlin in 1929. Brecht's radical revision of *The Mother* made it unacceptable at the Social Democratic Volksbühne and it had to be performed by a collective, the Young Actors' Group, which was subjected to police harassment in its efforts to stage the play for working-class audiences.

Pelagea Vlasova, the widowed Mother, starts out in 1905 as a solid citizen whose only concern is to cook her Communist son, Pavel, a decent bowl of soup. In trying to protect him she herself experiences the injustices he is fighting against. She learns to read, she is taught to distinguish between private property and the means of production. When Pavel comes back in 1912 from a spell in Siberia he has to slice his own bread because his mother is busy printing leaflets. Both now believe that these leaflets are the soup of the future. The domestic mother/son relationship has been transformed by the 'third cause' into the comradeship of the class war, and when her son is shot trying to reach Finland the cause sustains her; she no longer has a son but she is now the Mother to a whole militant class. For the final scene she rises from her sick bed to march with the revolutionaries, and she speaks the final exhortation in the play,

> When the ruling class has finished speaking
> Those they ruled will have their answer . . .
> For those defeated today will be the victors tomorrow
> And from 'never' comes our 'today'.

*The Mother* shows us Marxism in action: Vlasova starts as a law-abiding citizen at the mercy of the status quo. With experience she comes to understand her world and what it does to people like her, and as a changed woman she calls for changes in the world and actively works to effect these changes. Brecht's plays have moved from Brechtland to Marxland.

*The Mother* is a marvellous display of his didactic skills. The graphic simplicity with which he uses Vlasova's kitchen table to expound the Marxist theory of property foreshadows the lucid demonstrations of astronomical theory in *Life of Galileo*. The argumentation with which Vlasova confounds the hypocritical Landlady and the Poor Woman in the scene after Pavel's death, and the skill with which she confuses the patriots at the copper collection combine wit, cunning and logic in an irrefutable display of dramatic dialectics. In its own simplified terms the play turns a human drama into a faultlessly presented case for Communism which climaxes in a call for revolution. It does not however work only in these absolute terms. Di Trevis's 1986 production at Contact Theatre in Manchester riveted a string of full houses that didn't have a revolutionary thought in their heads, and used interpolated TV clips of the Scargill–Macgregor miners' strike to force the audience to make the connection between its liberal sympathy with the historical events and its own recent experience of controversial social issues.

Formally the play is a classic example of epic theatre. It tells a story which covers twelve years, and it presents it for our understanding, not our delectation. From Scene 1 in which Pavel does not speak and Vlasova turns directly to the audience to explain her domestic problems with no pretence of theatrical illusion through to the last scene, the play is a sociological experiment, a live demonstration of social issues. Scene 5 is an epic set piece. The bloody demonstration is presented in cool report, the participants offering eye-witness accounts as one might to a jury, punctuated here and there by Vlasova and Smilgin speaking the words they had spoken on the day. Smilgin also introduces himself to the audience, so that the significance of his part will be apparent. The mechanism is exposed and the viewer forced to think about it.

In the three plays in this volume Brecht travels from absolute sensual anarchism to absolute intellectual socialism. The volumes that follow show how the position he reached at the end of the Weimar Republic was refined and elaborated in the years of exile that were to follow.

Hugh Rorrison

Baal

*To my friend George Pfanzelt*

*Translator:* PETER TEGEL

*Characters*

Baal, poet · Mech, merchant and publisher · Emilie, his wife ·
Dr Piller, critic · Johannes Schmidt · Pschierer, director of the
water rates · a young man · a young woman · Johanna · Ekart ·
Luise, a waitress · the two sisters · the landlady · Sophie
Barger · the tramp · Lupu · Mjurk · the nightclub singer · a
pianist · the parson · Bolleboll · Gougou · the old beggar ·
Maja, the beggarwoman · the young woman · Watzmann · a
waitress · two policemen · drivers · peasants · woodcutters

Baal grew up within the whiteness of the-womb
With the sky already large and pale and calm
Naked, young, endlessly marvellous
As Baal loved it when he came to us.

And that sky remained with him through joy and care
Even when Baal slept, blissful and unaware.
Nights meant violet sky and drunken Baal
Dawns, Baal good, sky apricottish-pale.

So through hospital, cathedral, bar
Baal trots coolly on, and learns to let them go.
When Baal's tired, boys, Baal will not fall far:
Baal will drag his whole sky down below.

Where the sinners herd in shame together
Baal lies naked, soaking up the calm.
Just the sky, but sky to last for *ever*
Hides his nakedness with its strong arm.

And that lusty girl, the world, who laughs when yielding
To the man who'll stand the pressure of her thighs
Gives him instants of a sweet ecstatic feeling.
Baal survives it; he just looks and sees.

And when Baal sees corpses all around
Then a double pleasure comes to him.
Lots of space, says Baal; they're not enough to count.
Lots of space inside this woman's womb.

Once a woman, Baal says, gives her all
She'll have nothing more, so let her go!
Other men would represent no risk at all.
Even Baal is scared of babies, though.

Vice, says Baal, is bound to help a bit
And so are the men who practise it.
Vices leave their mark on all they touch.
Stick to two, for one will be too much.

Slackness, softness – that's what you should shun.
Nothing's tougher than pursuing fun.
Powerful limbs are needed, and experience too
Swollen bellies may discourage you.

Baal watches the vultures in the star-shot sky
Hovering patiently to see when Baal will die.
Sometimes Baal shams dead. The vultures swoop.
Baal, without a word, will dine on vulture soup.

Under mournful stars in our sad vale of trouble
Munching, Baal can graze broad pastures down to stubble.
When they're cropped, into the forest deep
Baal trots, singing, to enjoy his sleep.

And when Baal's dragged down to be the dark womb's
    prize
What's the world to Baal? Baal has been fed.
Sky enough still lurks behind Baal's eyes
To make just enough sky when he's dead.

Baal decayed within the darkness of the womb
With the sky once more as large and pale and calm
Naked, young, endlessly marvellous
As Baal loved it when he came to us.

## Dining Room

*Mech, Emilie Mech, Pschierer, Johannes Schmidt, Dr Piller, Baal
and other guests enter through the revolving door.*

MECH *to Baal:* Would you like some wine, Mr Baal? *All take
seats, Baal in the place of honour.* Do you like crab? That's a
dead eel.

PILLER *to Mech:* I'm very glad that the immortal poems of
Mr Baal, which I had the honour of reading to you, have
earned your approval. *To Baal:* You must publish your
poetry. Mr Mech pays like a real patron of the arts. You'll
be able to leave your attic.

MECH: I buy cinnamon wood. Whole forests of cinnamon
float down the rivers of Brazil for my benefit. But I'll also
publish your poetry.

EMILIE: You live in an attic?

BAAL *eating and drinking:* 64 Klauckestrasse.

MECH: I'm really too fat for poetry. But you've got the same-
shaped head as a man in the Malayan Archipelago, who
used to have himself driven to work with a whip. If he
wasn't grinding his teeth he couldn't work.

PSCHIERER: Ladies and gentlemen. I admit it frankly: I was
shattered to find a man like him in such modest circumstances. As you know, I discovered our dear poet in my
office, a simple clerk. I have no hesitation in calling it a
disgrace to our city that personalities of his calibre should
be allowed to work for a daily wage. May I congratulate
you, Mr Mech! Your salon will be famous as the cradle of
this genius's, yes genius's, worldwide reputation. Your
health, Mr Baal!

*Baal wards off the speech with a gesture; he eats.*

PILLER: I shall write an essay about you. Have you any manuscripts? I have the backing of the press.

A YOUNG MAN: How, my friend, do you get that accursed
naïve effect? It's positively homeric. I consider Homer one,

or rather one of several, highly civilized adapters with a penetrating delight in the naïveté of the original folk sagas.

A YOUNG LADY: You remind me more of Walt Whitman. But you're more significant. That's what I think.

ANOTHER MAN: I'd say he had something rather more of Verhaeren.

PILLER: Verlaine! Verlaine! Even in physiognomy. Don't forget our Lombroso.

BAAL: Some more of the eel, please.

THE YOUNG LADY: But you have the advantage of greater indecency.

JOHANNES: Mr Baal sings his songs to the lorry-drivers. In a café down by the river.

THE YOUNG MAN: Good God, none of those poets are even in the same category. My friend, you're streets ahead of any living poet.

THE OTHER MAN: At any rate he's promising.

BAAL: Some more wine please.

THE YOUNG MAN: I consider you a precursor of the great Messiah of European literature whom we can undoubtedly expect within the very near future.

THE YOUNG LADY: Dear poet, ladies, and gentlemen. Permit me to read you a poem from the periodical 'Revolution' which will also be of interest to you. *She rises and reads:*

The poet shuns shining harmonies.
He blows trombones, shrilly whips the drum.
He incites the people with chopped sentences.

The new world
Exterminating the world of pain,
Island of rapturous humanity.
Speeches. Manifestos.
Songs from grandstands.
Let there be preached the new,
The holy state, inoculated into the blood of the people,
Blood of their blood.

Paradise sets in.
– Let us spread a stormy climate!
Learn! Prepare! Practise!

*Applause.*
THE YOUNG LADY *quickly:* Permit me! I shall turn to another
poem in the same issue. *She reads:*

Sun had made him shrivel
And wind had blown him dry.
By every tree rejected
He simply fell away.

Only a single rowan
With berries on every limb,
Red as flaming tongues, would
Receive and shelter him.

So there he hung suspended,
His feet lay on the grass.
The blood-red sunset splashed him
As through his ribs it passed.

It moved across the landscape
And struck all the olive groves.
God in his cloud-white raiment
Was manifest above.

Within the flowering forest
There sang a thousand snakes
While necks of purest silver
With slender murmurs shook.

And they were seized with trembling
All over that leafy domain
Obeying the hands of their Father
So light in their delicate veins.

*Applause.*

CRIES OF: Brilliant! Extreme but in good taste. Simply heavenly.

THE YOUNG LADY: In my opinion it comes closest to the Baalian conception of the world.

MECH: You should travel! The Abyssinian mountains. That's something for you.

BAAL: They won't come to me, though.

PILLER: Why? With your zest for life! Your poems had an enormous effect on me.

BAAL: The lorry-drivers pay if they like them.

MECH *drinking:* I'll publish your poems. I'll let the cinnamon logs float away, or do both.

EMILIE *to Mech:* You shouldn't drink so much.

BAAL: I haven't got any shirts. I could use some white shirts.

MECH: You're not interested in the publishing deal?

BAAL: But they'd have to be soft.

PILLER *ironic:* Oh, and what can I do for you?

EMILIE: You write such wonderful poems, Mr Baal. So sensitive.

BAAL *to Emilie:* Won't you play something on the harmonium?

*Emilie plays.*

MECH: I like eating to the harmonium.

EMILIE *to Baal:* Please don't drink so much, Mr Baal.

BAAL *looks at Emilie:* Do you have forests of cinnamon floating for you, Mech? Butchered forests?

EMILIE: You can drink as much as you like. I was only asking a favour.

PILLER: Even your drinking shows promise.

BAAL *to Emilie:* Play higher up! You've got lovely arms.

*Emilie stops playing and approaches the table.*

PILLER: Apparently you don't care for the music itself.

BAAL: I can't hear the music. You're talking too much.

PILLER: You're a queer fish, Baal. I gather you don't want to get published.

BAAL: Don't you trade in animals too, Mech?

MECH: Do you object?

BAAL *stroking Emilie's arm:* What's my poetry to you?

MECH: I wanted to do you a favour. Couldn't you be peeling some more apples, Emilie?

PILLER: He's afraid of being sucked dry. – Haven't you found a use for me yet?

BAAL: Do you always wear wide sleeves, Emilie?

PILLER: But now you really must stop drinking.

PSCHIERER: Perhaps you ought to go easy on the alcohol. Full many a genius —

MECH: Would you like to have a bath? Shall I have a bed made up for you? Have you forgotten anything?

PILLER: Your shirts are floating away, Baal. Your poetry has floated off already.

BAAL *drinks:* I'm against monopolies. Go to bed, Mech.

MECH *has risen:* I delight in all the animals on God's earth, but this is one animal you can't do business with. Come, Emilie! Shall we go, ladies and gentlemen?

*All have risen indignantly.*

CRIES: Sir! Astounding! That's the . . .!

PSCHIERER: I am shattered, Mr Mech . . .

PILLER: Your poetry has a malicious streak.

BAAL *to Johannes:* What is the gentleman's name?

JOHANNES: Piller.

BAAL: Well, Piller, *you* can send me some old newspapers.

PILLER *leaving:* You mean nothing to me. You mean nothing to literature.

*All go.*

SERVANT *entering:* Your coat, sir.


## Baal's Attic

*Starlit night. At the window Baal and the adolescent Johannes. They look at the sky.*


BAAL: When you lie stretched out on the grass at night you

can feel in your bones that the earth is round and that we're flying, and that there are beasts on this star that devour its plants. It's one of the smaller stars.

JOHANNES: Do you know anything about astronomy?

BAAL: No.

*Silence.*

JOHANNES: I'm in love with a girl. She's the most innocent creature alive, but I saw her once in a dream being made love to by a juniper tree. That is to say, her white body lay stretched out on the juniper tree and the gnarled branches twisted about her. I haven't been able to sleep since.

BAAL: Have you ever seen her white body?

JOHANNES: No. She's innocent. Even her knees . . . There are degrees of innocence, don't you think? And yet, there are times when I hold her, just for a second, at night, and she trembles like a leaf, but only at night. But I haven't the strength to do it. She's seventeen.

BAAL: In your dream, did she like love?

JOHANNES: Yes.

BAAL: She wears clean linen, a snow-white petticoat between her knees? Bed her and she may turn into a heap of flesh without a face.

JOHANNES: You're saying what I always felt. I thought I was a coward. I can see now that you also think intercourse is unclean.

BAAL: That's the grunting of the swine who are no good at it. When you embrace her virginal loins, the joy and fear of created man turns you into a god. As the juniper tree's many roots are entwined within the earth, so are your limbs in bed. Blood flows and hearts beat.

JOHANNES: But it's punishable by law, and by one's parents.

BAAL: Your parents – *he reaches for his guitar* – they're a thing of the past. How dare they open their mouths, filled with rotten teeth, to speak against love, which anybody may die of? If you can't take love, there's nothing left but vomit. *He tunes the guitar.*

JOHANNES: Do you mean if I make her pregnant?

BAAL *striking chords on his guitar:* When the pale mild summer ebbs and they're swollen with love like sponges, they turn back into beasts, evil and childish, shapeless with their fat stomachs and hanging breasts, their damp arms clinging like slimy tentacles, and their bodies collapse and grow heavy unto death. And with hideous shrieks as if they were bringing a new world into being, they yield a small fruit. They spew out with pain what they once sucked in with pleasure. *He plucks the strings.* You have to have teeth for it, then love is like biting into an orange, with the juice squirting into your teeth.

JOHANNES: Your teeth are like an animal's. They're yellow and large, sinister.

BAAL: And love is like putting your naked arm into a pond and letting it float with weeds between your fingers, like the pain in which the drunken tree groans and sings as the wild wind rides it, like drowning in wine on a hot day, her body surging like a cool wine into every crease of your skin, limbs soft as plants in the wind, and the weight of the collision to which you yield is like flying against a storm, and her body tumbles over you like cool pebbles. But love is also like a coconut, good while it is fresh but when the juice is gone and only the bitter flesh remains you have to spit it out. *He throws the guitar aside.* I'm sick of this hymn.

JOHANNES: Then you think it's something I ought to do, if it's so wonderful?

BAAL: I think it's something for *you* to avoid, Johannes.

## An Inn

*Morning. Lorry-drivers. Ekart at the back with Luise, the waitress. White clouds can be seen through the window.*

BAAL *talking to the lorry-drivers:* He threw me out of his nice clean room, because I threw up his wine. But his wife ran after me, and in the evening we celebrated. I'm lumbered with her and sick of it.

DRIVERS: She needs a good hiding . . . They're randy as cats but stupider. Tell her to go and eat figs! . . . I always beat mine before I give her what she wants.

JOHANNES *enters with Johanna:* This is Johanna.

BAAL *to the drivers, who go to the back:* I'll give you a song later.

JOHANNA: Johannes read me some of your poems.

BAAL: Ah. How old are you?

JOHANNES: She was seventeen in June.

JOHANNA: I'm jealous. He does nothing but talk about you.

BAAL: You're in love with your Johannes. It's spring. I'm waiting for Emilie . . . Better to love than make love.

JOHANNES: I can understand your winning a man's love, but how can you have any success with women?
*Emilie enters quickly.*

BAAL: Here she comes. And how are you, Emilie? Johannes is here with his fiancée. Sit down!

EMILIE: How could you ask me to come here! A cheap bar, only fit for drunken louts! Typical of your taste.

BAAL: Luise, a gin for the lady.

EMILIE: Do you want to make a laughing stock of me?

BAAL: No. You'll drink. We're all human.

EMILIE: But you're not.

BAAL: How do you know? *He holds the glass out to Luise.* Don't be so mean, Luise. *He takes hold of her.* You're devilishly soft today, like a plum.

EMILIE: How ill-bred you are!

BAAL: Tell the world, darling.

JOHANNES: It's interesting here, I must say. Ordinary people. Drinking and amusing themselves. And then, those clouds in the window!

EMILIE: He dragged you here too, I expect. For a view of the clouds.

JOHANNA: Wouldn't it be nicer to go for a walk in the meadows by the river, Johannes?

BAAL: Nothing doing! Stay here! *He drinks.* The sky is

purple, particularly if you happen to be drunk. Beds on the other hand are white. To begin with. That's where love is, between Heaven and Earth. *He drinks.* Why are you such cowards? The sky's free, you feeble shadows! Full of bodies! Pale with love!

EMILIE: You've had too much again and now you're babbling. And with that bloody wonderful babble he drags you to his sty.

BAAL: Sometimes – *drinks* – the sky is yellow. Full of vultures. Let's all get drunk. *He looks under the table.* Who's kicking my shins? Is it you, Luise? Ah, you, Emilie! Well, no matter. Drink up.

EMILIE *half rising:* I don't know what's wrong with you today. Perhaps I shouldn't have come here after all.

BAAL: Have you just noticed? You might as well stay now.

JOHANNA: Don't say things like that, Mr Baal.

BAAL: You've a good heart, Johanna. You'll never be unfaithful, will you?

DRIVER *winning:* Ace, you bastards! – Trumped!

SECOND DRIVER: Keep going, the tart said, the worst's over. *Laughter.* Tell her to go and eat figs.

THIRD DRIVER: How could you betray me, as the lady said to the butler when she found him in bed with the maid.

JOHANNES *to Baal:* Because of Johanna. She's a child.

JOHANNA *to Emilie:* Will you come with me? We can go together.

EMILIE *bursting into tears at the table:* I feel so ashamed now.

JOHANNA *putting her arm round Emilie:* I understand; it doesn't matter.

EMILIE: Don't look at me like that. You're still so young. You don't know anything yet.

BAAL *gets up forbiddingly:* Comedy, entitled Sisters in Hades! *He goes to the drivers, takes the guitar down from the wall and tunes it.*

JOHANNA: He's been drinking. He'll regret it tomorrow.

EMILIE: If only you knew. He's always like this. And I love
  him.
BAAL *sings:*

> Orge told me that:
>
> In all the world the place he liked the best
> Was not the grass mound where his loved ones rest
>
> Was not the altar, nor some harlot's room
> Nor yet the warm white comfort of the womb.
>
> Orge thought the best place known to man
> In this world was the lavatory pan.
>
> That was a place to set the cheeks aglow
> With stars above and excrement below.
>
> A place of refuge where you had a right
> To sit in private on your wedding night.
>
> A place of truth, for there you must admit
> You are a man; there's no concealing it.
>
> A place of wisdom, where the gut turns out
> To gird itself up for another bout.
>
> Where you are always doing good by stealth
> Exerting tactful pressure for your health.
>
> At that you realize how far you've gone:
> Using the lavatory – to eat on.

DRIVERS *clapping:* Bravo! . . . A good song! Give the gentleman a cherry brandy, if you'll accept the offer, sir! He made
  it up all on his own . . . What a man!
LUISE *in the middle of the room:* You're a one, Mr Baal!

DRIVER: If *you* did a real job, you'd do all right for yourself. You could end up running a transport business.

SECOND DRIVER: Wish I had brains like that!

BAAL: That's nothing. You have to have a backside and the rest. Your very good health, Luise. *He goes back to his table.* And yours, Emmi. Come on, drink up. Even if you can't do anything else. Drink, I said.

*Emilie, tears in her eyes, sips her drink.*

BAAL: That's better. There'll be some life in you yet.

EKART *gets up and comes round slowly from the bar to Baal. He is lean, a powerful man:* Baal! Brother! Come with me! Give it up! Out to the hard dusty highroad: at night the air grows purple. To bars full of drunks: let the women you've stuffed fall into the black rivers. To cathedrals with small, pale ladies: you ask, dare a man breathe here? To cowsheds where you bed down with the beasts. It's dark there and the cows moo. And into the forests where axes ring out above and you forget the light of day: God has forgotten you. Do you still remember what the sky looks like? A fine tenor you've turned into! *He spreads his arms.* Come, brother! To dance, to sing, to drink! Rain to drench us! Sun to scorch us! Darkness and light! Dogs and women! Are you that degenerate?

BAAL: Luise! Luise! An anchor! Don't let me go with him. *Luise goes to him.* Help me, everyone.

JOHANNES: Don't let him lead you astray!

BAAL: My dear chap!

JOHANNES: Think of your mother, remember your art! Resist! *To Ekart:* You ought to be ashamed. You're evil.

EKART: Come, brother! We'll fly in the open sky as blissful as two white doves. Rivers in the morning light! Graveyards swept by the wind and the smell of endless unmown fields.

JOHANNA: Be strong, Mr Baal.

EMILIE *holding him:* I won't allow it! Do you hear? You can't throw yourself away!

BAAL: Not yet, Ekart! There's still another way. They won't play, brother.

EKART: Then go to the devil, you with your soft, fat, sentimental heart! *He goes.*

DRIVERS: Out with the ten ... Damn it! Add up ... Let's pack it in.

JOHANNA: You've won this time, Mr Baal.

BAAL: I'm sweating all over. Got any time today, Luise?

EMILIE: Don't talk like that, Baal! You don't know what you do to me when you talk like that.

LUISE: Stop upsetting the lady, Mr Baal. A child could see she's not herself.

BAAL: Don't worry, Luise! Horgauer!

DRIVER: What do you want?

BAAL: There's a lady being badly treated here, she wants love. Give her a kiss, Horgauer.

JOHANNES: Baal!

*Johanna puts her arm round Emilie.*

DRIVERS *laughing and hitting the table with their fists:* Press on, Andreas ... Have a go ... high class, blow your nose first ... You're a bastard, Mr Baal.

BAAL: Are you frigid, Emilie? Do you love me? He's shy, Emmi. Give him a kiss. If you make a fool of me in front of these people, it's the finish. One, two ...

*The driver bends down. Emilie raises her tear-stained face. He kisses her vigorously. Loud laughter.*

JOHANNES: That was evil, Baal. Drink brings out the evil in him, and then he feels good. He's too strong.

DRIVERS: Well done! What's she come to a place like this for? ... That's the way to treat them ... her kind break up families! ... Serves her right! *They get up from their card game.* Tell her to go and eat figs!

JOHANNA: How disgusting! You ought to be ashamed!

BAAL *going up to her:* Why are your knees shaking, Johanna?

JOHANNES: What do you want with her?

BAAL *a hand on his shoulder:* Must you also write poetry? While life's so decent? When you shoot down a racing

stream on your back, naked under an orange sky, and you
see nothing except the sky turning purple, then black like a
hole . . . when you trample your enemy underfoot . . . or
burst with joy at a funeral . . . or sobbing with love you eat
an apple . . . or bend a woman across a bed. *Johannes leads
Johanna away without saying a word.*

BAAL *leaning on the table:* It's all a bloody circus. Did you feel
it? Did it get under your skin? You have to lure the beast
from its cage! Get the beast into the sun! My bill! Let love
see the light of day! Naked in the sunshine! Under a clear
sky!

DRIVERS *shaking him by the hand:* Be seeing you, Mr Baal! . . .
At your service, sir! . . . For my part I always did say Mr
Baal had a screw loose. What with those songs and the
rest! But one thing's certain, his heart's in the right place! –
You have to treat women the way they deserve. – Well,
somebody exposed their precious white bottom here today.
– Good-bye, Mr Circus. *They go.*

BAAL: And good-bye to you, my friends! *Emilie has thrown
herself sobbing down on the bench. Baal touches her forehead with
the back of his hand.* Emmi! You can calm down now. The
worst is over. *He raises her head and brushes her hair from her
tear-stained face.* Just forget it! *He throws himself heavily on her
and kisses her.*

## Baal's Attic

1 *Sunrise.*
*Baal and Johanna sitting on the edge of the bed.*

JOHANNA: Oh, what have I done! I'm wicked.
BAAL: Wash yourself instead.
JOHANNA: I still don't know how it happened.
BAAL: Johannes is to blame for everything. Drags you up
here and behaves like a clown when he sees why your
knees are shaking.

JOHANNA *gets up, lowers her voice:* When he comes back . . .

BAAL: Time for a bit of literature. *He lies down again.* First light over Mount Ararat.

JOHANNA: Shall I get up?

BAAL: After the flood. Stay in bed.

JOHANNA: Won't you open the window?

BAAL: I like the smell. – What about another helping? What's gone's gone.

JOHANNA: How can you be so vile?

BAAL *lazily on the bed:* White and washed clean by the flood, Baal lets his thoughts fly like doves over the dark waters.

JOHANNA: Where's my petticoat . . . I can't . . . like this . . .

BAAL *handing it to her:* Here! What can't you . . . like this, darling?

JOHANNA: Go home. *She drops it, but then she dresses.*

BAAL *whistling:* God, what a girl! I can feel every bone in my body. Give me a kiss!

JOHANNA *by the table in the middle of the room:* Say something! *Baal is silent.* Do you still love me? Say it. *Baal whistles.* Can't you say it?

BAAL *looking up at the ceiling:* I'm fed to the teeth!

JOHANNA: Then what was it last night? And before?

BAAL: Johannes could make things awkward. And Emilie's staggering around like a rammed schooner. I could die of starvation here! None of you would lift a finger for me. There's only one thing you're out for.

JOHANNA *confused, clearing the table:* And you – didn't you ever feel differently about me?

BAAL: Have you washed? Not an ounce of sense. Did you get nothing out of it? Go home! You can tell Johannes I took you home last night and spew gall at him. It's been raining. *Rolls himself up in his blanket.*

JOHANNA: Johannes? *She walks wearily to the door and goes.*

BAAL *suddenly turning:* Johanna! *Goes from his bed to the door.* Johanna! *At the window.* There she goes. There she goes.

2  *Noon.*
*Baal lies on his bed.*

BAAL *humming:*

> The evening sky grows dark as pitch
> With drink; or often fiery red.
> Naked I'll have you in a ditch . . .

*The two sisters come into the room arm in arm.*

THE OLDER SISTER: You said we were to come and visit you again.

BAAL *still humming:*

> Or on a white and spacious bed.

THE OLDER SISTER: Well, we came, Mr Baal.

BAAL: Now they come fluttering in pairs to the dove-cot. Take off your clothes.

THE OLDER SISTER: Mother heard the stairs creak last week. *She undoes her sister's blouse.*

THE YOUNGER SISTER: It was getting light on the landing when we got to our room.

BAAL: One day I'll be stuck with you.

THE YOUNGER SISTER: I'd drown myself, Mr Baal.

THE OLDER SISTER: We came together . . .

THE YOUNGER SISTER: I feel ashamed.

THE OLDER SISTER: It isn't the first time . . .

THE YOUNGER SISTER: But it was never so light. It's broad daylight outside.

THE OLDER SISTER: And it isn't the second time.

THE YOUNGER SISTER: You get undressed as well.

THE OLDER SISTER: I will.

BAAL: When you've done, come on in! It'll be dark all right.

THE YOUNGER SISTER: You go first today.

THE OLDER SISTER: I was first last time . . .

THE YOUNGER SISTER: No, it was me . . .

BAAL: You'll both get it at once.

THE OLDER SISTER *standing with her arms round the younger one*: We're ready. It's so light in here!

BAAL: Is it warm outside?

THE OLDER SISTER: It's only April.

THE YOUNGER SISTER: But the sun's warm today.

BAAL: Did you enjoy yourselves last time?

*The sisters do not answer.*

THE OLDER SISTER: A girl threw herself into the river. Johanna Reiher.

THE YOUNGER SISTER: Into the Laach. I wouldn't go in there. The current's too strong.

BAAL: Into the river? Does anyone know why?

THE OLDER SISTER: There are rumours. People talk . . .

THE YOUNGER SISTER: She went off one afternoon and stayed out all night.

BAAL: Didn't she go home in the morning?

THE YOUNGER SISTER: No, then she went in the river. They haven't found her yet.

BAAL: Still afloat . . .

THE YOUNGER SISTER: What's the matter?

THE OLDER SISTER: Nothing. A chill perhaps.

BAAL: I'm too lazy today. You can go home.

THE OLDER SISTER: You can't do that, Mr Baal. You shouldn't do that to her.

*Knocking at the door.*

THE YOUNGER SISTER: Somebody's knocking. It's mother.

THE OLDER SISTER: For God's sake, don't open!

THE YOUNGER SISTER: I'm frightened.

THE OLDER SISTER: Here's your blouse.

*Loud knocking.*

BAAL: If it's your mother you're in for it.

THE OLDER SISTER *dressing quickly*: Wait a minute, don't open yet. Bolt the door, please, for God's sake!

LANDLADY *fat, enters*: Ah ha! I thought as much. Two at a time now! Aren't you ashamed of yourselves? A pair of you in his fishpond? Night and day, that fellow's bed never gets cold. Now I'm going to have my say. My attic isn't a brothel.

*Baal turns to the wall.*

LANDLADY: You're sleepy, are you? My word, don't you ever get enough of it? I can see the daylight through you. You look like a ghost. You're nothing but a bag of bones.

BAAL *moving his arms:* Like swans they fly to my wood.

LANDLADY *clapping her hands:* Nice swans! The way you put things! You could be a poet, you! If your knees don't rot first.

BAAL: I indulge in white bodies.

LANDLADY: White bodies! You're a poet, you really are! Don't know what else you are though. And the poor young things! You're sisters, are you? And snivelling because you're poor orphans, I suppose. How about a good hiding? For your white bodies? *Baal laughs.* And he laughs. You ruin poor girls by the hundredweight, poor girls you drag here. You disgusting pig! I'm giving you notice. As for you, look sharp and back to your mother! I'm coming with you.

*The younger sister sobs loudly.*

THE OLDER SISTER: It isn't her fault.

LANDLADY *taking both by the hand:* Now for the waterworks! These girls! Oh well, you're not the only ones. That one's up to his neck in swans. There's plenty besides you he's made happy, then dumped on the rubbish heap. Off with you now, into the fresh air! There's no need for tears. *She puts her arms round them both.* I know what he's like. I know the make. Stop snivelling, else it'll show in your eyes. Go home to your mother like good girls and don't do it again. *She pushes them out.* And you, you've had your notice. You can set up your swan-sty somewhere else. *She pushes the girls out of the room and goes out herself.*

BAAL *gets up, stretches:* A bitch with a heart! . . . I'm dead lazy today anyway. *He throws paper down on the table and sits down.* I'll make the new Adam. *He sketches big letters on the paper.* I'll have a go at the inner man. I'm hollowed out, but hungry as a vulture. Nothing but a bag of bones. The bitch! *He leans back and stretches his arms and legs with emphasis.* I'll make summer. Red. Scarlet red. Greedy. *He hums again.*

3 *Evening.*
*Baal sits at his table.*

BAAL *picks up the bottle. The following speech to be delivered with pauses:* I've covered the paper with red summer for four days now: wild, pale, greedy; and fought the bottle. There have been defeats, but the bodies on the wall are beginning to retreat into the dark, into the Egyptian night. I nail them to the wall, but I must stop drinking. *He murmurs:* This white liquor is my rod and staff. It reflects my paper and has remained untouched since the snow began to drip from the gutter. But now my hands are shaking. As if the bodies were still in them. *He listens.* My heart's pounding like a horse's hoof. *With enthusiasm:* Oh Johanna, one more night in your aquarium, and I would have rottad among the fish. But now I smell the warm May nights. I'm a lover with no one to love. I give in. *He drinks and gets up.* I must move. First I'll get myself a woman. To move out alone is sad. *He looks out of the window.* No matter who. One with a face like a woman. *Humming, he goes out. Tristan is being played down below on the hurdy gurdy.*
*Johannes enters, wretched and pale. He riffles the papers on the table, picks up the bottle and goes shyly to the door.*
*He waits there.*
*Noise on the landing. Whistling.*
BAAL *pulling Sophie Barger into the room. Whistles:* Be nice to me, darling. That is my room. *He sits down, sees Johannes.* What are you doing here?
JOHANNES: I only wanted to . . .
BAAL: So you wanted to? What are you standing there for? A tombstone for my Johanna, who's been washed away? The ghost of Johannes from another world, is that it? I'll throw you out! Leave this room at once! *Runs round him.* It's

an impertinence! I'll knock you down. It's spring, anyway.
Get out!

*Johannes looks at him and goes.*

*Baal whistles.*

SOPHIE: What did the poor boy do to you? Let me go!

BAAL *opens the door wide:* When you get to the first floor, turn
to the right.

SOPHIE: They followed us after you picked me up in front of
the door. They'll find me.

BAAL: No one will find you here.

SOPHIE: I don't even know you. What do you want from
me?

BAAL: If you mean that, you may as well go.

SOPHIE: You rushed up to me in the street. I thought it was
an orangutan.

BAAL: It's spring, isn't it? I need something white in this
damned hole, a cloud. *He opens the door and listens.* Those
idiots, they've lost their way.

SOPHIE: I'll get thrown out if I come home late.

BAAL: Especially —

SOPHIE: Especially what?

BAAL: The way a woman looks when I've made love to her.

SOPHIE: I don't know why I'm still here.

BAAL: I can give you the information.

SOPHIE: You needn't think the worst of me, please!

BAAL: Why not? You're a woman like any other. The faces
vary, the knees are always weak.

*Sophie is half prepared to go; at the door she looks round.*

*Baal looks at her, astride a chair.*

SOPHIE: Good-bye!

BAAL *indifferently:* Do you feel faint?

SOPHIE *leans against the wall:* I don't know. I feel so weak.

BAAL: I know. It's April. It's growing dark, and you smell
me. That's how it is with animals. *Gets up.* Now you belong
to the wind, white cloud. *He goes to her quickly, slams the
door, and takes Sophie Barger into his arms.*

SOPHIE *breathlessly:* Let me go!

BAAL: My name's Baal.

SOPHIE: Let me go!

BAAL: You must console me. The winter left me weak. And you look like a woman.

SOPHIE *looks up at him:* Your name's Baal?

BAAL: That makes you want to stay?

SOPHIE *looking up at him:* You're so ugly, so ugly, it's frightening. – But then —

BAAL: Mm?

SOPHIE: Then it doesn't matter.

BAAL *kisses her:* Are your knees steady, mm?

SOPHIE: You don't even know my name. I'm Sophie Barger.

BAAL: Forget your name. *Kisses her.*

SOPHIE: Don't – don't – it's the first time anybody's ever . . .

BAAL: Untouched? Come! *He leads her to the bed. They sit down.* You see! Bodies have poured through this room like water. But now I want a face. We'll go out tonight. We'll lie down in the fields. You're a woman. I've become unclean. You must love me, for a while.

SOPHIE: Is that what you're like? . . . I love you.

BAAL *rests his head on her breasts:* Now the sky's above us, and we're alone.

SOPHIE: But you must lie still.

BAAL: Like a child.

SOPHIE *sitting up:* My mother's at home. I have to go home.

BAAL: Is she old?

SOPHIE: She's seventy.

BAAL: Then she's used to wickedness.

SOPHIE: What if the earth swallowed me up? What if I'm carried off at night and never return?

BAAL: Never? *Silence.* Have you any brothers or sisters?

SOPHIE: Yes, they need me.

BAAL: The air here is like milk. *Goes to the window.* The willows down by the river are soaking wet, and unkempt from the rain. *Takes hold of her.* Your thighs must be pale.

# Whitewashed Houses with Brown Tree Trunks

*Sombre ringing of bells. Baal. The tramp, a pale drunk individual.*

BAAL *striding in a half circle round the tramp, who sits on a stone, his pale face turned to the sky:* Who nailed the tree corpses to the wall?

TRAMP: The pale ivory wind around the corpses of trees. Corpus Christi.

BAAL: Not to mention ringing the bells when plants die!

TRAMP: Bells give me a moral uplift.

BAAL: Don't the trees depress you?

TRAMP: Pff! Tree carcases! *Drinks from a bottle.*

BAAL: Women's bodies aren't any better!

TRAMP: What have women's bodies to do with a religious procession?

BAAL: They're both obscene. There's no love in you.

TRAMP: There's love in me for the white body of Jesus. *Passes him the bottle.*

BAAL *calmer:* I wrote songs down on paper. They get hung up in lavatories these days.

TRAMP *transfigured:* To serve the Lord Jesus! I see the white body of Jesus. Jesus loves sinners.

BAAL *drinking:* Like me.

TRAMP: Do you know the story about him and the dead dog? They all said, it's a stinking mess. Fetch the police! It's unbearable! But, he said, it has nice white teeth.

BAAL: Perhaps I'll turn Catholic.

TRAMP: He didn't. *Takes the bottle from him.*

BAAL *runs about enraged:* But the women's bodies he nails to the wall. I wouldn't do that.

TRAMP: Nailed to the wall! They never floated down the river. They were slaughtered for him, for the white body of Jesus.

BAAL *takes the bottle from him, turns away:* There's too much religion or too much gin in your blood. *Walks away with the bottle.*

TRAMP *beside himself, shouting after him:* So you won't defend your ideals, sir! You won't join the procession? You love plants and won't do anything for them?

BAAL: I'm going down to the river to wash myself. I can't be bothered with corpses. *Goes.*

TRAMP: But I'm full of drink, I can't bear it. I can't bear the damned dead plants. If I had more gin in me, perhaps I could bear it.


## Spring Night Beneath Trees

*Baal. Sophie.*

BAAL *lazily:* It's stopped raining. The grass must still be wet . . . it never came through the leaves of our tree. The young leaves are dripping wet, but here among the roots it's dry! *Angrily.* Why can't a man make love to a plant?

SOPHIE: Listen!

BAAL: The wild roaring of the wind through the damp, black foliage. Can you hear the rain drip from the leaves?

SOPHIE: I can feel a drop on my neck . . . Oh, let me go!

BAAL: Love rips the clothes from a man like a whirlpool and buries him naked among the corpses of leaves, after he's seen the sky.

SOPHIE: I should like to hide in you, Baal, because I'm naked.

BAAL: I'm drunk and you're staggering. The sky is black and we're on a swing with love in our bodies and the sky is black. I love you.

SOPHIE: Oh, Baal, my mother'll be weeping over my dead body, she'll think I drowned myself. How many weeks is it now? It wasn't even May then. It must be nearly three weeks.

BAAL: It must be nearly three weeks, said the beloved among the roots of the tree, after thirty years had passed and she was half rotted by then.

SOPHIE: It's good to lie here like a captive, with the sky above, and never be alone again.

BAAL: I'm going to take your petticoat off again.


# A Club Called 'The Night Cloud'

*A small, swinish café; whitewashed dressing-room; at the back on the left a dark brown curtain; to the side on the right a whitewashed door made of boards leading to the lavatory. At the back on the right a door. When it is open blue night sky is seen. A woman entertainer sings at the back of the café.*
*Baal walks around, chest and shoulders bare, drinking and humming. Lupu, a fat, pale boy with black glossy hair gummed down in two strips on to his sweaty, pale face and a prominent back to his head, stands in the doorway right.*


LUPU: The lamp has been knocked down again.

BAAL: Only pigs come here. Where's my gin ration?

LUPU: You've drunk it all.

BAAL: You watch your step!

LUPU: Mjurk said something about a sponge.

BAAL: Does that mean I don't get a drink?

LUPU: No more gin for you until you've done your number, Mjurk said. I'm sorry for you.

MJURK *by the curtain:* Make yourself scarce, Lupu!

BAAL: No drink, no song.

MJURK: You shouldn't drink so much, or one of these days you won't be able to sing at all.

BAAL: Why else do I sing?

MJURK: Next to Savettka, you're the 'Night Cloud's' most brilliant attraction. You're my personal discovery. Was there ever such a delicate talent in such a fat lump? The fat lump makes the success, not the songs. Your drinking'll ruin me.

BAAL: I'm sick of haggling every night for gin that's my contractual right. I'm clearing out.

MJURK: I've got police backing. You should try sleeping one of these nights, you crawl around as if you'd been hamstrung. Tell your sweetheart to go to hell! *Applause in the café.* You're on now, anyway.

BAAL: I'm fed to the teeth.

*Savettka with the pianist, a pale apathetic individual, coming from behind the curtain:*

SAVETTKA: That's my lot. I'm off now.

MJURK *forcing a tail-coat on Baal:* You don't go half naked on to the stage in my club.

BAAL: Moron! *He throws down the tail-coat and goes off behind the curtain, dragging the guitar.*

SAVETTKA *sits down and drinks:* He only works for that woman he's living with. He's a genius. Lupu imitates him shamelessly. He has taken his tone as well as his girl.

PIANIST *leaning on the lavatory door:* His songs are divine but he's been haggling with Lupu for his drink for the last ten days.

SAVETTKA *drinking:* Life's hell!

BAAL *from behind the curtain:* Small am I, pure am I, a jolly little boy am I. *Applause. Baal continues, accompanying himself on the guitar:*

Through the room the wild wind comes.
What's the child been eating? Plums.
Soft and white its body lay
Helping pass the time away.

*Applause and whistles. Baal goes on singing, and the noise gets rowdier as the song gets more and more shameless. Finally, uproar in the café.*

PIANIST *phlegmatically:* My God, he's packing up. Call a doctor! Now Mjurk's talking, they'll tear him to pieces. No one censored that!

*Baal comes from behind the curtain, dragging his guitar.*

MJURK *following him:* You bastard! I'll have the hide off you!

You are going to sing! As stated in the contract! Or I'll get
the police. *He goes back behind the curtain.*

PIANIST: You'll ruin us, Baal.

*Baal raises a hand to his throat and goes to the lavatory door.*

PIANIST *not letting him pass:* Where are you off to?

*Baal pushes him aside and goes through the door, dragging his guitar
after him.*

SAVETTKA: Taking your guitar to the lavatory? Lovely!

GUESTS *peering in:* Where's that bastard? Go on with the
song – don't stop now! The filthy bastard! *They return to the
room.*

MJURK: I spoke like a Salvation Army general. We can rely
on the police. But they're shouting for him again. Where is
he? He'll have to go on.

PIANIST: The main attraction's sitting on the lavatory.

*Cry from behind the scenes: Baal!*

MJURK *drumming on the door:* You. Answer me! Damn it, I
forbid you to lock yourself in! While I'm paying you! I've
got it in writing. You swindler! *Thumps wildly.*

LUPU *in the door on the right. Blue night sky outside:* The lavatory
window's open. The bird has flown. No drink, no song!

MJURK: Empty! Gone? Out through the lavatory? The cut-
throat! Police! I want the police! *He rushes out. Calls in
rhythm from behind the curtain: Baal! Baal! Baal!*


# Green Fields. Blue Plum Trees

*Baal. Ekart.*


BAAL *slowly coming through the fields:* Since the sky turned green
and pregnant, summertime, wind, no shirt in my trousers.
*Back to Ekart.* They rub my backside, my skull's blown up
with the wind, and the smell of the fields hangs in the hair of
my armpits. The air trembles as if it were drunk.

EKART *behind him:* Why are you running away from the plum
trees like an elephant?

BAAL: Put your hand on my head. It swells with every pulse-beat and goes down like a balloon. Can't you feel it?

EKART: No.

BAAL: You don't understand my soul.

EKART: Let's go and lie in the river.

BAAL: My soul, brother, is the groaning of the cornfields as they bend in the wind, and the gleam in the eyes of two insects who want to devour each other.

EKART: A mad summer boy with immortal intestines, that's what you are! A dumpling, who'll leave a grease spot on the sky.

BAAL: Only words. But it doesn't matter.

EKART: My body's light as a little plum in the wind.

BAAL: That's because of the pale summer sky, brother. Shall we soak up the warm water of a blue pond? Otherwise the white roads that lead across the land will draw us like angels' ropes up to heaven.


## Village Inn

*Evening. Farmers. Baal. Ekart on his own in a corner.*

BAAL: I'm glad I've got you all here together. My brother will be here tomorrow evening. The bulls have to be here by then.

FARMER *gaping:* How can we see if a bull's the right sort for your brother?

BAAL: Only my brother can see. They all have to be strong, fine beasts. Or they're no use. Another gin!

SECOND FARMER: Will you buy the bull on the spot?

BAAL: The one with the strongest legs.

THIRD FARMER: For your price they'll bring them from eleven villages.

FIRST FARMER: Come and have a look at *my* bull.

BAAL: A gin!

FARMERS: My bull is the best! Tomorrow evening, you said?
*They separate.* – Are you staying the night here?

BAAL: Yes, in a bed.

*The farmers go.*

EKART: What are you trying to do? Have you gone mad?

BAAL: Wasn't it wonderful, the way they gawped and gaped, and then they got the idea and began to add up.

EKART: It brought in a few gins! But now we'd better get out quickly.

BAAL: Go now? Are you mad?

EKART: You're crazy! Think of the bulls!

BAAL: And just why did I jockey the boys?

EKART: Well – for the drinks?

BAAL: Wake up! I wanted to give you a treat, Ekart. *He opens the window behind him. It grows dark. He sits down again.*

EKART: You're drunk on six gins. You should be ashamed.

BAAL: It's going to be tremendous. I love these simple people. You're going to see an impressive sight, Ekart. Your health!

EKART: You love pretending to be more naïve than you are. Those poor fellows will beat me up – and you.

BAAL: It'll be part of their education. I'm thinking about them now on this warm evening with a certain tenderness. They come, in their own simple way, to swindle, and that pleases me.

EKART: All right, the bulls or me! I'm going, before the landlord catches on.

BAAL: The evening is so warm. Stay another hour. Then I'll go with you. You know I love you. One can even smell the dung on the fields from here. Do you think the landlord would stand the promoters of the bull business another gin?

EKART: There's someone coming!

PARSON *enters:* Good evening! Are you the man with the bulls?

BAAL: I am.

PARSON: What is the object of this hoax?

BAAL: Because we have nothing else in the world! How strong the smell of the hay is! Is it always like this in the evenings?

PARSON: Your world seems to be very impoverished, my friend.

BAAL: My heaven is full of trees and naked bodies.

PARSON: Don't talk like that. The world isn't a circus for your entertainment.

BAAL: What is the world, then?

PARSON: Just clear out. I'm a very good-natured person, you know. I don't want to make things difficult for you. I've dealt with the matter.

BAAL: The man of God has no sense of humour, Ekart.

PARSON: Don't you realize how childish your plan was? *To Ekart:* What does your friend want?

BAAL *leaning back:* In the evening when it gets dark – of course, it has to be evening and of course the sky must be cloudy – when the air is warm and the wind gentle, the bulls come. They come trotting from every direction, an impressive sight. And the poor farmers stand in the middle and don't know what to do with the bulls, and they've miscalculated: all they get is an impressive sight. I like people who miscalculate. And where else can you see so many animals together?

PARSON: And just for this you wanted to mobilize seven villages?

BAAL: What are seven villages compared with an impressive sight?

PARSON: Now I understand. You're just a poor fellow. With a particular liking for bulls, I suppose?

BAAL: Come, Ekart, he's spoilt it all. Christians don't love animals any more.

PARSON *laughs, then seriously:* I can't agree with you there. Be off now, and don't make yourselves conspicuous. I think I'm rendering you a considerable service.

BAAL: Let's go, Ekart. You've missed your treat, brother. *He slowly leaves with Ekart.*

PARSON: Good evening! I'll settle the gentlemen's bill.

LANDLORD *behind the table:* Eleven gins, your reverence.

# Trees in the Evening

*Six or seven woodcutters are sitting on the ground leaning against a tree, among them Baal. A corpse in the grass.*

FIRST WOODCUTTER: It was an oak tree. It didn't kill him at once. He suffered.

SECOND WOODCUTTER: Only this morning he said the weather seemed to be getting better. This is how he liked it, green and a bit of rain. And the wood not too dry.

THIRD WOODCUTTER: He was a good lad, Teddy. He used to keep a small shop somewhere. In the old days. Used to be as fat as a priest. He ruined his business on account of a woman, and he came up here. Lost a bit of his paunch every year.

ANOTHER WOODCUTTER: Didn't he ever say anything about the woman?

THIRD WOODCUTTER: No. And I don't know that he wanted to go back. He saved quite a bit, but maybe that was because he was abstemious. Nobody tells the truth up here. It's better that way.

A WOODCUTTER: Last week he said he was going north this winter. It seems he had a cabin somewhere up there. Didn't he tell you where, elephant? *To Baal:* You were talking about it, weren't you?

BAAL: Leave me alone. I don't know anything.

THE PREVIOUS ONE: You wouldn't be thinking of moving in yourself, eh?

SECOND WOODCUTTER: You can't trust that one. Remember how he put our boots in the water that night, so we couldn't go to the forest the next day. Only because he was lazy as usual.

ANOTHER WOODCUTTER: He does nothing for his money.

BAAL: It's not a day for wrangling. Can't you spare a thought for poor Teddy?

A WOODCUTTER: Where were you when he packed in?
*Baal gets up, sways over the grass to Teddy. He sits there.*

THE PREVIOUS ONE: Look, he can't walk straight!

ANOTHER: Leave him alone! The elephant had a shock!

THE THIRD: Can't you keep it quiet just for today while he's lying there.

THE OTHER: What are you doing to Teddy, elephant?

BAAL *by the corpse:* Teddy is at peace, and we are the opposite. Both are good. The sky is black. The trees shudder. Somewhere clouds gather. That is the setting. One eats. After sleep one wakes. Not him. Us. And that's doubly good.

THE OTHER: What did you say the sky was like?

BAAL: The sky is black.

THE OTHER: You're not all there. The good ones always cop it first.

BAAL: How right you are, my dear chap!

A WOODCUTTER: It couldn't happen to Baal. He's never around where there's work.

BAAL: But Teddy, he was a hard worker. Teddy was generous. Teddy was friendly. One thing's certain: Teddy *was.*

THE SECOND: Wonder where he is now?

BAAL *points to the dead man:* There he is.

THE THIRD: I always get the feeling that the wind is made of dead souls, especially on spring evenings. But I get the feeling in autumn too.

BAAL: And in summer, in the sun, over the cornfields.

THE THIRD: That doesn't fit. It has to be dark.

BAAL: It has to be dark, Teddy.
*Silence.*

FOURTH WOODCUTTER: What are we going to do with him?

THE THIRD: He's got nobody who wants him.

THE OTHER: He was just on his own in the world.

A WOODCUTTER: What about his things?

THE THIRD: There isn't much. He carried his money off somewhere, to a bank. It'll stay there even if he doesn't turn up. Got any idea, Baal?

BAAL: He doesn't stink yet.

A WOODCUTTER: I've just had a good idea.

THE OTHER: Out with it!

THE MAN WITH THE IDEA: The elephant's not the only one with ideas, mate. What about drinking Teddy's good health?

BAAL: That's indecent, Bergmeier.

THE OTHERS: Rot, indecent. What shall we drink? Water? What a lousy idea!

THE MAN WITH THE IDEA: Gin!

BAAL: I vote in favour. Gin is decent. Whose gin?

THE MAN WITH THE IDEA: Teddy's gin.

THE OTHERS: Teddy's! – Sounds all right. – Teddy's ration! – Teddy was careful. – Not a bad idea for an idiot.

THE MAN WITH THE IDEA: A brainwave, what! Something for you blockheads! Teddy's gin at Teddy's funeral! Cheap and fitting! Anybody made a speech yet? Isn't that the proper thing to do?

BAAL: I did.

SOME: When?

BAAL: Earlier. Before you began to talk rubbish. It began with 'Teddy is at peace' . . . You don't notice anything until it's over.

THE OTHERS: Blockhead! Let's get the gin!

BAAL: It's a disgrace!

THE OTHERS: Oho! – Why, you big elephant.

BAAL: It's Teddy's property. The bottles must not be opened. Teddy's got a wife and five poor orphans.

A WOODCUTTER: Four! Four orphans!

ANOTHER: It's all coming out now.

BAAL: Do you want to drink the gin that belongs to Teddy's five poor orphans? Is that Christian?

THE PREVIOUS ONE: Four! Four orphans!

BAAL: Taking gin out of the mouths of Teddy's four orphans.

A WOODCUTTER: Teddy hasn't any family at all.

BAAL: But orphans, my friend, orphans.

ANOTHER: Do you think these orphans the elephant keeps

kidding you about are going to drink Teddy's gin? All right, it's Teddy's property . . .

BAAL *interrupts:* It was . . .

THE OTHER: What are you getting at?

A WOODCUTTER: He's jabbering. He's not all there.

THE OTHER: As I said, it was Teddy's property and so we'll pay for it. In cash. That'll fix the orphans.

EVERYBODY: A good suggestion. So much for the elephant. He must be mad, not to want any gin. Let's leave him and get Teddy's drink!

BAAL *calls after them:* Come back, you bloody scavengers! *To Teddy:* Poor Teddy! And the trees are pretty strong today and the air is good and soft, and I feel fortified within. Poor Teddy, don't you feel a tickle? You're through, I'm telling you, soon you'll stink, and everything will go on as before, the wind will blow, and I know where your cabin is, and your property will be taken over by the living, and you abandoned it and only wanted peace. Your body wasn't so bad, Teddy, it isn't so bad now, only a little damaged on one side and the legs . . . it would have finished you with women, you can't put that on top of a woman. *He lifts the dead man's leg.* With a bit more luck you could have gone on living, though, in that body, but your soul was too bloody choosy, the building was condemned, and the rats left the sinking ship. You were just a victim of your own habits, Teddy.

THE OTHERS *returning:* Hey, elephant! You're in for it! Where's the gin Teddy kept under his old bed? – Where were you when we were looking after Teddy? Teddy wasn't even dead then. – Where were you then, you son of a bitch, robbing the dead, protecting Teddy's poor orphans, eh?

BAAL: You've got no proof, my friends!

THE OTHERS: Where's the gin, then? In your esteemed opinion, did the bottle drink it? – This is a serious matter, old chap! – Stand up, you, get up! Walk in a straight line and then try and tell us it's the shock, it's because you're completely rotten, body and soul, you swine! – Get him on his legs! Liven him up, boys. Besmirching Teddy's poor old name! *They put Baal on his feet.*

BAAL: Bastards! Don't trample on poor Teddy! *He sits down and takes the arm of the corpse under his arm.* If you do anything to me, Teddy'll fall flat on his face. Is that piety? Anything I do will be in self-defence. There are seven of you, seven, and sober. And I'm on my own and drunk. Is that right, is that honourable? Seven against one! Calm down! Teddy's calmed down.

SOME *sad and indignant:* Nothing's sacred to him. – God forgive his drunken soul! – He's the blackest sinner on God's earth.

BAAL: Sit down, I don't like this preacher's cant. There are some with brains and some without. It makes for a better division of labour. Now you've seen for yourselves. I work with my brains. *He smokes.* You've always been too irreverent, friends! And what effect would it have if you sank that good gin? Me, I make discoveries, let me say. I was telling Teddy some most important things. *He takes papers from Teddy's jacket and looks at them.* But you had to run after that wretched gin. Sit down. Look at the sky growing dark between the trees. Is that nothing? There's no religion in your blood!


# A Hut

*You can hear the rain. Baal. Ekart.*


BAAL: This is the winter sleep of white bodies in the black mud.

EKART: You still haven't been to fetch the meat?

BAAL: You're working on your mass, I suppose?

EKART: Why worry about my mass? Worry about your woman! Where have you driven her to this time, in the rain?

BAAL: She runs after us like a mad woman and hangs round my neck.

EKART: You're sinking lower and lower.

BAAL: I'm too heavy.

EKART: You're not reckoning to peg out, I suppose?

BAAL: I'll fight it to the last ditch. I'll live without a skin. I'll retreat into my toes. I'll fall like a bull. On the grass, where it's softest. I'll swallow death and know nothing.

EKART: You've got fatter while we've been lying here.

BAAL *putting his right hand under his left armpit:* My shirt has got bigger. The dirtier it gets the bigger it gets. There's room for someone else, but no one fat. What are you lolling about for, you lazy bag of bones?

EKART: There's a kind of sky in my head, very green and vast, where my thoughts drift like featherweight clouds in the wind. They're completely undecided in their course. All that's inside me.

BAAL: It's delirium. You're an alcoholic. You see, it gets you in the end.

EKART: When I'm delirious I can feel it by my face.

BAAL: Your face has room for the four winds. Concave! *He looks at him.* You haven't a face. You're nothing. You're transparent.

EKART: I'm growing more and more mathematical.

BAAL: Nobody knows your history. Why don't you ever talk about yourself?

EKART: I shan't ever have one. Who's that outside?

BAAL: You've got a good ear! There's something in you that you hide. You're a bad man, like me, a devil. But one day you'll see rats. Then you'll be a good man again.
*Sophie at the door.*

EKART: Is that you, Sophie?

BAAL: What do you want this time?

SOPHIE: May I come in now, Baal?

# A Plain. Sky

*Evening. Baal, Ekart, Sophie.*

SOPHIE: My knees are giving way. Why are you running like
a mad man?

BAAL: Because you're hanging round my neck like a mill-
stone.

EKART: How can you treat her like this? You made her
pregnant.

SOPHIE: I wanted it, Ekart.

BAAL: She wanted it, and now she's hanging round my neck.

EKART: You behave like an animal! Sit down, Sophie.

SOPHIE *sits down heavily:* Let him go.

EKART: If you throw her out I'll stay with her.

BAAL: She won't stay with you. But you'd desert me!
Because of her? That's like you.

EKART: Twice you took my place in bed. You didn't want
my women. They left you cold, but you stole them from
me although I loved them.

BAAL: Because you loved them. Twice I defiled corpses to
keep you clean. I need that. God knows, it gave me no
pleasure.

EKART *to Sophie:* Are you still in love with this depraved
animal?

SOPHIE: I can't help it, Ekart. I'd love his corpse. I even love
his fists. I can't help it, Ekart.

BAAL: Don't ever tell me what you two were up to while I
was inside!

SOPHIE: We stood together in front of the white prison wall
and looked up at your window.

BAAL: You were together.

SOPHIE: Beat me for it.

EKART *shouts:* Didn't you throw her at me?

BAAL: You might have been stolen from me.

EKART: I haven't got your elephant's hide.

BAAL: I love you for it.

EKART: Keep your damned mouth shut about it while she's still with us!

BAAL: Tell her to get lost! She's turning into a bitch! *He puts his hands up to his throat.* She's washing her dirty laundry in your tears. Can you still not see that she's running naked between us? I have the patience of a lamb, but I can't change my skin.

EKART *sits down beside Sophie:* Go home to your mother.

SOPHIE: I can't.

BAAL: She can't, Ekart.

SOPHIE: Beat me if you want, Baal. I won't ask you to walk slowly again. I didn't mean to. Let me keep up with you, as long as I can. Then I'll lie down in the bushes and you needn't look. Don't drive me away, Baal.

BAAL: Throw your fat body into the river. I'm sick of you, and it's your own doing.

SOPHIE: Do you want to leave me here or don't you? You're still uncertain, Baal. You're like a child, to talk like that.

BAAL: I'm fed to the teeth with you.

SOPHIE: But not at night, Baal, not at night! I'm afraid alone. I'm afraid of the dark. I'm frightened of it.

BAAL: In your condition? No one will touch you.

SOPHIE: But tonight! Just wait both of you tonight.

BAAL: Go to the bargemen! It's midsummer night. They'll be drunk.

SOPHIE: A few minutes!

BAAL: Come on, Ekart!

SOPHIE: Where shall I go?

BAAL: To heaven, darling!

SOPHIE: With my child?

BAAL: Bury it.

SOPHIE: I pray that you'll never have cause to remember what you've just said to me, under this beautiful sky you love. I pray for it on my knees.

EKART: I'll stay with you. And then I'll take you to your mother, if you say you'll stop loving this swine.

BAAL: She loves me.

SOPHIE: I love him.

EKART: Are you still on your feet, you swine! Haven't you got knees? Are you besotted with drink or poetry? Depraved swine! Depraved swine!

BAAL: Simpleton.

*Ekart attacks him, they fight.*

SOPHIE: Mother of God! They're like wild animals!

EKART *fighting:* Did you hear what she said? Back there! And it's getting dark now. Depraved animal! Depraved animal!

BAAL *against him, pressing Ekart to himself:* Now you're close to me. Can you smell me? Now I'm holding you. There's more than the closeness of women. *He stops.* Look, you can see the stars above the trees now, Ekart.

EKART *looks hard at Baal, who gazes up into the sky:* I can't strike this thing!

BAAL *his arm round Ekart:* It's getting dark. We must find a place for the night. There are hollows in the wood where the wind never penetrates. Come, I'll tell you about the animals. *He draws him away.*

SOPHIE *alone in the dark, screams:* Baal!


## Brown Wooden Bar

*Night. Wind. At tables, Gougou, Bolleboll. The old beggar and Maja with a child in a box.*

BOLLEBOLL *playing cards with Gougou:* I've no more money. Let's play for our souls.

THE BEGGAR: Brother wind wants to come in. But we don't know our cold brother wind. Heh, heh, heh!

*The child cries.*

MAJA *the beggar woman:* Listen! Something's prowling round the house. Pray God it's no wild beast!

BOLLEBOLL: Why? Are you feeling randy again?

*Knocking at the door.*

MAJA: Listen! I won't open.

THE BEGGAR: You will open.

MAJA: No, no, Mother of God, no!

THE BEGGAR: Bouque la Madonne! Open up!

MAJA *crawls to the door:* Who's outside?
  *The child cries. Maja opens the door.*

BAAL *enters with Ekart, soaked to the skin:* Is this where they look after the sick?

MAJA: Yes, but there's no bed free. *More insolently:* And I'm ill.

BAAL: We've brought champagne. *Ekart has gone to warm himself by the stove.*

BOLLEBOLL: Come here! The man who knows what champagne is, is good enough for us.

THE BEGGAR: There's high society here today, my boy!

BAAL *goes up to the table and pulls two bottles from his pocket:* Mmm?

THE BEGGAR: That's fishy.

BOLLEBOLL: I know where you got that champagne. But I won't give you away.

BAAL: Here, Ekart! Any glasses?

MAJA: Cups, kind gentlemen. Cups. *She brings some.*

GOUGOU: I need a cup of my own.

BAAL *doubtful:* Are you allowed to drink champagne?

GOUGOU: Please! *Baal pours him some.*

BAAL: What's wrong with you?

GOUGOU: Bronchitis. Nothing bad. A little inflammation. Nothing serious.

BAAL *to Bolleboll:* And you?

BOLLEBOLL: Stomach ulcers. Won't kill me!

BAAL *to the beggar:* There's something wrong with you too, I trust?

THE BEGGAR: I'm mad.

BAAL: Here's to you! We understand each other. I'm healthy.

THE BEGGAR: I knew a man who said he was healthy too. He believed it. He came from the forest and one day he went back there as there was something he had to think over. He found the forest very strange and no longer familiar, he walked for many days. Always deeper into the forest, because he wanted to see how independent he was and how much endurance there was left in him. But there wasn't much. *He drinks.*

BAAL *uneasy:* What a wind! We have to move on tonight, Ekart.

THE BEGGAR: Yes, the wind. One evening, at sunset, when he was no longer alone, he went through the great stillness between the trees and stood beneath one of the highest. *Drinks.*

BOLLEBOLL: That was the ape in him.

THE BEGGAR: Yes, perhaps it was the ape. He leant against it, very closely, and felt the life in it, or thought so. And he said, you are higher than I am and stand firm and you know the earth beneath you, and it holds you. I can run and move better, but I do not stand firm and I do not reach into the depths of the earth and nothing holds me up. Nor do I know the quiet of the endless sky above the still tree-tops. *He drinks.*

GOUGOU: What did the tree say?

THE BEGGAR: Yes. And the wind blew. A shudder ran through the tree. And the man felt it. He threw himself down on the ground and he clutched the wild, hard roots and cried bitterly. But he did it to many trees.

EKART: Did it cure him?

THE BEGGAR: No. He had an easier death, though.

MAJA: I don't understand that.

THE BEGGAR: Nothing is understood. But some things are felt. If one understands a story it's just that it's been told badly.

BOLLEBOLL: Do you believe in God?

BAAL *with an effort:* I've always believed in myself. But a man *could* turn atheist.

BOLLEBOLL *laughs loudly:* Now I feel happy. God! Champagne! Love! Wind and rain! *He reaches for Maja.*

MAJA: Leave me alone. Your breath stinks.

BOLLEBOLL: And I suppose you haven't got the pox? *He takes her on his lap.*

THE BEGGAR: Watch it! *To Bolleboll:* I'm getting drunker and drunker. If I get completely drunk you can't go out in the rain tonight.

GOUGOU *to Ekart:* He used to be better looking, that's how he got her.

EKART: What about your intellectual superiority? Your psychic ascendancy?

GOUGOU: She wasn't like that. She was completely innocent.

EKART: And what did you do?

GOUGOU: I was ashamed.

BOLLEBOLL: Listen! The wind. It's asking God for peace.

MAJA *sings:*

Lullaby baby, away from the storm
Here we are sheltered and drunken and warm.

BAAL: Whose child is that?

MAJA: My daughter, sir.

THE BEGGAR: A virgo dolorosa.

BAAL *drinks:* That's how it used to be, Ekart. And it was all right too.

EKART: What?

BOLLEBOLL: He's forgotten what.

BAAL: Used to be! That's a strange phrase!

GOUGOU *to Ekart:* The best of all is nothingness.

BOLLEBOLL: Pst! We're going to have Gougou's aria. A song from the old bag of worms.

GOUGOU: It's as if the air was quivering on a summer evening. Sunshine. But it isn't quivering. Nothing. Nothing at all. You just stop. The wind blows, and you don't feel cold. It rains, and you don't get wet. Funny things happen, and you don't laugh with the others. You rot, and you don't need to wait. General strike.

THE BEGGAR: That's Hell's Paradise.

GOUGOU: Yes, that's paradise. No wish unfulfilled. You have none left. You learn to abandon all your habits. Even wishing. That's how you become free.

MAJA: What happened in the end?

GOUGOU *grins:* Nothing. Nothing at all. There is no end. Nothingness lasts for ever.

BOLLEBOLL: Amen.

BAAL *gets up, to Ekart:* Ekart, get up. We've fallen among murderers. *He supports himself by putting his arm round Ekart's shoulders.* The vermin multiply. The rot sets in. The maggots sing and show off.

EKART: It's the second time that's happened to you. I wonder if it's just the drink.

BAAL: My guts are hanging out . . . this is no mud bath.

EKART: Sit down. Get drunk. Warm yourself.

MAJA *drunk, sings:*

Summer and winter and snowstorms and rain
If we aren't sober we won't feel the pain.

BOLLEBOLL *takes hold of Maja and pummels her:* Your aria tickles me, little Gougou. Itsiwitsi, little Maja.
*The child cries.*

BAAL *drinks:* Who are you? *Amused, to Gougou:* Your name's bag of worms. Are you a candidate for the mortuary? Your health! *He sits down.*

THE BEGGAR: Watch out, Bolleboll! Champagne doesn't agree with me.

MAJA *hanging on to Bolleboll, sings:*

Seeing is suffering, keep your eyes shut
All go to sleep now, and nothing will hurt.

BAAL *brutally:*

Float down the river with rats in your hair
Everything's lovely, the sky is still there.

*He gets up, glass in hand.* The sky is black! Did that scare you? *Drums on the table.* You have to stand the roundabout. It's wonderful. *He sways.* I want to be an elephant in a circus and pee when things go wrong . . . *He begins to dance and sing.* Dance with the wind, poor corpse! Sleep with a cloud, you degenerate God! *He goes up to the table, swaying.*

EKART *gets up, drunk:* I'm not going with you any farther. I've got a soul too. You corrupted my soul. You corrupt everything. And then I shall start on my Mass again.

BAAL: Your health! I love you.

EKART: But I'm not going with you any farther. *He sits down.*

THE BEGGAR *to Bolleboll:* Hands off, you pig!

MAJA: What's it got to do with you?

THE BEGGAR: Shut up, you poor thing!

MAJA: You're raving!

BOLLEBOLL *venomously:* He's a fraud. There's nothing wrong with him. That's right. It's all a fraud!

THE BEGGAR: And you've got cancer.

BOLLEBOLL *uncannily quiet:* I've got cancer?

THE BEGGAR *turning coward:* I didn't say anything. Leave her alone! *Maja laughs.*

BAAL: Why's it crying? *Sways to the box.*

THE BEGGAR *angry:* What do you want?

BAAL *leans over the box:* Why are you crying? Have you never seen them at it before? Or do you cry every time?

THE BEGGAR: Leave it alone, you! *He throws his glass at Baal.*

MAJA: You pig!

BOLLEBOLL: He's only having a peep under her skirt!

BAAL *gets up slowly:* Oh you swine! You don't know what's human any more. Come on, Ekart! We'll wash ourselves in the river. *He leaves with Ekart.*

# Green Thicket. River Beyond

*Baal. Ekart.*

BAAL *sitting in the thicket:* The water's warm. You can lie like
  a crab on the sand. And the shrubs and white clouds in the
  sky. Ekart!
EKART *concealed:* What do you want?
BAAL: I love you.
EKART: I'm too comfortable here.
BAAL: Did you see the clouds earlier?
EKART: Yes, they're shameless. *Silence.* A while ago a woman
  went by on the other side.
BAAL: I don't care for women any longer . . .

# Country Road. Willows

*Wind. Night. Ekart asleep in the grass. Baal comes across the fields
as if drunk, his clothes open, like a sleepwalker.*

BAAL: Ekart! Ekart! I've got it! Wake up!
EKART: What's the matter? Are you talking in your sleep
  again?
BAAL *sits down by him:* This:

When she had drowned, and started her slow descent
Down the streams to where the rivers broaden
The opal sky shone most magnificent
As if it had to be her body's guardian.

Wrack and seaweed cling to her as she swims
Slowly their burden adds to her weight.
Coolly fishes play about her limbs
Creatures and growths encumber her in her final state.

And in the evening the sky grew dark as smoke
And at night the stars kept the light still soaring.
But soon it cleared as dawn again broke
To preserve her sequence of evening and morning.

As her pale body decayed in the water there
It happened (very slowly) that God gradually forgot it
First her face, then the hands, and right at the last her hair
Then she rotted in rivers where much else rotted.

*The wind.*

EKART: Has the ghost risen? It's not as wicked as you. Now
   sleep's gone to the devil and the wind is groaning in the
   willows like an organ. Nothing left but the white breast of
   philosophy, darkness, cold, and rain right up to our
   blessed end, and even for old women nothing left but their
   second sight.

BAAL: You don't need gin to be drunk in this wind. I see the
   world in a soft light: it is the excrement of the Almighty.

EKART: The Almighty, who made himself known once and
   for all through the association of the urinary passage with
   the sexual organ.

BAAL *lying down:* It's all so beautiful.
*Wind.*

EKART: The willows are like rotten teeth in the black mouth
   of the sky. I shall start work on my Mass soon.

BAAL: Is the quartet finished?

EKART: When did I have the time?
*Wind.*

BAAL: It's that redhead, the pale one, that you drag everywhere.

EKART: She has a soft white body, and at noon she brings it
   with her under the willows. They've drooping branches
   like hair, behind which we fuck like squirrels.

BAAL: Is she more beautiful than me?
*Darkness. The wind blows on.*

## Young Hazel Shrubs

*Long red switches hanging down. In the middle of them, Baal, sitting.
Noon.*

BAAL: I'll satisfy her, the white dove . . . *He looks at the place.*
You get a good view of the clouds here through the willow
. . . when he comes there'll only be skin left. I'm sick of his
love affairs. Be calm!
*A young woman comes out of the thicket. Red hair, a full figure.*
BAAL *without looking round:* Is that you?
THE YOUNG WOMAN: Where's your friend?
BAAL: He's doing a Mass in E flat minor.
THE YOUNG WOMAN: Tell him I was here.
BAAL: He's too thin. He's transparent. He defiles himself.
He's regressing into zoology. Do sit down! *He looks round.*
THE YOUNG WOMAN: I prefer to stand.
BAAL: He's been eating too many eggs lately. *He pulls himself
up by the red switches.*
THE YOUNG WOMAN: I love him.
BAAL: You're no concern of mine. *He takes her in his arms.*
THE YOUNG WOMAN: Don't touch me! You're too dirty!
BAAL *slowly reaches for her throat:* Is that your throat? Do you
know how they put down pigeons, or wild ducks in the
wood?
THE YOUNG WOMAN: Mother of God! Leave me alone! *She
struggles.*
BAAL: With your weak knees? You're falling over already.
You want to be laid in the willows. A man's a man, in this
respect most of them are equal. *He takes her in his arms.*
THE YOUNG WOMAN *shaking:* Please, let me go!
BAAL: A shameless bird! I'll have it. Act of rescue by
desperate man! *He takes her by both arms and drags her into the
thicket.*

## Maple Trees in the Wind

*Clouded sky. Baal and Ekart, sitting among the roots.*

BAAL: Drink's needed, Ekart. Any money left?
EKART: No. Look at the maple in the wind!
BAAL: It's trembling.
EKART: Where's that girl you used to go around the bars with?
BAAL: Turn into a fish and look for her.
EKART: You overeat, Baal. You'll burst.
BAAL: I'd like to hear the bang.
EKART: Do you ever look into water when it's black and deep and got no fish in it? Don't ever fall in. Watch out for yourself. You're so very heavy, Baal.
BAAL: I'll watch out for somebody else. I've written a song. Do you want to hear it?
EKART: Read it, then I'll know you.
BAAL: It's called Death in the Forest.

And a man died deep in the primaeval woods
While the storm blew in torrents around him –
Died like an animal scrabbling for roots
Stared up through the trees, as the wind skimmed the woods
And the roar of the thunderclap drowned him.

Several of them stood to watch him go
And they strove to make his passage smoother
Telling him: We'll take you home now, brother.
But he forced them from him with a blow
Spat, and cried: and where's my home, d'you know?
That was home, and he had got no other.

Is your toothless mouth choking with pus?
How's the rest of you: can you still tell?
Must you die so slowly and with so much fuss?
We've just had your horse chopped into steaks for us.
Hurry up! They're waiting down in hell.

Then the forest roared above their head
And they watched him clasp a tree and stagger
And they heard his screams and what he said.
Each man felt an overwhelming dread
Clenched his fist or, trembling, drew his dagger:
So like them, and yet so nearly dead!

You're foul, useless, mad, you mangy bear!
You're a sore, a chancre, filthy creature!
Selfish beast, you're breathing up our air!
So they said. And he, the cancer there:
Let me live! Your sun was never sweeter!
– Ride off in the light without a care!

That's what none of them could understand:
How the horror numbed and made them shiver.
There's the earth holding his naked hand.
In the breeze from sea to sea lies land:
Here I lie in solitude for ever.

Yes, mere life, with its abundant weight
Pinned him so that even half-decayed
He pressed his dead body ever deeper.
At dawn he fell dead in the grassy shade.
Numb with shock, they buried him, and cold with hate
Covered him with undergrowth and creeper.

Then they rode in silence from that place
Turning round to see the tree again
Under which his body once had lain
Who felt dying was too sharp a pain:
The tree stood in the sun ablaze.
Each made the mark of the cross on his face
And rode off swiftly over the plain.

EKART: Well, well! I suppose it's come to that now.
BAAL: When I can't sleep at night I look up at the stars. It's
just as good.

EKART: Is it?

BAAL *suspiciously:* But I don't do it often. It makes you weak.

EKART *after a pause:* You've made up a lot of poetry recently. You haven't had a woman for a long time, have you?

BAAL: Why?

EKART: I was thinking. Say no.

*Baal gets up, stretches, looks at the top of the maple and laughs.*


# Inn

*Evening. Ekart. The waitress. Watzmann. Johannes, in a shabby coat with a turned-up collar, hopelessly gone to seed. The waitress has the features of Sophie.*


EKART: It's been eight years.

*They drink. Wind.*

JOHANNES: They say life only begins at twenty-five. That's when they get broader and have children.

*Silence.*

WATZMANN: His mother died yesterday. So he runs around trying to borrow money for the funeral. When he gets it he comes here. Then we can pay for the drinks. The landlord's a good man. He gives credit on a corpse which was a mother. *Drinks.*

JOHANNES: Baal! There's no wind left in his sails.

WATZMANN *to Ekart:* You must have to put up with a lot from him?

EKART: One can't spit in his face. The man's done for.

WATZMANN *to Johannes:* Does it distress you? Do you think about it?

JOHANNES: It's a waste of a man, I tell you. *Drinks.*

*Silence.*

WATZMANN: He's getting more and more disgusting.

EKART: Don't say that. I don't want to hear it. I love him. I don't resent him, because I love him. He's a child.

WATZMANN: He only does what he has to. Because he's so lazy.

EKART *goes to the door:* It's a mild night. The wind's warm. Like milk. I love all this. One should never drink. Or not so much. *Back to the table:* It's a mild night. Now and for another three weeks into the autumn a man can live on the road all right. *He sits down.*

WATZMANN: Do you want to leave tonight? You'd like to get rid of him, I suppose? He's a burden.

JOHANNES: You'd better be careful.

*Baal enters slowly.*

WATZMANN: Is that you, Baal?

EKART *hard:* What do you want now?

BAAL *enters, sits down:* What a miserable hole this place has turned into! *The waitress brings drink.*

WATZMANN: Nothing's changed here. Only you, it would appear, have got more refined.

BAAL: Is that still you, Luise?

*Silence.*

JOHANNES: Yes, it's agreeable here. – I have to drink, you see, drink a lot. It makes one strong. Even then one makes one's way to hell along a path of razors. But not in the same way. As if your legs were giving way under you, yielding, you know. So that you don't feel the razors at all. With springy loose joints. Besides, I never used to have ideas of this sort, really peculiar ones. Not while everything went well, when I lived a good bourgeois life. But now I have ideas, now that I've turned into a genius. Hm.

EKART *bursting out:* I'd like to be back in the forest, at dawn! The light between the trees is the colour of lemons! I want to go back up into the forest.

JOHANNES: That's something I don't understand, you must buy me another drink, Baal. It's really agreeable here.

BAAL: A gin for —

JOHANNES: No names! We know each other. I have such fearful dreams at night, you know, now and then. But only now and then. It really is agreeable here.

*The wind. They drink.*

WATZMANN *hums:*

The trees come in avalanches
Each very conveniently made.
You can hang yourself from their branches
Or loll underneath in their shade.

BAAL: Where was it like that? It was like that once.

JOHANNES: She's still afloat, you see. Nobody's found her. But sometimes I get a feeling she's being washed down my throat with all the drink, a very small corpse, half rotted. And she was already seventeen. Now there are rats and weed in her green hair, rather becoming . . . a little swollen and whitish, and filled with the stinking ooze from the river, completely black. She was always so clean. That's why she went into the river and began to stink.

WATZMANN: What is flesh? It decays just like the spirit. Gentlemen, I am completely drunk. Twice two is four. Therefore I am not drunk. But I have intimations of a higher world. Bow! . . . be hup! . . . humble! Put the old Adam aside! *Drinks heavily and shakily.* I've not reached rock bottom yet, not while I have my intimations, not while I can add up properly that twice two . . . What is this thing called two? Two – oo, curious word! Two! *Sits down. Baal reaches for his guitar and smashes the light with it.*

BAAL: Now I'll sing. *Sings:*

Sick from the sun, and eaten raw by the weather
A looted wreath crowning his tangled head
He called back the dreams of a childhood he had lost altogether
Forgot the roof, but never the sky overhead.

*Then speaks:* My voice is not entirely clear as a bell. *Tunes the guitar.*

EKART: Go on singing, Baal.

BAAL *goes on singing:*

O you whose life it has been always to suffer
You murderers they threw out from heaven and hell
Why did you not stay in the arms of your mother
Where it was quiet, and you slept, and all was well?

*Speaks.* The guitar's not in tune either.

WATZMANN: A good song. Very apt in my case. Romantic.

BAAL *goes on singing:*

Still he explores and scans the absinthe-green ocean
Though his mother give him up for lost
Grinning and cursing, or weeping at times with contrition
Always in search of that land where life is best.

WATZMANN: I can't find my glass. The table's rocking stupidly. Put the light on. How's a man to find his mouth?

EKART: Idiot! Can you see anything, Baal?

BAAL: No. I don't want to. It's good in the dark. With champagne in the blood and homesickness without memory. Are you my friend Ekart?

EKART *with an effort:* Yes, but sing!

BAAL *sings:*

Loafing through hells and flogged through paradises
Calm and grinning, with expressionless stare
Sometimes he dreams of a small field he recognizes
With blue sky overhead and nothing more.

JOHANNES: I'll always stay with you. You could take me with you. I hardly ever eat.

WATZMANN *has lit the lamp, with an effort:* Let there be light. Heh heh heh heh.

BAAL: It's blinding. *Gets up.*

*Ekart, with the waitress on his lap, gets up with an effort and tries to take her arm from his neck.*

EKART: What's the matter? This is nothing. It's ridiculous.

*Baal gets ready to leap.*

EKART: You're not jealous of her?
*Baal gropes, a glass falls to the floor.*
EKART: Why shouldn't I have women?
*Baal looks at him.*
EKART: Am I your lover?
*Baal throws himself at him, chokes him.*
*The light goes out. Watzmann laughs drunkenly, the waitress screams. Other guests from the adjoining room enter with a lamp.*
WATZMANN: He's got a knife.
THE WAITRESS: He's killing him. Oh God!
TWO MEN *hurl themselves on the wrestlers:* Blast you, man! Let go! – He's stabbed him! God Almighty!
*Baal gets up. Sunset suddenly bursts into the room. The lamp goes out.*
BAAL: Ekart!

## 10° E. of Greenwich

*Forest. Baal with guitar, his hands in his pockets, walks off into the distance.*

BAAL: The pale wind in the black trees! They're like Lupu's wet hair. At eleven the moon'll rise. It'll be light enough then. This is a small wood. I'll go where there are forests. I can move now that I'm on my own again. I must bear north. Follow the ribbed side of the leaves. I'll have to shrug off that little matter. Forward! *Sings:*

Baal will watch the vultures in the star-shot sky
Hovering patiently to see when Baal will die.

*Disappearing.*

Sometimes Baal shams dead. The vultures swoop.
Baal, without a word, will dine on vulture soup.

*Gust of wind.*

# A Country Road

*Evening. Wind. Rain. Two policemen struggle against the wind.*

FIRST POLICEMAN: The black rain and this wailing wind!
The bloody tramp!

SECOND POLICEMAN: It seems to me he keeps moving
northwards towards the forests. It'll be impossible to find
him there.

FIRST POLICEMAN: What is he?

SECOND POLICEMAN: Above all, a murderer. Before that,
revue actor and poet. Then roundabout proprietor, woods-
man, lover of a millionairess, convict and pimp. When he
did the murder they caught him, but he's got the strength of
an elephant. It was because of a waitress, a registered
whore. He knifed his best and oldest friend because of her.

FIRST POLICEMAN: A man like that has no soul. He belongs
to the beasts.

SECOND POLICEMAN: And he's childish too. He carries
wood for old women, and nearly gets caught. He never had
anything. Except for the waitress. That must have been
why he killed his friend, another dubious character.

FIRST POLICEMAN: If only we could get some gin somewhere or a woman! Let's go! It's eerie. And there's something moving over there. *Both go.*

BAAL *comes out of the undergrowth with rucksack and guitar. He
whistles through his teeth:* So he's dead? Poor little animal!
Getting in my way. Now things are getting interesting. *He
follows the men.*
*Wind.*

## Hut in the Forest

*Night. Wind. Baal on a dirty bed. Men at cards and drink.*

A MAN *by Baal:* What do you want? You're at your last gasp.
A child could see that. And who's going to look after you?
Have you got anyone? That's it! That's it! Grit your teeth!
Got any teeth left? Now and then it even gets the ones that
could go on enjoying themselves, millionaires! But you
don't even have any papers. Don't you be afraid, the
world'll keep rolling, round as a ball, tomorrow morning
the wind'll whistle. See the situation in a more reasonable
light. Tell yourself it's a rat that's on the way out. That's it!
Don't move! You've no teeth left.

THE MEN: Is it still pissing? We'll have to spend the night
with the corpse. – Shut your mouth! Trumped! – Got any
breath left, fatty? Sing us a song! 'Baal grew up within
the . . .' – Let him be! He'll be a cold man before the black
rain's stopped. On with the game! – He drank like a sieve
but there's something about that pale hunk that makes you
think about yourself. That's something he didn't have
crooned over his cradle. – Ten of clubs! Keep your cards
up, please! That's no way to play; if you're not going to be
serious, you can't get a good game going.

*Silence, except for a few curses.*

BAAL: What's the time?

ONE OF THE MEN: Eleven. Are you going?

BAAL: Soon. Are the roads bad?

THE MAN: Rain.

THE MEN *getting up:* It's stopped raining. Time to· go. –
Everything'll be soaking wet. – Another excuse for him to
do nothing.

*They pick up the axes.*

A MAN *stops in front of Baal and spits:* Good night and good-
bye. Have you had it?

ANOTHER MAN: Are you on the way out? Incognito?

A THIRD MAN: Arrange your smelly periods better tomorrow, if you don't mind. We'll be working till twelve
and then we want to eat.

BAAL: Can't you stay a little longer?

ALL *amid loud laughter:* Do you want us to play mother? – Do
you want to sing us your swan song? – Do you want to confess, you old soak? – Can't you throw up on your own?

BAAL: If you could stay half an hour.

ALL *amid loud laughter:* You know what? Snuff out on your
own! – Let's get moving! The wind's died down. – What's
the matter?

THE MAN: I'll follow.

BAAL: It can't last much longer, gentlemen. *Laughter.* You
won't like dying on your own, gentlemen! *Laughter.*

ANOTHER MAN: Old woman! Here's a souvenir! *Spits in his
face.*

*They go.*

BAAL: Twenty minutes.

*The men leave by the open door.*

THE MAN *in the door:* Stars.

BAAL: Wipe the spit away!

THE MAN *to him:* Where?

BAAL: On my forehead.

THE MAN: Done! What are you laughing at?

BAAL: I like the taste.

THE MAN *indignant:* You're done for. Good-bye! *With his axe
to the door.*

BAAL: Thanks.

THE MAN: Is there anything else . . . but I have to go to work.
Jesus. Corpses!

BAAL: You! Come closer! *The man bends down.* It was very
beautiful . . .

THE MAN: What was, you crazy hen? I nearly said capon.

BAAL: Everything.

THE MAN: Snob! *Laughs loudly, goes, the door remains open, one
sees the blue night.*

BAAL *uneasy:* You! You there!

THE MAN *at the window* : Mmmm?

BAAL: Are you going?

THE MAN: To work.

BAAL: Where?

THE MAN: What's that got to do with you?

BAAL: What's the time?

THE MAN: A quarter past eleven. *Goes*.

BAAL: He's gone.

> *Silence*.

Mother! Tell Ekart to go away, the sky's so damned near too, you can touch it, everything's soaking wet again. Sleep. One. Two. Three. Four. It's suffocating in here. It must be light outside. I want to go out. *Raises himself*. I will go out. Dear Baal. *Sharply*. I'm not a rat. It must be light outside. Dear Baal. You can get to the door. You've still got knees, it's better in the door. Damn it! Dear Baal! *He crawls on all fours to the threshold*. Stars ... mmm. *He crawls out*.


# Early Morning in the Forest

*Woodcutters*.


A WOODCUTTER: Give me the bottle! Listen to the birds!

ANOTHER: It'll be a hot day.

A THIRD: There's plenty of trees left standing that'll have to be down before nightfall.

A FOURTH: He'll be cold by now.

THE THIRD: Yes. Yes. He'll be cold by now.

THE SECOND: Yes. Yes.

THE THIRD: We could have had the eggs now if he hadn't eaten them all. There's a man for you, stealing eggs on his deathbed. First he kept moaning at me, I got sick of that. He never got a whiff of the bottle in all three days, thank God. It's inconsiderate. Eggs in a corpse.

THE FIRST: He had a way of laying himself down in the dirt,

and then he never got up again, and he knew it. It was like a
ready-made bed to him. He lay down carefully. Did anybody know him? What's his name? What did he do?

THE FOURTH: We'll have to bury him, anyway. Give me the
bottle!

THE THIRD: I asked him, as the death-rattle was in his
throat, what are you thinking about? I always want to
know what goes on in a man's head then. I'm still listening
to the rain, he said. I went cold all over. I'm still listening to
the rain, he said.

The Threepenny Opera

*after John Gay*: The Beggar's Opera

*Collaborators:* ELISABETH HAUPTMANN, KURT WEILL

*Translators:* RALPH MANHEIM, JOHN WILLETT

*Characters*
MACHEATH, *called Mac the Knife*
JONATHAN JEREMIAH PEACHUM, *proprietor of the Beggar's Friend Ltd*
CELIA PEACHUM, *his wife*
POLLY PEACHUM, *his daughter*
BROWN, *High Sheriff of London*
LUCY, *his daughter*
LOW-DIVE JENNY
SMITH
THE REVEREND KIMBALL
FILCH
A BALLAD SINGER
THE GANG
Beggars
Whores
Constables

# PROLOGUE

## The Ballad of Mac the Knife

*Fair in Soho.*

*The beggars are begging, the thieves are stealing, the whores are whoring. A ballad singer sings a ballad.*

See the shark with teeth like razors.
All can read his open face.
And Macheath has got a knife, but
Not in such an obvious place.

See the shark, how red his fins are
As he slashes at his prey.
Mac the Knife wears white kid gloves which
Give the minimum away.

By the Thames's turbid waters
Men abruptly tumble down.
Is it plague or is it cholera?
Or a sign Macheath's in town?

On a beautiful blue Sunday
See a corpse stretched in the Strand.
See a man dodge round the corner . . .
Mackie's friends will understand.

And Schmul Meier, reported missing
Like so many wealthy men:
Mac the Knife acquired his cash box.
God alone knows how or when.

*Peachum goes walking across the stage from left to right with his wife and daughter.*

Jenny Towler turned up lately
With a knife stuck through her breast
While Macheath walks the Embankment
Nonchalantly unimpressed.

Where is Alfred Gleet the cabman?
Who can get that story clear?
All the world may know the answer
Just Macheath has no idea.

And the ghastly fire in Soho –
Seven children at a go –
In the crowd stands Mac the Knife, but he
Isn't asked and doesn't know.

And the child-bride in her nightie
Whose assailant's still at large
Violated in her slumbers –
Mackie, how much did you charge?

*Laughter among the whores. A man steps out from their midst and walks quickly away across the square.*

LOW-DIVE JENNY: That was Mac the Knife!

# ACT ONE

I

To combat the increasing callousness of mankind, J. Peachum, a man of business, has opened a shop where the poorest of the poor can acquire an exterior that will touch the hardest of hearts.

*Jonathan Jeremiah Peacham's outfitting shop for beggars.*

### PEACHUM'S MORNING HYMN

You ramshackle Christian, awake!
Get on with your sinful employment
Show what a good crook you could make.
The Lord will cut short your enjoyment.

Betray your own brother, you rogue
And sell your old woman, you rat.
You think the Lord God's just a joke?
He'll give you His Judgement on that.

PEACHUM *to the audience:* Something new is needed. My business is too hard, for my business is arousing human sympathy. There are a few things that stir men's souls, just a few, but the trouble is that after repeated use they lose their effect. Because man has the abominable gift of being able to deaden his feelings at will, so to speak. Suppose, for instance, a man sees another man standing on the corner with a stump for an arm; the first time he may be shocked enough to give him tenpence, but the second time it will only be fivepence, and if he sees him a third time he'll hand him over to the police without batting an eyelash. It's the same with the spiritual approach. *A large sign saying 'It is more blessed to give than to receive' is lowered from the grid.* What good are the most beautiful, the most poignant sayings, painted on the most enticing little signs, when they get expended so quickly? The Bible has four or five sayings that stir the heart; once a man has expended them, there's nothing for it but starvation. Take this one, for instance – 'Give and it shall be given unto you' – how threadbare it is after hanging here a mere three weeks. Yes, you have to keep on offering something new. So it's back to the good old Bible again, but how long can it go on providing? *Knocking. Peachum opens. Enter a young man by the name of Filch.*

FILCH: Messrs Peachum & Co.?

PEACHUM: Peachum.

FILCH: Are you the proprietor of The Beggar's Friend Ltd.? I've been sent to you. Fine slogans you've got there! Money in the bank, those are. Got a whole library full of them, I suppose? That's what I call really something. What chance has a bloke like me got to think up ideas like that; and how can business progress without education?

PEACHUM: What's your name?

FILCH: It's this way, Mr Peachum, I've been down on my luck since a boy. Mother drank, father gambled. Left to my own resources at an early age, without a mother's tender hand, I sank deeper and deeper into the quicksands of the big city. I've never known a father's care or the blessings of a happy home. So now you see me . . .

PEACHUM: So now I see you . . .

FILCH *confused:* . . . bereft of all support, a prey to my baser instincts.

PEACHUM: Like a derelict on the high seas and so on. Now tell me, derelict, which district have you been reciting that fairy story in?

FILCH: What do you mean, Mr Peachum?

PEACHUM: You deliver that speech in public, I take it?

FILCH: Well, it's this way, Mr Peachum, yesterday there was an unpleasant little incident in Highland Street. There I am, standing on the corner quiet and miserable, holding out my hat, no suspicion of anything nasty . . .

PEACHUM *leafs through a notebook:* Highland Street. Yes, yes, right. You're the bastard that Honey and Sam caught yesterday. You had the impudence to be molesting passers-by in District 10. We let you off with a thrashing because we had reason to believe you didn't know what's what. But if you show your face again it'll be the chop for you. Got it?

FILCH: Please, Mr Peachum, please. What can I do, Mr Peachum? The gentlemen beat me black and blue and then they gave me your business card. If I took off my coat, you'd think you were looking at a fish on a slab.

PEACHUM: My friend, if you're not flat as a kipper, then my men weren't doing their job properly. Along come these young whipper-snappers who think they've only got to hold out their paw to land a steak. What would you say if someone started fishing the best trout out of your pond?

FILCH: It's like this, Mr Peachum – I haven't got a pond.

PEACHUM: Licences are delivered to professionals only. *Points in a businesslike way to a map of the city.* London is divided into fourteen districts. Any man who intends to practise the craft of begging in any one of them needs a licence from Jonathan Jeremiah Peachum & Co. Why, anybody could come along – a prey to his baser instincts.

FILCH: Mr Peachum, only a few shillings stand between me and utter ruin. Something must be done. With two shillings in my pocket I . . .

PEACHUM: One pound.

FILCH: Mr Peachum!

*Points imploringly at a sign saying 'Do not turn a deaf ear to misery!' Peachum points to the curtain over a showcase, on which is written: 'Give and it shall be given unto you!'*

FILCH: Ten bob.

PEACHUM: Plus fifty per cent of your take, settle up once a week. With outfit seventy per cent.

FILCH: What does the outfit consist of?

PEACHUM: That's for the firm to decide.

FILCH: Which district could I start in?

PEACHUM: Baker Street. Numbers 2 to 104. That comes even cheaper. Only fifty per cent, including the outfit.

FILCH: Very well. *He pays.*

PEACHUM: Your name?

FILCH: Charles Filch.

PEACHUM: Right. *Shouts.* Mrs Peachum! *Mrs Peachum enters.* This is Filch. Number 314. Baker Street district. I'll do his entry myself. Trust you to pick this moment to apply, just before the Coronation, when for once in a lifetime there's a chance of making a little something. Outfit C. *He opens a linen curtain before a showcase in which there are five wax dummies.*

FILCH: What's that?

PEACHUM: Those are the five basic types of misery, those most likely to touch the human heart. The sight of such types puts a man into the unnatural state where he is willing to part with money. Outfit A: Victim of vehicular progress. The merry paraplegic, always cheerful – *He acts it out.* – always carefree, emphasised by arm-stump. Outfit B: Victim of the Higher Strategy. The Tiresome Trembler, molests passers-by, operates by inspiring nausea – *He acts it out.* – attenuated by medals. Outfit C: Victim of advanced Technology. The Pitiful Blind Man, the Cordon Bleu of Beggary.

*He acts it out, staggering toward Filch. The moment he bumps into Filch, Filch cries out in horror. Peachum stops at once, looks at him with amazement and suddenly roars.*

He's *sorry* for me! You'll never be a beggar as long as you live! You're only fit to be begged from! Very well, outfit D! Celia, you've been drinking again. And now you can't see straight. Number 136 has complained about his outfit. How often do I have to tell you that a gentleman doesn't put on filthy clothes? The only thing about it that could inspire pity was the stains and they should have been added by just ironing in candle wax. Use your head! Have I got to do everything myself? *To Filch:* Take off your clothes and put this on, but mind you, look after it!

FILCH: What about my things?

PEACHUM: Property of the firm. Outfit E: young man who has seen better days or, if you'd rather, never thought it would come to this.

FILCH: Oh, you use them again? Why can't *I* do the better days act?

PEACHUM: Because nobody can make his own suffering sound convincing, my boy. If you have a bellyache and say so, people will simply be disgusted. Anyway, you're not here to ask questions but to put these things on.

FILCH: Aren't they rather dirty? *After Peachum has given him a penetrating look.* Excuse me, sir, please excuse me.

MRS PEACHUM: Shake a leg, son, I'm not standing here holding your trousers till Christmas.

FILCH *suddenly emphatic:* But I'm not taking my shoes off! Absolutely not. I'd sooner pack the whole thing in. They're the only present my poor mother ever gave me, I may have sunk pretty low, but never . . .

MRS PEACHUM: Stop drivelling. We all know your feet are dirty.

FILCH: Where am I supposed to wash my feet? In midwinter?

*Mrs Peachum leads him behind a screen, then she sits down on the left and starts ironing candle wax into a suit.*

PEACHUM: Where's your daughter?

MRS PEACHUM: Polly? Upstairs.

PEACHUM: Has that man been here again? The one who's always coming round when I'm out?

MRS PEACHUM: Don't be so suspicious, Jonathan, there's no finer gentleman. The Captain takes a real interest in our Polly.

PEACHUM: I see.

MRS PEACHUM: And if I've got half an eye in my head, Polly thinks he's very nice too.

PEACHUM: Celia, the way you chuck your daughter around anyone would think I was a millionaire. Wanting to marry her off? The idea! Do you think this lousy business of ours would survive a week if those ragamuffins our customers had nothing better than *our* legs to look at? A husband! He'd have us in his clutches in three shakes! In his clutches! Do you think your daughter can hold her tongue in bed any better than you?

MRS PEACHUM: A fine opinion of your daughter you have.

PEACHUM: The worst. The very worst. A lump of sensuality, that's what she is.

MRS PEACHUM: If so, she didn't get it from you.

PEACHUM: Marriage! I expect my daughter to be to me as bread to the hungry. *He leafs in the Book.* It even says so in the Bible somewhere. Anyway marriage is disgusting. I'll teach her to get married.

MRS PEACHUM: Jonathan, you're just a barbarian.

PEACHUM: Barbarian! What's this gentleman's name?

MRS PEACHUM: They never call him anything but 'the Captain'.

PEACHUM: So you haven't even asked him his name? Interesting.

MRS PEACHUM: You don't suppose we'd ask for a birth certificate when such a distinguished gentleman invites Polly and me to the Cuttlefish Hotel for a little hop.

PEACHUM: Where?

MRS PEACHUM: To the Cuttlefish Hotel for a little hop.

PEACHUM: Captain? Cuttlefish Hotel? Hm, hm, hm . . .

MRS PEACHUM: A gentleman who has always handled me and my daughter with kid gloves.

PEACHUM: Kid gloves!

MRS PEACHUM: Honest, he always does wear gloves, white ones: white kid gloves.

PEACHUM: I see. White gloves and a cane with an ivory handle and spats and patent-leather shoes and a charismatic personality and a scar . . .

MRS PEACHUM: On his neck. Isn't there anyone you don't know?

*Filch crawls out from behind the screen.*

FILCH: Mr Peachum, couldn't you give me a few tips, I've always believed in having a system and not just shooting off my mouth any old how.

MRS PEACHUM: A system!

PEACHUM: He can be a half-wit. Come back this evening at six, we'll teach you the rudiments. Now piss off!

FILCH: Thank you very much indeed, Mr Peachum. Many thanks. *Goes out.*

PEACHUM: Fifty per cent! – And now I'll tell you who this

gentleman with the gloves is – Mac the Knife! *He runs up the stairs to Polly's bedroom.*

MRS PEACHUM: God in Heaven! Mac the Knife! Jesus! Gentle Jesus meek and mild – Polly! Where's Polly?
*Peachum comes down slowly.*

PEACHUM: Polly? Polly's not come home. Her bed has not been slept in.

MRS PEACHUM: She'll have gone to supper with that wool merchant. That'll be it, Jonathan.

PEACHUM: Let's hope to God it is the wool merchant!
*Mr and Mrs Peachum step before the curtain and sing. Song lighting: golden glow. The organ is lit up. Three lamps are lowered from above on a pole, and the signs say:*


THE 'NO THEY CAN'T' SONG

No, they can't
Bear to be at home all tucked up tight in bed.
It's fun they want
You can bet they've got some fancy notions brewing up
    instead.

So that's your Moon over Soho
That is your infernal 'd'you feel my heart beating?' line.
That's the old 'wherever you go I shall be with you,
    honey'
When you first fall in love and the moonbeams shine.

No, they can't
See what's good for them and set their mind on it.
It's fun they want
So they end up on their arses in the shit.

Then where's your Moon over Soho?
What's come of your infernal 'd'you feel my heart beat-
    ing?' bit?
Where's the old 'wherever you go I shall be with you,
    honey'?
When you're no more in love, and you're in the shit?

2

Deep in the heart of Soho the bandit Mac the Knife is celebrating his marriage to Polly Peachum, the beggar king's daughter.

*Bare stable.*

MATTHEW, *known as Matt of the Mint, holds out his revolver and searches the stable with a lantern:* Hey, hands up, anybody that's here!
*Macheath enters and makes a tour of inspection along the footlights.*
MACHEATH: Well, is there anybody?
MATTHEW: Not a soul. Just the place for our wedding.
POLLY *enters in wedding dress:* But it's a stable!
MAC: Sit on the feed-bin for the moment, Polly. *To the audience:* Today this stable will witness my marriage to Miss Polly Peachum, who has followed me for love in order to share my life with me.
MATTHEW: All over London they'll be saying this is the most daring job you've ever pulled, Mac, enticing Mr Peachum's only child from his home.
MAC: Who's Mr Peachum?
MATTHEW: He'll tell you he's the poorest man in London.
POLLY: But you can't be meaning to have our wedding here? Why, it is a common stable. You can't ask the vicar to a place like this. Besides, it isn't even ours. We really oughtn't to start our new life with a burglary, Mac. Why, this is the biggest day of our life.
MAC: Dear child, everything shall be done as you wish. We can't have you embarrassed in any way. The trimmings will be here in a moment.
MATTHEW: That'll be the furniture.
*Large vans are heard driving up. Half a dozen men come in, carry-*

*ing carpets, furniture, dishes, etc., with which they transform the*
*stable into an exaggeratedly luxurious room.*

MAC: Junk.

*The gentlemen put their presents down left, congratulate the bride*
*and report to the bridegroom.*

JAKE *known as Crook-fingered Jake*: Congratulations! At 14
Ginger Street there were some people on the second floor.
We had to smoke them out.

BOB *known as Bob the Saw*: Congratulations! A copper got done
in the Strand.

MAC: Amateurs.

NED: We did all we could, but three people in the West End
were past saving. Congratulations!

MAC: Amateurs and bunglers.

JIMMY: An old gent got hurt a bit, but I don't think it's anything serious. Congratulations.

MAC: My orders were: avoid bloodshed. It makes me sick to
think of it. You'll never make business men! Cannibals,
perhaps, but not business men!

WALTER *known as Dreary Walt*: Congratulations. Only half an
hour ago, Madam, that harpsichord belonged to the
Duchess of Somerset.

POLLY: What is this furniture anyway?

MAC: How do you like the furniture, Polly?

POLLY *in tears*: Those poor people, all for a few sticks of
furniture.

MAC: And what furniture! Junk! You have a perfect right to
be angry. A rosewood harpsichord along with a renaissance
sofa. That's unforgivable. What about a table?

WALTER: A table?

*They lay some planks over the bins.*

POLLY: Oh, Mac, I'm so miserable! I only hope the vicar
doesn't come.

MATTHEW: Of course he'll come. We gave him exact
directions.

WALTER *introduces the table*: A table!

MAC *seeing Polly in tears*: My wife is very much upset. Where
are the rest of the chairs? A harpsichord and the happy

couple has to sit on the floor! Use your heads! For once I'm having a wedding, and how often does that happen? Shut up, Dreary! And how often does it happen that I leave you to do something on your own? And when I do you start by upsetting my wife.

NED: Dear Polly . . .

MAC *knocks his hat off his head* : 'Dear Polly'! I'll bash your head through your kidneys with your 'dear Polly', you squirt. Have you ever heard the like? 'Dear Polly!' I suppose you've been to bed with her?

POLLY: Mac!

NED: I swear . . .

WALTER: Dear madam, if any items of furniture should be lacking, we'll be only too glad to go back and . . .

MAC: A rosewood harpsichord and no chairs. *Laughs.* Speaking as a bride, what do you say to that?

POLLY: It could be worse.

MAC: Two chairs and a sofa and the bridal couple has to sit on the floor.

POLLY: Something new, I'd say.

MAC *sharply:* Get the legs sawn off this harpsichord! Go on!

FOUR MEN *saw the legs off the harpsichord and sing:*

Bill Lawgen and Mary Syer
Were made man and wife a week ago.
When it was over and they exchanged a kiss
He was thinking 'Whose wedding dress was this?'
While his name was one thing she'd rather like to
     know.
Hooray!

WALTER: The finished article, madam: there's your bench.

MAC: May I now ask the gentlemen to take off those filthy rags and put on some decent clothes? This isn't just anybody's wedding, you know. Polly, may I ask you to look after the fodder?

POLLY: Is this our wedding feast? Was the whole lot stolen, Mac?

MAC: Of course. Of course.

POLLY: I wonder what you will do if there's a knock at the door and the sheriff steps in.

MAC: I'll show you what your husband will do in that situation.

MATTHEW: It couldn't happen today. The mounted police are all sure to be in Daventry. They'll be escorting the Queen back to town for Friday's Coronation.

POLLY: Two knives and fourteen forks! One knife per chair.

MAC: What incompetence! That's the work of apprentices, not experienced men! Haven't you any sense of style? Fancy not knowing the difference between Chippendale and Louis Quatorze.

*The gang comes back. The gentlemen are now wearing fashionable evening dress, but unfortunately their movements are not in keeping with it.*

WALTER: We only wanted to bring the most valuable stuff. Look at that wood! Really first class.

MATTHEW: Ssst! Ssst! Permit us, Captain . . .

MAC: Polly, come here a minute.

*Mac and Polly assume the pose of a couple prepared to receive congratulations.*

MATTHEW: Permit us, Captain, on the greatest day of your life, in the full bloom of your career, or rather the turning point, to offer you our heartiest and at the same time most sincere congratulations, etcetera. That posh talk don't half make me sick. So to cut a long story short – *Shakes Mac's hand.* – keep up the good work, old mate.

MAC: Thank you, that was kind of you, Matthew.

MATTHEW *shaking Polly's hand after embracing Mac with emotion:* It was spoken from the heart, all right! So as I was saying, keep it up, old china, I mean – *Grinning* – the good work of course.

*Roars of laughter from the guests. Suddenly Mac with a deft movement sends Matthew to the floor.*

MAC: Shut your trap. Keep that filth for Kitty, she's the kind of slut that appreciates it.

POLLY: Mac, don't be so vulgar.

MATTHEW: Here, I don't like that. Calling Kitty a slut . . . *Stands up with difficulty.*

MAC: Oh, so you don't like that?

MATTHEW: And besides, I never use filthy language with her.
I respect Kitty too much. But maybe you wouldn't understand that, the way you are. You're a fine one to talk about
filth. Do you think Lucy didn't tell me the things you've
told her? Compared to that, I'm driven snow.
*Mac looks at him.*

JAKE: Cut it out, this is a wedding. *They pull him away.*

MAC: Fine wedding, isn't it, Polly? Having to see trash like
this around you on the day of your marriage. You wouldn't
have thought your husband's friends would let him down.
Think about it.

POLLY: I think it's nice.

ROBERT: Blarney. Nobody's letting you down. What's a
difference of opinion between friends? Kitty's as good as
the next girl. But now bring out your wedding present,
mate.

ALL: Yes, hand it over!

MATTHEW *offended:* Here.

POLLY: Oh, a wedding present. How kind of you, Mr Matt of
the Mint. Look, Mac, what a lovely nightgown.

MATTHEW: Another bit of filth, eh, Captain?

MAC: Forget it. I didn't mean to hurt your feelings on this
festive occasion.

WALTER: What do you say to this? Chippendale!
*He unveils an enormous Chippendale grandfather clock.*

MAC: Quatorze.

POLLY: It's wonderful. I'm so happy. Words fail me. You're
so unbelievably kind. Oh, Mac, isn't it a shame we've no
flat to put it in?

MAC: Hm, it's a start in the right direction. The great thing is
to get started. Thank you kindly, Walter. Go on, clear the
stuff away now. Food!

JAKE *while the others start setting the table:* Trust me to come
empty-handed again. *Intensely to Polly:* Believe me, young
lady, I find it most distressing.

POLLY: It doesn't matter in the least, Mr Crook-finger Jake.

JAKE: Here are the boys flinging presents right and left, and
me standing here like a fool. What a situation to be in! It's

always the way with me. Situations! It's enough to make your hair stand on end. The other day I meet Low-Dive Jenny; well, I say, you old cow . . .

*Suddenly he sees Mac standing behind him and goes off without a word.*

MAC *leads Polly to her place:* This is the best food you'll taste today, Polly. Gentlemen!

*All sit down to the wedding feast.*

NED *indicating the china:* Beautiful dishes. Savoy Hotel.

JAKE: The plover's eggs are from Selfridge's. There was supposed to be a bucket of foie gras. But Jimmy ate it on the way, he was mad because it had a hole in it.

WALTER: We don't talk about holes in polite society.

JIMMY: Don't bolt your eggs like that, Ned, not on a day like this.

MAC: Couldn't somebody sing something? Something splendiferous?

MATTHEW *choking with laughter:* Something splendiferous? That's a first-class word. *He sits down in embarrassment under Mac's withering glance.*

MAC *knocks a bowl out of someone's hand:* I didn't mean us to start eating yet. Instead of seeing you people wade straight into the trough, I would have liked something from the heart. That's what other people do on this sort of occasion.

JAKE: What, for instance?

MAC: Am I supposed to think of everything myself? I'm not asking you to put on an opera. But you might have arranged for something else besides stuffing your bellies and making filthy jokes. Oh well, it's a day like this that you find out who your friends are.

POLLY: The salmon is marvellous, Mac.

NED: I bet you've never eaten anything like it. You get that every day at Mac the Knife's. You've landed in the honey pot all right. That's what I've always said: Mac is the right match for a girl with a feeling for higher things. As I was saying to Lucy only yesterday.

POLLY: Lucy? Mac, who is Lucy?

JAKE *embarrassed:* Lucy? Oh, nothing serious, you know.

*Matthew has risen; standing behind Polly, he is waving his arms to shut Jake up.*

POLLY *sees him:* Do you want something? Salt perhaps . . .?
What were you saying, Mr Jake?

JAKE: Oh, nothing, nothing at all. The main thing I wanted
to say really was nothing at all. I'm always putting my foot
in it.

MAC: What have you got in your hand, Jake?

JAKE: A knife, Boss.

MAC: And what have you got on your plate?

JAKE: A trout, Boss.

MAC: I see. And with the knife you are eating the trout, are
you not? It's incredible. Did you ever see the like of it,
Polly? Eating his fish with a knife! Anybody who does that
is just a plain swine, do you get me, Jake? Think about it.
You'll have your hands full, Polly, trying to turn trash like
this into a human being. Have you boys got the least idea
what that is?

WALTER: A human being or a human pee-ing?

POLLY: Really, Mr Walter!

MAC: So you won't sing a song, something to brighten up the
day? Has it got to be a miserable gloomy day like any
other? And come to think of it, is anybody guarding the
door? I suppose you want me to attend to that myself too?
Do you want me on this day of days to guard the door so
you lot can stuff your bellies at my expense?

WALTER *sullenly:* What do you mean at your expense?

JIMMY: Stow it, Walter boy. I'm on my way. Who's going to
come here anyway? *Goes out.*

JAKE: A fine joke on a day like this if all the wedding guests
were pulled in.

JIMMY *rushes in:* Hey, Captain. The cops!

WALTER: Tiger Brown!

MATTHEW: Nonsense, it's the Reverend Kimball.
*Kimball enters.*

ALL *roar:* Good evening, Reverend Kimball!

KIMBALL: So I've found you after all. I find you in a lowly
hut, a humble place but your own.

MAC: Property of the Duke of Devonshire.

POLLY: Good evening, Reverend. Oh, I'm so glad that on the
happiest day of our life you . . .

MAC: And now I request a rousing song for the Reverend Kimball.

MATTHEW: How about Bill Lawgen and Mary Syer?

JAKE: Good. Bill Lawgen might be just the thing.

KIMBALL: Be nice if you'd do a little number, boys.

MATTHEW: Let's have it, gentlemen.

*Three men rise and sing hesitantly, weakly and uncertainly:*

### WEDDING SONG FOR THE LESS WELL-OFF

Bill Lawgen and Mary Syer
Were made man and wife a week ago
(Three cheers for the happy couple: hip, hip, hooray!)
When it was over and they exchanged a kiss
He was thinking 'Whose wedding dress was this?'
While his name was one thing she'd rather like to know.
Hooray!

Do you know what your wife's up to? No!
Do you like her sleeping round like that? No!
Three cheers for the happy couple: Hip, hip, hooray!
Billy Lawgen told me recently
Just one part of her will do for me.
The swine.
Hooray!

MAC: Is that all? Penurious!

MATTHEW *chokes again:* Penurious is the word, gentlemen.

MAC: Shut your trap!

MATTHEW: Oh, I only meant no gusto, no fire, and so on.

POLLY: Gentlemen, if none of you wishes to perform, I myself will sing a little song; it's an imitation of a girl I saw once in some twopenny-halfpenny dive in Soho. She was washing the glasses, and everybody was laughing at her, and then she turned to the guests and said things like the things I'm going to sing to you. Right. This is a little bar, I want you to think of it as filthy. She stood behind it morning and night. This is the bucket and this is the rag she washed the glasses with. Where you are sitting, the customers were sitting laughing at her. You can laugh too, to make it exactly the same; but if you don't want to, you don't have to. *She starts pretending to wash glasses, muttering to herself.* Now, for instance, one of them – it might be you – *Pointing at Walter* – says: Well, when's your ship coming in, Jenny?

WALTER: Well, when's your ship coming in, Jenny?

POLLY: And another says – you, for instance: Still washing up glasses, Jenny the pirate's bride?

MATTHEW: Still washing up glasses, Jenny the pirate's bride?

POLLY: Good. And now I'll begin.

*Song lighting: golden glow. The organ is lit up. Three lamps are lowered from above on a pole, and the signs say:*

### PIRATE JENNY

Now you gents all see I've the glasses to wash.
When a bed's to be made I make it.
You may tip me with a penny, and I'll thank you very
    well
And you see me dressed in tatters, and this tatty old hotel
And you never ask how long I'll take it.
But one of these evenings there will be screams from the
    harbour
And they'll ask: what can all that screaming be?
And they'll see me smiling as I do the glasses
And they'll say: how she can smile beats me.
    And a ship with eight sails and
    All its fifty guns loaded
    Has tied up at the quay.

They say: get on, dry your glasses, my girl
And they tip me and don't give a damn.
And their penny is accepted, and their bed will be made
(Although nobody is going to sleep there, I'm afraid)
And they still have no idea who I am.
But one of these evenings there will be explosions from
    the harbour,
And they'll ask: what kind of a bang was that?

And they'll see me as I stand beside the window
And they'll say: what has she got to smile at?
   And that ship with eight sails and
   All its fifty guns loaded
   Will lay siege to the town.


Then you gents, you aren't going to find it a joke
For the walls will be knocked down flat
And in no time the town will be rased to the ground.
Just one tatty old hotel will be left standing safe and
   sound
And they'll ask: did someone special live in that?
Then there'll be a lot of people milling round the hotel
And they'll ask: what made them let that place alone?
And they'll see me as I leave the door next morning
And they'll say: don't tell us she's the one.
   And that ship with eight sails and
   All its fifty guns loaded
   Will run up its flag.


And a hundred men will land in the bright midday sun
Each stepping where the shadows fall.
They'll look inside each doorway and grab anyone they
   see
And put him in irons and then bring him to me
And they'll ask: which of these should we kill?
In that noonday heat there'll be a hush round the harbour
As they ask which has got to die.
And you'll hear me as I softly answer: the lot!
And as the first head rolls I'll say: hoppla!
   And that ship with eight sails and
   All its fifty guns loaded
   Will vanish with me.


MATTHEW: Very nice. Cute, eh? The way the missus puts it
across!
MAC: What do you mean nice? It's not nice, you idiot! It's
art, it's not nice. You did that marvellously, Polly. But it's
wasted on trash like this, if you'll excuse me, your Rever-

ence. *In an undertone to Polly:* Anyway, I don't like you play-acting; let's not have any more of it.

*Laughter at the table. The gang is making fun of the parson.*

What you got in your hand, your Reverence?

JAKE: Two knives, Captain.

MAC: What you got on your plate, your Reverence?

KIMBALL: Salmon, I think.

MAC: And with that knife you are eating the salmon, are you not?

JAKE: Did you ever see the like of it, eating fish with a knife? Anybody who does that is just a plain . . .

MAC: Swine. Do you understand me, Jake? Think about it.

JIMMY *rushing in:* Hey, Captain, coppers. The sheriff in person.

WALTER: Brown. Tiger Brown!

MAC: Yes, Tiger Brown, exactly. It's Tiger Brown himself, the Chief Sheriff of London, pillar of the Old Bailey, who will now enter Captain Macheath's humble abode. Think about it.

*The bandits creep away.*

JAKE: It'll be the drop for us!

*Brown enters.*

MAC: Hullo, Jackie.

BROWN: Hullo, Mac! I haven't much time, got to be leaving in a minute. Does it have to be somebody else's stable? Why, this is breaking and entering again!

MAC: But Jackie, it's such a good address. I'm glad you could come to old Mac's wedding. Let me introduce my wife, née Peachum. Polly, this is Tiger Brown, what do you say, old man? *Slaps him on the back.* And these are my friends, Jackie, I imagine you've seen them all before.

BROWN *pained:* I'm here unofficially, Mac.

MAC: So are they. *He calls them. They come in with their hands up.* Hey, Jake.

BROWN: That's Crook-fingered Jake. He's a dirty dog.

MAC: Hey, Jimmy; hey, Bob; hey, Walter!

BROWN: Well, just for today I'll turn a blind eye.

MAC: Hey, Ned; hey, Matthew.

BROWN: Be seated, gentlemen, be seated.

ALL: Thank you, sir.

BROWN: I'm delighted to meet my old friend Mac's charming wife.

POLLY: Don't mention it, sir.

MAC: Sit down, you old bugger, and pitch into the whisky! – Polly and gentlemen! You have today in your midst a man whom the king's inscrutable wisdom has placed high above his fellow men and who has none the less remained my friend throughout the storms and perils, and so on. You know who I mean, and you too know who I mean, Brown. Ah, Jackie, do you remember how we served in India together, soldiers both of us? Ah, Jackie, let's sing the Cannon Song right now.

*They sit down on the table.*

*Song lighting: golden glow. The organ is lit up. Three lamps are lowered from above on a pole, and the signs say:*


### THE CANNON SONG

John was all present and Jim was all there
And Georgie was up for promotion.
Not that the army gave a bugger who they were
When confronting some heathen commotion.
    The troops live under
    The cannon's thunder
    From the Cape to Cooch Behar.
    Moving from place to place
    When they come face to face
    With a different breed of fellow
    Whose skin is black or yellow
    They quick as winking chop him into beefsteak tartare.


Johnny found his whisky too warm
And Jim found the weather too balmy
But Georgie took them both by the arm
And said: never let down the army.
    The troops live under
    The cannon's thunder

From the Cape to Cooch Behar.
Moving from place to place
When they come face to face
With a different breed of fellow
Whose skin is black or yellow
They quick as winking chop him into beefsteak
    tartare.

John is a write-off and Jimmy is dead
And they shot poor old Georgie for looting
But young men's blood goes on being red
And the army goes on recruiting.
    The troops live under
    The cannon's thunder
    From the Cape to Cooch Behar.
    Moving from place to place
    When they come face to face
    With a different breed of fellow
    Whose skin is black or yellow
    They quick as winking chop him into beefsteak
        tartare.

MAC: Though life with its raging torrent has carried us boyhood friends far apart, although our professional interests
are very different, some people would go so far as to say
diametrically opposed, our friendship has come through
unimpaired. Think about it. Castor and Pollux, Hector and
Andromache, etcetera. Seldom have I, the humble bandit,
well, you know what I mean, made even the smallest haul
without giving him, my friend, a share, a substantial share,
Brown, as a gift and token of my unswerving loyalty, and
seldom has he, take that knife out of your mouth, Jake, the
all-powerful police chief, staged a raid without sending me,
his boyhood friend, a little tip-off. Well, and so on and so
forth, it's all a matter of give and take. Think about it. *He
takes Brown by the arm.* Well, Jackie, old man, I'm glad
you've come, I call that real friendship. *Pause, because Brown
has been looking sadly at a carpet.* Genuine Shiraz.
BROWN: From the Oriental Carpet Company.

MAC: Yes, we never go anywhere else. Do you know, Jackie, I had to have you here today, I hope it's not awkward for you in your position?

BROWN: You know, Mac, that I can't refuse you anything. I must be going, I've really got so much on my plate; if the slightest thing should go wrong at the Queen's Coronation . . .

MAC: See here, Jackie, my father-in-law is a revolting old bastard. If he tries to make trouble for me, is there anything on record against me at Scotland Yard?

BROWN: There's nothing whatsoever on record against you at Scotland Yard.

MAC: I knew it.

BROWN: I've taken care of that. Good night.

MAC: Aren't you fellows going to stand up?

BROWN *to Polly:* Best of luck. *Goes out accompanied by Mac.*

JAKE *who along with Matthew and Walter has meanwhile been conferring with Polly:* I must admit I couldn't repress a certain alarm a while ago when I heard Tiger Brown was coming.

MATTHEW: You see, dear lady, we have contacts in the highest places.

WALTER: Yes, Mac always has some iron in the fire that the rest of us don't even suspect. But we have our own little iron in the fire. Gentlemen, it's half-past nine.

MATTHEW: And now comes the *pièce de résistance.*

*All go upstage behind the carpet that conceals something. Mac enters.*

MAC: I say, what's going on?

MATTHEW: Hey, Captain, another little surprise.

*Behind the curtain they sing the Bill Lawgen song softly and with much feeling. But at 'his name was one thing she'd rather like to know' Matthew pulls down the carpet and all go on with the song, bellowing and pounding on the bed that has been disclosed.*

MAC: Thank you, friends, thank you.

WALTER: And now we shall quietly take our leave.

*The gang go out.*

MAC: And now the time has come for softer sentiments. Without them man is a mere beast of burden. Sit down, Polly.

*Music.*

MAC: Look at the moon over Soho.

POLLY: I see it, dearest. Feel my heart beating, my beloved.

MAC: I feel it, beloved.

POLLY: Where'er you go I shall be with you.

MAC: And where you stay, there too shall I be.

BOTH:
And though we've no paper to say we're wed
And no altar covered with flowers
And nobody knows for whom your dress was made
And even the ring is not ours –
The platter off which you've been eating your bread
Give it one brief look; fling it far.
For love will endure or not endure
Regardless of where we are.

3

## To Peachum, conscious of the hardness of the world, the loss of his daughter means utter ruin.

*Peachum's Outfitting Emporium for Beggars.*

*To the right Peachum and Mrs Peachum. In the doorway stands Polly in her coat and hat, holding her travelling bag.*

MRS PEACHUM: Married? First you rig her fore and aft in dresses and hats and gloves and parasols, and when she's cost as much as a sailing ship, she throws herself in the garbage like a rotten pickle. Are you really married?
*Song lighting: golden glow. The organ is lit up. Three lamps are lowered from above on a pole and the signs say:*

IN A LITTLE SONG POLLY GIVES HER PARENTS TO
UNDERSTAND THAT SHE HAS MARRIED THE
BANDIT MACHEATH:

I once used to think, in my innocent youth
(And I once was as innocent as you)
That someone someday might come my way
And then how should I know what's best to do?
And if he'd got money
And seemed a nice chap
And his workday shirts were white as snow
And if he knew how to treat a girl with due respect
I'd have to tell him: No.
    That's where you must keep your head screwed on
    And insist on going slow.
    Sure, the moon will shine throughout the night
    Sure, the boat is on the river, tied up tight.
    That's as far as things can go.
    Oh, you can't lie back, you must stay cold at heart
    Oh, you must not let your feelings show.
    Oh, whenever you feel it might start
    Ah, then your only answer's: No.

The first one that came was a man of Kent
And all that a man ought to be.
The second one owned three ships down at Wapping
And the third was crazy about me.
And as they'd got money
And all seemed nice chaps
And their workday shirts were white as snow
And as they knew how to treat a girl with due respect
Each time I told them: No.
    That's where I still kept my head screwed on
    And I chose to take it slow.
    Sure, the moon could shine throughout the night
    Sure, the boat was on the river, tied up tight
    That's as far as things could go.
    Oh, you can't lie back, you must stay cold at heart

> Oh, you must not let your feelings show.
> Oh, whenever you feel it might start
> Ah, then your only answer's: No.
>
> But then one day, and that day was blue
> Came someone who didn't ask at all
> And he went and hung his hat on the nail in my little
> attic
> And what happened I can't quite recall.
> And as he'd got no money
> And was not a nice chap
> And his Sunday shirts, even, were not like snow
> And as he'd no idea of treating a girl with due respect
> I could not tell him: No.
>> That's the time my head was not screwed on
>> And to hell with going slow.
>> Oh, the moon was shining clear and bright
>> Oh, the boat kept drifting downstream all that night
>> That was how it simply had to go.
>> Yes, you must lie back, you can't stay cold at heart
>> In the end you have to let your feelings show.
>> Oh, the moment you know it must start
>> Ah, then's no time for saying: No.

PEACHUM: So she's associating with criminals. That's lovely. That's delightful.

MRS PEACHUM: If you're immoral enough to get married, did it have to be a horse-thief and a highwayman? That'll cost you dear one of these days! I ought to have seen it coming. Even as a child she had a swollen head like the Queen of England.

PEACHUM: So she's really got married!

MRS PEACHUM: Yes, yesterday, at five in the afternoon.

PEACHUM: To a notorious criminal. Come to think of it, it shows that the fellow is really audacious. If I give away my daughter, the sole prop of my old age, why, my house will cave in and my last dog will run off. I'd think twice about giving away the dirt under my fingernails, it would mean risking starvation. If the three of us can get through the winter on one log of wood, maybe we'll live to see the new year. Maybe.

MRS PEACHUM: What got into you? This is our reward for all we've done, Jonathan. I'm going mad. My head is swimming. I'm going to faint. Oh! *She faints.* A glass of Cordial Médoc.

PEACHUM: You see what you've done to your mother. Quick! Associating with criminals, that's lovely, that's delightful! Interesting how the poor woman takes it to heart. *Polly brings in a bottle of Cordial Médoc.* That's the only consolation your poor mother has left.

POLLY: Go ahead, give her two glasses. *My* mother can take twice as much when she's not quite herself. That will put her back on her feet. *During the whole scene she looks very happy.*

MRS PEACHUM *wakes up:* Oh, there she goes again, pretending to be so loving and sympathetic!
*Five men enter.*

BEGGAR: I'm making a complaint, see, this thing is a mess, it's not a proper stump, it's a botch-up, and I'm not wasting my money on it.

PEACHUM: What do you expect? It's as good a stump as any other; it's just that you don't keep it clean.

BEGGAR: Then why don't I take as much money as the others? Naw, you can't do that to me. *Throws down the stump.* If I wanted crap like this, I could cut off my real leg.

PEACHUM: What do you fellows want anyway? Is it my fault if people have hearts of flint? I can't make you five stumps. In five minutes I can turn any man into such a pitiful wreck it would make a dog weep to see him. Is it my fault if people don't weep? Here's another stump for you if one's not enough. But look after your equipment!

BEGGAR: This one will do.

PEACHUM *tries a false limb on another:* Leather is no good, Celia; rubber is more repulsive. *To the third:* That swelling is going down and it's your last. Now we'll have to start all over again. *Examining the fourth:* Of course natural scabies is never as good as the artificial kind. *To the fifth:* You're a sight! You've been eating again. I'll have to make an example of you.

BEGGAR: Mr Peachum, I really haven't eaten anything much. I'm just abnormally fat, I can't help it.

PEACHUM: Nor can I. You're fired. *Again to the second beggar:* My dear man, there's an obvious difference between 'tugging at people's heart strings' and 'getting on people's nerves'. Yes, artists, that's what I need. Only an artist can tug at anybody's heart strings nowadays. If you fellows performed properly, your audience would be forced to applaud. You just haven't any ideas! Obviously I can't extend your engagement.

*The beggars go out.*

POLLY: Look. Is he particularly handsome? No. But he makes a living. He can support me. He is not only a first-class burglar but a far-sighted and experienced stick-up man as well. I've been into it, I can tell you the exact amount of his savings to date. A few successful ventures and we shall be able to retire to a little house in the country just like that Mr Shakespeare father admires so much.

PEACHUM: It's quite simple. You're married. What does a girl do when she's married? Use your head. Well, she gets divorced, see. Is that so hard to figure out?

POLLY: I don't know what you're talking about.

MRS PEACHUM: Divorce.

POLLY: But I love him. How can I think of divorce?

MRS PEACHUM: Really, have you no shame?

POLLY: Mother, if you've ever been in love . . .

MRS PEACHUM: In love! Those damn books you've been reading have turned your head. Why, Polly, everybody's doing it.

POLLY: Then I'm an exception.

MRS PEACHUM: Then I'm going to tan your behind, you exception.

POLLY: Oh yes, all mothers do that, but it doesn't help because love goes deeper than a tanned behind.

MRS PEACHUM: Don't strain my patience.

POLLY: I won't let my love be taken away from me.

MRS PEACHUM: One more word out of you and you'll get a clip on the ear.

POLLY: But love is the finest thing in the world.

MRS PEACHUM: Anyway, he's got several women, the black-guard. When he's hanged, like as not half a dozen widows will turn up, each of them like as not with a brat in her arms. Oh, Jonathan!

PEACHUM: Hanged, what made you think of that, that's a good idea. Run along, Polly. *Polly goes out.* Quite right. That'll earn us forty pounds.

MRS PEACHUM: I see. Report him to the sheriff.

PEACHUM: Naturally. And besides, that way we get him hanged free of charge . . . Two birds with one stone. Only we've got to find out where he's holed up.

MRS PEACHUM: I can tell you that, my dear, he's holed up with his tarts.

PEACHUM: But they won't turn him in.

MRS PEACHUM: Just let me attend to that. Money rules the world. I'll go to Turnbridge right away and talk to the girls. Give us a couple of hours, and after that if he meets a single one of them he's done for.

POLLY *has been listening behind the door:* Dear Mama, you can spare yourself the trip. Mac will go to the Old Bailey of his own accord sooner than meet any of those ladies. And even if he did go to the Old Bailey, the sheriff would serve him a cocktail; they'd smoke their cigars and have a little chat about a certain shop in this street where a little more goes on than meets the eye. Because, Papa dear, the sheriff was very cheerful at my wedding.

PEACHUM: What's this sheriff called?

POLLY: He's called Brown. But you probably know him as Tiger Brown. Because everyone who has reason to fear him calls him Tiger Brown. But my husband, you see, calls him Jackie. Because to him he's just dear old Jackie. They're boyhood friends.

PEACHUM: Oh, so they're friends, are they? The sheriff and Public Enemy No. 1, ha, they must be the only friends in this city.

POLLY *poetically:* Every time they drank a cocktail together, they stroked each other's cheeks and said: 'If you'll have the same again, I'll have the same again.' And every time one of them left the room, the other's eyes grew moist and he said: 'Where'er you go I shall be with you.' There's nothing on record against Mac at Scotland Yard.

PEACHUM: I see. Between Tuesday evening and Thursday morning Mr Macheath, a gentleman who has assuredly been married many times, lured my daughter from her home on pretext of marriage. Before the week is out, he will be taken to the gallows on that account, and deservedly so. 'Mr Macheath, you once had white kid gloves, a cane with an ivory handle, and a scar on your neck, and frequented the Cuttlefish Hotel. All that is left is your scar, undoubtedly the least valuable of your distinguishing marks, and today you frequent nothing but prison cells, and within the foreseeable future no place at all . . .'

MRS PEACHUM: Oh, Jonathan, you'll never bring it off. Why, he's Mac the Knife, whom they call the biggest criminal in London. He takes what he pleases.

PEACHUM: Who's Mac the Knife? Get ready, we're going to see the Sheriff of London. And you're going to Turnbridge.

MRS PEACHUM: To see his whores.

PEACHUM: For the villainy of the world is great, and a man needs to run his legs off to keep them from being stolen from under him.

POLLY: I, Papa, shall be delighted to shake hands with Mr Brown again.

*All three step forward and sing the first finale. Song lighting. On the signs is written:*

### FIRST THREE-PENNY FINALE
#### CONCERNING THE INSECURITY OF THE HUMAN CONDITION

POLLY:
Am I reaching for the sky?
All I'm asking from this place is
To enjoy a man's embraces.
Is that aiming much too high?

PEACHUM *with a Bible in his hand:*
Man has a right, in this our brief existence
To call some fleeting happiness his own

Partake of worldly pleasures and subsistence
And have bread on his table rather than a stone.
Such are the basic rights of man's existence.
But do we know of anything suggesting
That when a thing's a right one gets it? No!
To get one's rights would be most interesting
But our condition's such it can't be so.

MRS PEACHUM:

How I want what's best for you
How I'd teach you airs and graces
Show you things and take you places
As a mother likes to do.

PEACHUM:

Let's practise goodness: who would disagree?
Let's give our wealth away: is that not right?
Once all are good His Kingdom is at hand
Where blissfully we'll bask in His pure light.
Let's practise goodness: who would disagree?
But sadly on this planet while we're waiting
The means are meagre and the morals low.
To get one's record straight would be elating
But our condition's such it can't be so.

POLLY AND MRS PEACHUM:

So that is all there is to it.
The world is poor, and man's a shit.

PEACHUM:

Of course that's all there is to it.
The world is poor, and man's a shit.
Who wouldn't like an earthly paradise?
Yet our condition's such it can't arise.
Out of the question in our case.
Let's say your brother's close to you
But if there's not enough for two
He'll kick you smartly in the face.
You think that loyalty's no disgrace?
But say your wife is close to you
And finds she's barely making do
She'll kick you smartly in the face.
And gratitude: that's no disgrace

But say your son is close to you
And finds your pension's not come through
He'll kick you smartly in the face.
And so will all the human race.

POLLY AND MRS PEACHUM:
That's what you're all ignoring
That's what's so bloody boring.
The world is poor, and man's a shit
And that is all there is to it.

PEACHUM:
Of course that's all there is to it
The world is poor, and man's a shit.
We should aim high instead of low
But our condition's such this can't be so.

ALL THREE:
Which means He has us in a trap:
The whole damn thing's a load of crap.

PEACHUM:
The world is poor, and man's a shit
And that is all there is to it.

ALL THREE:
That's what you're all ignoring
That's what's so bloody boring.
That's why He's got us in a trap
And why it's all a load of crap.

# ACT TWO

## 4

Thursday afternoon: Mac the Knife takes leave of his wife and flees from his father-in-law to the heaths of Highgate.

*The stable.*

POLLY *enters:* Mac! Mac, don't be frightened.

MAC *lying on the bed:* Well, what's up? Polly, you look a wreck.

POLLY: I've been to see Brown, my father went too, they decided to pull you in; my father made some terrible threats and Brown stood up for you, but then he weakened, and now he thinks too that you'd better stir yourself and make yourself scarce for a while, Mac. You must pack right away.

MAC: Pack? Nonsense. Come here, Polly. You and I have got better things to do than pack.

POLLY: No, we mustn't now. I'm so frightened. All they talked about was hanging.

MAC: I don't like it when you're moody, Polly. There's nothing on record against me at Scotland Yard.

POLLY: Perhaps there wasn't yesterday, but suddenly today there's an awful lot. You — I've brought the charges with me, I don't even know if I can get them straight, the list goes on so. You've killed two shopkeepers, more than thirty burglaries, twenty-three hold-ups, and God knows how many acts of arson, attempted murder, forgery and perjury, all within eighteen months. You're a dreadful man. And in Winchester you seduced two sisters under the age of consent.

MAC: They told me they were over twenty. What did Brown say?

*He stands up slowly and goes whistling to the right along the footlights.*

POLLY: He caught up with me in the corridor and said there was nothing he could do for you now. Oh, Mac! *She throws herself on his neck.*

MAC: All right, if I've got to go away, you'll have to run the business.

POLLY: Don't talk about business now, Mac, I can't bear it. Kiss your poor Polly again and swear that you'll never never be . . .

*Mac interrupts her brusquely and leads her to the table where he pushes her down in a chair.*

MAC: Here are the ledgers. Listen carefully. This is a list of the personnel. *Reads.* Hm, first of all, Crook-finger Jake, a year and a half in the business. Let's see what he's brought in. One, two, three, four, five gold watches, not much, but clean work. Don't sit on my lap, I'm not in the mood right now. Here's Dreary Walter, an unreliable sod. Sells stuff on the side. Give him three weeks, grace, then get rid of him. Just turn him in to Brown.

POLLY *sobbing:* Just turn him in to Brown.

MAC: Jimmy II, cheeky bastard; good worker but cheeky. Swipes bed sheets right out from under ladies of the best society. Give him a rise.

POLLY: I'll give him a rise.

MAC: Robert the Saw: small potatoes, not a glimmer of genius. Won't end on the gallows, but he won't leave any estate either.

POLLY: Won't leave any estate either.

MAC: In all other respects you will carry on exactly the same as before. Get up at seven, wash, have your weekly bath and so on.

POLLY: You're perfectly right, I'll have to grit my teeth and look after the business. What's yours is mine now, isn't it, Mackie? What about your chambers, Mac? Should I let them go? I don't like having to pay the rent.

MAC: No, I still need them.

POLLY: What for, it's just a waste of our money!

MAC: Oh, so you think I won't be coming back at all, do you?

POLLY: What do you mean? You can rent other rooms. Mac
.⌐. Mac, I can't go on. I keep looking at your lips and then
I don't hear what you say. Will you be faithful to me, Mac?

MAC: Of course I'll be faithful, I'll do as I'm done by. Do you
think I don't love you? It's only that I see farther ahead
than you.

POLLY: I'm so grateful to you, Mac. Worrying about me
when they're after you like bloodhounds . . .
*Hearing the word 'bloodhounds' he goes stiff, stands up, goes to the
right, throws off his coat and washes his hands.*

MAC *hastily:* You will go on sending the profits to Jack
Poole's banking house in Manchester. Between ourselves
it's only a matter of weeks before I go over to banking
altogether. It's safer and it's more profitable. In two weeks
at the most the money will have to be taken out of this
business, then off you go to Brown and give the list to the
police. Within four weeks all that human scum will be
safely in the cells at the Old Bailey.

POLLY: Why, Mac! How can you look them in the eye when
you've written them off and they're as good as hanged?
How can you shake hands with them?

MAC: With who? Robert the Saw, Matt of the Mint, Crook-
fingered Jake? Those gaol-birds?
*Enter the gang.*

MAC: Gentlemen, it's a pleasure to see you.

POLLY: Good evening, gentlemen.

MATTHEW: I've got hold of the Coronation programme,
Captain. It looks to me like we're going to be very busy in
the next few days. The Archbishop of Canterbury is arriv-
ing in half an hour.

MAC: When?

MATTHEW: Five thirty. We'd better be shoving off, Captain.

MAC: Yes, you'd better be shoving off.

ROBERT: What do you mean: you?

MAC: For my part, I'm afraid I'm obliged to take a little trip.

ROBERT: Good God, are they out to nab you?

MATTHEW: It would be just now, with the Coronation com-

ing up! A Coronation without you is like porridge without
a spoon.

MAC: Shut your trap! In view of that, I am temporarily handing over the management of the business to my wife.

*He pushes her forward and goes to the rear where he observes her.*

POLLY: Well, boys, I think the Captain can go away with an
easy mind. We'll swing this job, you bet. What do you say,
boys?

MATTHEW: It's no business of mine. But at a time like this
I'm not so sure that a woman . . . I'm not saying anything
against you, Ma'am.

MAC *from upstage:* What do you say to that, Polly?

POLLY: You shit, that's a fine way to start in. *Screaming.* Of
course you're not saying anything against me! If you were,
these gentlemen would have ripped your pants off long ago
and tanned your arse for you. Wouldn't you, gentlemen?
*Brief pause, then all clap like mad.*

JAKE: Yes, there's something in that, you can take her word
for it.

WALTER: Hurrah, the missus knows how to lay it on! Hurrah for Polly!

ALL: Hurrah for Polly!

MAC: The rotten part of it is that I won't be here for the
Coronation. There's a gilt-edged deal for you. In the day
time nobody's home and at night the toffs are all drunk.
That reminds me, you drink too much, Matthew. Last
week you suggested it was you set the Greenwich Children's
Hospital on fire. If such a thing occurs again, you're out.
Who set the Children's Hospital on fire?

MATTHEW: I did.

MAC *to the others:* Who set it on fire?

THE OTHERS: You, Mr Macheath.

MAC: So who did it?

MATTHEW *sulkily:* You, Mr Macheath. At this rate our sort
will never rise in the world.

MAC *with a gesture of stringing up:* You'll rise all right if you
think you can compete with me. Who ever heard of one of
those professors at Oxford College letting some assistant
put his name to his mistakes? He puts his own.

ROBERT: Ma'am, while your husband is away, you're the boss. We settle up every Thursday, ma'am.

POLLY: Every Thursday, boys.

*The gang goes out.*

MAC: And now farewell, my heart. Look after your complexion, and don't forget to make up every day, exactly as if I were here. That's very important, Polly.

POLLY: And you, Mac, promise me you won't look at another woman and that you'll leave town right away. Believe me, it's not jealousy that makes your little Polly say that; no, it's very important, Mac.

MAC: Oh, Polly, why should I go round drinking up the empties? I love only you. As soon as the twilight is deep enough I'll take my black stallion from somebody's stable and before you can see the moon from your window, I'll be the other side of Highgate Heath.

POLLY: Oh, Mac, don't tear the heart out of my body. Stay with me and let us be happy.

MAC: But I must tear my own heart out of my body, for I must go away and no one knows when I shall return.

POLLY: It's been such a short time, Mac.

MAC: Does it have to be the end?

POLLY: Oh, last night I had a dream. I was looking out the window and I heard laughter in the street, and when I looked out I saw our moon and the moon was all thin like a worn-down penny. Don't forget me, Mac, in strange cities.

MAC: Of course I won't forget you, Polly. Kiss me, Polly.

POLLY: Goodbye, Mac.

MAC: Goodbye, Polly. *On his way out:*

> For love will endure or not endure
> Regardless of where we are.

POLLY *alone:* He never will come back. *She sings:*

> Nice while it lasted, and now it is over
> Tear out your heart, and goodbye to your lover!
> What's the use of grieving, when the mother that bore
>     you
> (Mary, pity women!) knew it all before you?

*The bells start ringing.*

POLLY:
> Into this London the Queen now makes her way.
> Where shall we be on Coronation Day?

## Interlude

*Mrs Peachum and Low-Dive Jenny step out before the curtain.*

MRS PEACHUM: So if you see Mac the Knife in the next few days, run to the nearest constable and turn him in; it'll earn you ten shillings.

JENNY: Shall we see him, though, if the constables are after him? If the hunt is on, he won't go spending his time with us.

MRS PEACHUM: Take it from me, Jenny, even with all London at his heels, Macheath is not the man to give up his habits. *She sings:*

### THE BALLAD OF SEXUAL OBSESSION

> There goes a man who's won his spurs in battle
> The butcher, he. And all the others, cattle.
> The cocky sod! No decent place lets him in.
> Who does him down, that's done the lot? The women.
> Want it or not, he can't ignore that call.
> Sexual obsession has him in its thrall.
>> He doesn't read the Bible. He sniggers at the law
>> Sets out to be an utter egoist
>> And knows a woman's skirts are what he must resist
>> So when a woman calls he locks his door.
>> So far, so good, but what's the future brewing?
>> As soon as night falls he'll be up and doing.

> Thus many a man watched men die in confusion:
> A mighty genius, stuck on prostitution!
> The watchers claimed their urges were exhausted
> But when they died who paid the funeral? Whores did.
> Want it or not, they can't ignore that call.
> Sexual obsession has them in its thrall.

Some fall back on the Bible. Some stick to the law
Some turn to Christ and some turn anarchist.
At lunch you pick the best wine on the list
Then meditate till half-past four.
At tea: what high ideals you are pursuing!
Then soon as night falls you'll be up and doing.

5

Before the Coronation bells had died away, Mac
the Knife was sitting with the whores of Turnbridge! The whores betray him. It is Thursday
evening.

*Whorehouse in Turnbridge.*

*An afternoon like any other; the whores, mostly in their shifts, are
ironing clothes, playing draughts, or washing: a bourgeois idyll.
Crook-fingered Jake is reading the newspaper. No one pays any
attention to him. He is rather in the way.*

JAKE: He won't come today.
WHORE: No?
JAKE: I don't think he'll ever come again.
WHORE: That would be a pity.
JAKE: Think so? If I know him, he's out of town by now.
    This time he's really cleared out.
    *Enter Macheath, hangs his hat on a nail, sits down on the sofa
    behind the table.*
MAC: My coffee!
VIXEN *repeats admiringly:* 'My coffee!'
JAKE *horrified:* Why aren't you in Highgate?
MAC: It's my Thursday. Do you think I can let such trifles
    interfere with my habits? *Throws the warrant on the floor.*
    Anyhow, it's raining.

JENNY *reads the warrant:* In the name of the King, Captain Macheath is charged with three . . .

JAKE *takes it away from her:* Am I in it too?

MAC: Naturally, the whole team.

JENNY *to the other whore:* Look, that's the warrant. *Pause.* Mac, let's see your hand. *He gives her his hand.*

DOLLY: That's right, Jenny, read his palm, you do it so well. *Holds up an oil lamp.*

MAC: Coming into money?

JENNY: No, not coming into money.

BETTY: What's that look for, Jenny? It gives me the shivers.

MAC: A long journey?

JENNY: No, no long journey.

VIXEN: What *do* you see?

MAC: Only the good things, not the bad, please.

JENNY: Oh well, I see a narrow dark place and not much light. And then I see a big T, that means a woman's treachery. And then I see . . .

MAC: Stop. I'd like some details about that narrow dark place and the treachery. What's this treacherous woman's name?

JENNY: All I see is it begins with a J.

MAC: Then you've got it wrong. It begins with a P.

JENNY: Mac, when the Coronation bells start ringing at Westminster, you'll be in for a sticky time.

MAC: Go on! *Jake laughs uproariously.* What's the matter? *He runs over to Jake, and reads.* They've got it wrong, there were only three of them.

JAKE *laughs:* Exactly.

MAC: Nice underwear you've got there.

WHORE: From the cradle to the grave, underwear first, last and all the time.

OLD WHORE: I never wear silk. Makes gentlemen think you've got something wrong with you.
*Jenny slips stealthily out the door.*

SECOND WHORE *to Jenny:* Where are you going, Jenny?

JENNY: You'll see. *Goes out.*

DOLLY: But homespun underwear can put them off too.

OLD WHORE: I've had very good results with homespun underwear.

VIXEN: It makes the gentlemen feel they're at home.

MAC *to Betty:* Have you still got the black lace trimming?

BETTY: Still the black lace trimming.

MAC: What kind of lingerie do you have?

SECOND WHORE: Oh, I don't like to tell you. I can't take anybody to my room because my aunt is so crazy about men, and in doorways, you know, I just don't wear any.
*Jake laughs.*

MAC: Finished?

JAKE: No, I just got to the rapes.

MAC *back to the sofa:* But where's Jenny? Ladies, long before my star rose over this city . . .

VIXEN: 'Long before my star rose over this city . . .'

MAC: . . . I lived in the most impecunious circumstances with one of you dear ladies. And though today I am Mac the Knife, my good fortune will never lead me to forget the companions of my dark days, especially Jenny, whom I loved the best of all. Now listen, please.
*While Mac sings, Jenny stands to the right outside the window and beckons to Constable Smith. Then Mrs Peachum joins her. The three stand under the street lamp and watch the house.*

### BALLAD OF IMMORAL EARNINGS

There was a time, now very far away
When we set up together, I and she.
I'd got the brain, and she supplied the breast.
I saw her right, and she looked after me –
A way of life then, if not quite the best.
And when a client came I'd slide out of our bed
And treat him nice, and go and have a drink instead
And when he paid up I'd address him: Sir
Come any night you feel you fancy her.
That time's long past, but what would I not give
To see that whorehouse where we used to live?
*Jenny appears in the door, with Smith behind her.*

JENNY:
That was the time, now very far away
He was so sweet and bashed me where it hurt.

And when the cash ran out the feathers really flew
He'd up and say: I'm going to pawn your skirt.
A skirt is nicer, but no skirt will do.
Just like his cheek, he had me fairly stewing
I'd ask him straight to say what he thought he was doing
Then he'd lash out and knock me headlong down the
    stairs.
I had the bruises off and on for years.

BOTH:

That time's long past, but what would I not give
To see that whorehouse where we used to live?

BOTH *together and alternating*:

That was the time, now very far away

MAC:

Not that the bloody times seem to have looked up.

JENNY:

When afternoons were all I had for you

MAC:

I told you she was generally booked up.
(The night's more normal, but daytime will do.)

JENNY:

Once I was pregnant, so the doctor said.

MAC:

So we reversed positions on the bed.

JENNY:

He thought his weight would make it premature.

MAC:

But in the end we flushed it down the sewer.
That could not last, but what would I not give
To see that whorehouse where we used to live?
*Dance. Mac picks up his sword stick, she hands him his hat, he
is still dancing when Smith lays a hand on his shoulder.*

SMITH: Coming quietly?

MAC: Is there only one way out of this dump?

*Smith tries to put the handcuffs on Macheath; Mac gives him a
push in the chest and he reels back. Mac jumps out of the window.
Outside stands Mrs Peachum with constables.*

MAC *with poise, very politely*: Good afternoon, ma'am.

MRS PEACHUM: My dear Mr Macheath. My husband says the

greatest heroes in history have tripped over this humble threshold.

MAC: May I ask how your husband is doing?

MRS PEACHUM: Better, thank you. I'm so sorry, you'll have to be bidding the charming ladies goodbye now. Come, constable, escort the gentleman to his new home. *He is led away. Mrs Peachum through the window:* Ladies, if you wish to visit him, you'll invariably find him in. From now on the gentleman's address will be the Old Bailey. I knew he'd be round to see his whores. I'll settle the bill. Goodbye, ladies. *Goes out.*

JENNY: Wake up, Jake, something has happened.

JAKE *who has been too immersed in his reading to notice anything:* Where's Mac?

JENNY: The rozzers were here.

JAKE: Good God! And me just reading, reading, reading . . . Well, I never! *Goes out.*

# 6

Betrayed by the wnores, Macheath is freed from prison by the love of yet another woman.

*The cells in the Old Bailey.*
*A cage.*

*Enter Brown.*

BROWN: If only my men don't catch him! Let's hope to God he's riding out beyond Highgate Heath, thinking of his Jackie. But he's so frivolous, like all great men. If they bring him in now and he looks at me with his faithful friendly eyes, I won't be able to bear it. Thank God, anyway, the moon is shining; if he is riding across the heath, at least he won't stray from the path. *Sounds backstage.* What's that? Oh, my God, they're bringing him in.

MAC *tied with heavy ropes, accompanied by six constables, enters with head erect.* Well, flatfeet, thank God we're home again. *He notices Brown who has fled to the far corner of the cell.*

BROWN *after a long pause, under the withering glance of his former friend:* Oh, Mac, it wasn't me . . . I did everything . . . don't look at me like that, Mac . . . I can't stand it . . . Your silence is killing me. *Shouts at one of the constables:* Stop tugging at that rope, you swine . . . Say something, Mac. Say something to your poor Jackie . . . A kind word in his tragic . . . *Rests his head against the wall and weeps.* He doesn't deem me worthy even of a word. *Goes out.*

MAC: That miserable Brown. The living picture of a bad conscience. And he calls himself a chief of police. It was a good idea not shouting at him. I was going to at first. But just in time it occurred to me that a deep withering stare would send much colder shivers down his spine. It worked. I looked at him and he wept bitterly. That's a trick I got from the Bible.

*Enter Smith with handcuffs.*

MAC: Well, Mr Warder, I suppose these are the heaviest you've got? With your kind permission I should like to apply for a more comfortable pair. *He takes out his cheque book.*

SMITH: Of course, Captain, we've got them here at every price. It all depends how much you want to spend. From one guinea to ten.

MAC: How much would none at all be?

SMITH: Fifty.

MAC *writes a cheque:* But the worst of it is that now this business with Lucy is bound to come out. If Brown hears that I've been carrying on with his daughter behind his friendly back, he'll turn into a tiger.

SMITH: You've made your bed, now lie on it.

MAC: I bet the little tart is waiting outside right now. I can see happy days between now and the execution.

Is this a life for one of my proud station?
I take it, I must frankly own, amiss.
From childhood up I heard with consternation:

One must live well to know what living is!
*Song lighting: golden glow. The organ is lit up. Three lamps are
lowered on a pole, and the signs say:*


BALLADE OF GOOD LIVING

I've heard them praising single-minded spirits
Whose empty stomachs show they live for knowledge
In rat-infested shacks awash with ullage.
I'm all for culture, but there are some limits.
The simple life is fine for those it suits.
I don't find, for my part, that it attracts.
There's not a bird from here to Halifax
Would peck at such unappetising fruits.
What use is freedom? None, to judge from this.
One must live well to know what living is.


The dashing sort who cut precarious capers
And go and risk their necks just for the pleasure
Then swagger home and write it up at leisure
And flog the story to the Sunday papers –
If you could see how cold they get at night
Sullen, with chilly wife, climbing to bed
And how they dream they're going to get ahead
And see the future stretching out of sight –
Now tell me, who would choose to live like this?
One must live well to know what living is.


There's plenty that they have. I know I lack it
And ought to join their splendid isolation
But when I gave it more consideration
I told myself: my friend, that's not your racket.
Suffering ennobles, but it can depress.
The paths of glory lead but to the grave.
You once were poor and lonely, wise and brave.
You ought to try to bite off rather less.
The search for happiness boils down to this:
One must live well to know what living is.

*Enter Lucy.*

LUCY: You dirty dog, you – how can you look me in the face after all there's been between us?

MAC: Have you no bowels, no tenderness, my dear Lucy, seeing a husband in such circumstances?

LUCY: A husband! You monster! So you think I haven't heard about your goings-on with Miss Peachum! I could scratch your eyes out!

MAC: Seriously, Lucy, you're not fool enough to be jealous of Polly?

LUCY: You're married to her, aren't you, you beast?

MAC: Married! It's true, I go to the house, I chat with the girl. I kiss her, and now the silly jade goes about telling everyone that I'm married to her. I am ready, my dear Lucy, to give you satisfaction – if you think there is any in marriage. What can a man of honour say more? He can say nothing more.

LUCY: Oh, Mac, I only want to become an honest woman.

MAC: If you think marriage with me will . . . all right. What can a man of honour say more? He can say nothing more.
*Enter Polly.*

POLLY: Where is my dear husband? Oh, Mac, there you are. Why do you turn away from me? It's your Polly. It's your wife.

LUCY: Oh, you miserable villain!

POLLY: Oh, Mackie in prison! Why didn't you ride across Highgate Heath? You told me you weren't going to see those women any more. I knew what they'd do to you; but I said nothing, because I believed you. Mac, I'll stay with you till death us do part. – Not one kind word, Mac? Not one kind look? Oh, Mac, think what your Polly must be suffering to see you like this.

LUCY: Oh, the slut.

POLLY: What does this mean, Mac? Who on earth is that? You might at least tell her who I am. Please tell her I'm your wife. Aren't I your wife? Look at me. Tell me, aren't I your wife?

LUCY: You low-down sneak! Have you got two wives, you monster?

POLLY: Say something, Mac. Aren't I your wife? Haven't I done everything for you? I was innocent when I married, you know that. Why, you even put me in charge of the gang, and I've done it all the way we arranged, and Jake wants me to tell you that he . . .

MAC: If you two would kindly shut your traps for one minute I'll explain everything.

LUCY: No, I won't shut my trap, I can't bear it. It's more than flesh and blood can stand.

POLLY: Yes, my dear, naturally the wife has . . .

LUCY: The wife!!

POLLY: . . . the wife is entitled to some preference. Or at least the appearance of it, my dear. All this fuss and bother will drive the poor man mad.

LUCY: Fuss and bother, that's a good one. What have you gone and picked up now? This messy little tart! So this is your great conquest! So this is your Rose of old Soho!
*Song lighting: golden glow. The organ is lit up. Three lamps are lowered on a pole and the signs say:*

### JEALOUSY DUET

#### LUCY:
Come on out, you Rose of Old Soho!
Let us see your legs, my little sweetheart!
I hear you have a lovely ankle
And I'd love to see such a complete tart.
They tell me that Mac says your behind is so provoking.

#### POLLY:
Did he now, did he now?

#### LUCY:
If what I see is true he must be joking.

#### POLLY:
Is he now, is he now?

#### LUCY:
Ho, it makes me split my sides!

#### POLLY:
Oh, that's how you split your side?

LUCY:

Fancy you as Mackie's bride!

POLLY:

Mackie fancies Mackie's bride.

LUCY:

Ha ha ha! Catch him sporting
With something that the cat brought in.

POLLY:

Just you watch your tongue, my dear.

LUCY:

Must I watch my tongue, my dear?

BOTH:

Mackie and I, see how we bill and coo, man
He's got no eye for any other woman.
The whole thing's an invention
You mustn't pay attention
To such a bitch's slanders.
Poppycock!

POLLY:

Oh, they call me Rose of Old Soho
And Macheath appears to find me pretty.

LUCY:

Does he now?

POLLY:

They say I have a lovely ankle
And the best proportions in the city.

LUCY:

Little whippersnapper!

POLLY:

Who's a little whippersnapper?
Mac tells me that he finds my behind is most provoking.

LUCY:

Doesn't he? Doesn't he?

POLLY:

I do not suppose that he is joking.

LUCY:

Isn't he, isn't he?

POLLY:

Ho, it makes me split my sides!

LUCY:

Oh, that's how you split your side?

POLLY:

Being Mackie's only bride!

LUCY:

Are you Mackie's only bride?

POLLY *to the audience:*

Can you really picture him sporting
With something that the cat brought in?

LUCY:

Just you watch your tongue, my dear.

POLLY:

Must I watch my tongue, my dear?

BOTH:

Mackie and I, see how we bill and coo, man
He's got no eye for any other woman.
The whole thing's an invention
You cannot pay attention
To such a bitch's slanders.
Poppycock!

MAC: All right, Lucy. Calm down. You see it's just a trick of Polly's. She wants to come between us. I'm going to be hanged and she wants to parade as my widow. Really, Polly, this isn't the moment.

POLLY: Have you the heart to disclaim me?

MAC: And have you the heart to go on about my being married? Oh, Polly, why do you have to add to my misery? *Shakes his head reproachfully:* Polly! Polly!

LUCY: It's true, Miss Peachum. You're putting yourself in a bad light. Quite apart from the fact that it's uncivilised of you to worry a gentleman in his situation!

POLLY: The most elementary rules of decency, my dear young lady, ought to teach you, it seems to me, to treat a man with a little more reserve when his wife is present.

MAC: Seriously, Polly, that's carrying a joke too far.

LUCY: And if, my dear lady, you start raising a row here in this prison, I shall be obliged to send for the screw to show you the door. I'm sorry, my dear Miss Peachum.

POLLY: Mrs, if you please! Mrs Macheath. Just let me tell you this, young lady. The airs you give yourself are most unbecoming. My duty obliges me to stay with my husband.

LUCY: What's that? What's that? Oh, she won't leave! She stands there and we throw her out and she won't leave! Must I speak more plainly?

POLLY: You – you just hold your filthy tongue, you slut, or I'll knock your block off, my dear young lady.

LUCY: You've been thrown out, you interloper! I suppose that's not clear enough. You don't understand nice manners.

POLLY: You and your nice manners! Oh, I'm forgetting my dignity! I shouldn't stoop to . . . no, I shouldn't.
*She starts to bawl.*

LUCY: Just look at my belly, you slut! Did I get that from out of nowhere? Haven't you eyes in your head?

POLLY: Oh! So you're in the family way! And you think that gives you rights? A fine lady like you, you shouldn't have let him in!

MAC: Polly!

POLLY *in tears:* This is really too much. Mac, you shouldn't have done that. Now I don't know what to do.
*Enter Mrs Peachum.*

MRS PEACHUM: I knew it. She's with her man. You little trollop, come here immediately. When they hang your man, you can hang yourself too. A fine way to treat your respectable mother, making her come and get you out of jail. And he's got two of them, what's more – the Nero!

POLLY: Leave me here, mama; you don't know . . .

MRS PEACHUM: You're coming home this minute.

LUCY: There you are, it takes your mama to tell you how to behave.

MRS PEACHUM: Get going.

POLLY: Just a second. I only have to . . . I only have to tell him something . . . Really . . . it's very important.

MRS PEACHUM *giving her a box on the ear:* Well, this is important too. Get going!

POLLY: Oh, Mac! *She is dragged away.*

MAC: Lucy, you were magnificent. Of course I felt sorry for her. That's why I couldn't treat the slut as she deserved. Just for a moment you thought there was some truth in what she said. Didn't you?

LUCY: Yes, my dear, so I did.

MAC: If there were any truth in it, her mother wouldn't have put me in this situation. Did you hear how she laid into me? A mother might treat a seducer like that, not a son-in-law.

LUCY: It makes me happy to hear you say that from the bottom of your heart. I love you so much I'd almost rather see you on the gallows than in the arms of another. Isn't that strange?

MAC: Lucy, I should like to owe you my life.

LUCY: It's wonderful the way you say that. Say it again.

MAC: Lucy, I should like to owe you my life.

LUCY: Shall I run away with you, dearest?

MAC: Well, but you see, if we run away together, it won't be easy for us to hide. As soon as they stop looking, I'll send for you post haste, you know that.

LUCY: What can I do to help you?

MAC: Bring me my hat and cane.

*Lucy comes back with his hat and cane and throws them into his cage.*

Lucy, the fruit of our love which you bear beneath your heart will hold us forever united.

*Lucy goes out.*

SMITH *enters, goes into the cell, and says to Mac:* Let's have that cane.

*After a brief chase, in which Smith pursues Mac with a chair and a crow bar, Mac jumps over the bars. Constables run after him. Enter Brown.*

BROWN *off:* Hey, Mac! – Mac, answer me, please. It's Jackie. Mac, please be a good boy, answer me, I can't stand it any longer. *Comes in.* Mackie! What's this? He's gone, thank God.

*He sits down on the bed.*

*Enter Peachum.*

PEACHUM *to Smith:* My name is Peachum. I've come to col-

lect the forty pounds reward for the capture of the bandit
Macheath. *Appears in front of the cage.* Excuse me! Is that
Mr Macheath? *Brown is silent.* Oh. I suppose the other
gentleman has gone for a stroll? I come here to visit a
criminal and who do I find sitting here but Mr Brown!
Tiger Brown is sitting here and his friend Macheath is not
sitting here.

BROWN *groaning:* Oh, Mr Peachum, it wasn't my fault.

PEACHUM: Of course not. How could it be? You'd never
have dreamt . . . considering the situation it'll land you in
. . . it's out of the question, Brown.

BROWN: Mr Peachum, I'm beside myself.

PEACHUM: I believe you. Terrible, you must feel.

BROWN: Yes, it's this feeling of helplessness that ties one's
hands so. Those fellows do just as they please. It's dreadful,
dreadful.

PEACHUM: Wouldn't you care to lie down awhile? Just close
your eyes and pretend nothing has happened. Imagine
you're on a lovely green meadow with little white clouds
overhead. The main thing is to forget all about those
ghastly things, those that are past, and most of all, those
that are still to come.

BROWN *alarmed:* What do you mean by that?

PEACHUM: I'm amazed at your fortitude. In your position I
should simply collapse, crawl into bed and drink hot tea.
And above all, I'd find someone to lay a soothing hand on
my forehead.

BROWN: Damn it all, it's not my fault if the fellow escapes.
There's not much the police can do about it.

PEACHUM: I see. There's not much the police can do about
it. You don't believe we'll see Mr Macheath back here
again? *Brown shrugs his shoulders.* In that case your fate will
be hideously unjust. People are sure to say – they always do
– that the police shouldn't have let him escape. No, I can't
see that glittering Coronation procession just yet.

BROWN: What do you mean?

PEACHUM: Let me remind you of a historical incident which,
though it caused a great stir at the time, in the year 1400 BC,
is unknown to the public of today. On the death of the

Egyptian king Rameses II, the police captain of Nineveh, or was it Cairo, committed some minor offence against the lower classes of the population. Even at that time the consequences were terrible. As the history books tell us, the coronation procession of Semiramis, the new Queen, 'developed into a series of catastrophes thanks to the unduly active participation of the lower orders'. Historians still shudder at the cruel way Semiramis treated her police captain. I only remember dimly, but there was some talk of snakes she fed on his bosom.

BROWN: Really?

PEACHUM: The Lord be with you, Brown. *Goes out.*

BROWN: Now only the mailed fist can help. Sergeants! Report to me at the double!

*Curtain. Macheath and Low-Dive Jenny step before the curtain and sing to song lighting:*

### SECOND THREEPENNY FINALE
### WHAT KEEPS MANKIND ALIVE?

You gentlemen who think you have a mission
To purge us of the seven deadly sins
Should first sort out the basic food position
Then start your preaching: that's where it begins.
You lot, who preach restraint and watch your waist as
    well
Should learn for all time how the world is run:
However much you twist, whatever lies you tell
Food is the first thing. Morals follow on.
So first make sure that those who now are starving
Get proper helpings when we do the carving.
    What keeps mankind alive? The fact that millions
    Are daily tortured, stifled, punished, silenced,
        oppressed.
    Mankind can keep alive thanks to its brilliance
    In keeping its humanity repressed.
    For once you must try not to shirk the facts:
    Mankind is kept alive by bestial acts.

You say that girls may strip with your permission.
You draw the lines dividing art from sin.
So first sort out the basic food position
Then start your preaching: that's where we begin.
You lot, who bank on your desires and our disgust
Should learn for all time how the world is run:
Whatever lies you tell, however much you twist
Food is the first thing. Morals follow on.
So first make sure that those who now are starving
Get proper helpings when we do the carving.

> What keeps mankind alive? The fact that millions
> Are daily tortured, stifled, punished, silenced,
> oppressed.
> Mankind can keep alive thanks to its brilliance
> In keeping its humanity repressed.
> For once you must try not to shirk the facts:
> Mankind is kept alive by bestial acts.

# ACT THREE

## 7

That night Peachum prepares his campaign. He plans to disrupt the Coronation procession by a demonstration of human misery.

*Peachum's Outfitting Emporium for Beggars.*

*The beggars paint little signs with inscriptions such as 'I gave my eye for my king', etc.*

PEACHUM: Gentlemen, at this moment, in our eleven branches from Drury Lane to Turnbridge, one thousand four hundred and thirty-two gentlemen are working on signs like these with a view to attending the Coronation of our Queen.

MRS PEACHUM: Get a move on! If you won't work, you can't beg. Call yourself a blind man and can't even make a proper K? That's supposed to be child's writing, anyone would think it was an old man's.

*A drum rolls.*

BEGGAR: That's the Coronation guard presenting arms. Little do they suspect that today, the biggest day in their military careers, they'll have us to deal with.

FILCH *enters and reports:* Mrs Peachum, there's a dozen sleepy-looking hens traipsing in. They claim there's some money due them.

*Enter the whores.*

JENNY: Madam . . .

MRS PEACHUM: Hm, you do look as if you'd fallen off your perches. I suppose you've come to collect the money for that Macheath of yours? Well, you'll get nothing, you understand, nothing.

JENNY: How are we to understand that, Ma'am?

MRS PEACHUM: Bursting in here in the middle of the night! Coming to a respectable house at three in the morning! With the work you do, I should think you'd want some sleep. You look like sicked-up milk.

JENNY: Then you won't give us the stipulated fee for turning in Macheath, ma'am?

MRS PEACHUM: Exactly. No thirty pieces of silver for you.

JENNY: Why not, ma'am?

MRS PEACHUM: Because your fine Mr Macheath has scattered himself to the four winds. And now, ladies, get out of my parlour.

JENNY: Well, I call that the limit. Just don't you try that on us. That's all I've got to say to you. Not on us.

MRS PEACHUM: Filch, the ladies wish to be shown the door. *Filch goes towards the ladies, Jenny pushes him away.*

JENNY: I would be grateful if you would be so good as to hold your filthy tongue. If you don't, I'm likely to . . . *Enter Peachum.*

PEACHUM: What's going on, you haven't given them any money, I hope? Well, ladies how about it? Is Mr Macheath in jail, or isn't he?

JENNY: Don't talk to me about Mr Macheath. You're not fit to black his boots. Last night I had to let a customer go because it made me cry into my pillow thinking how I had sold that gentleman to you. Yes, ladies, and what do you think happened this morning? Less than an hour ago, just after I had cried myself to sleep, I heard somebody whistle, and out on the street stood the very gentleman I'd been crying about, asking me to throw down the key. He wanted to lie in my arms and make me forget the wrong I had done him. Ladies, he's the last sportsman left in London. And if our friend Suky Tawdry isn't here with us now, it's because he went on from me to her to console her too.

PEACHUM *muttering to himself:* Suky Tawdry . . .

JENNY: So now you know that you're not fit to black that gentleman's boots. You miserable sneak.

PEACHUM: Filch, run to the nearest police station, tell them Mr Macheath is at Miss Suky Tawdry's place. *Filch goes out.* But ladies, what are we arguing for? The money will be paid out, that goes without saying. Celia dear, you'd do better to make the ladies some coffee instead of slanging them.

MRS PEACHUM *on her way out:* Suky Tawdry! *She sings the third stanza of the Ballad of Sexual Obsession:*

> There stands a man. The gallows loom above him.
> They've got the quicklime mixed in which to shove him.
> They've put his neck just under where the noose is
> And what's he thinking of, the idiot? Floozies.
> They've all but hanged him, yet he can't ignore that call.
> Sexual obsession has him in its thrall.
> > She's sold him down the river heart and soul
> > He's seen the dirty money in her hand
> > And bit by bit begins to understand:
> > The pit that covers him is woman's hole.
> > Then he may rant and roar and curse his ruin –
> > But soon as night falls he'll be up and doing.

PEACHUM: Get a move on, you'd all be rotting in the sewers of Turnbridge if in my sleepless nights I hadn't worked out how to squeeze a penny out of your poverty. I discovered that though the rich of this earth find no difficulty in creating misery, they can't bear to see it. Because they are weaklings and fools just like you. They may have enough to eat till the end of their days, they may be able to wax their floors with butter so that even the crumbs from their tables grow fat. But they can't look on unmoved while a man is collapsing from hunger, though of course that only applies so long as he collapses outside their own front door. *Enter Mrs Peachum with a tray full of coffee cups.*

MRS PEACHUM: You can come by the shop tomorrow and pick up your money, but only once the Coronation's over.

JENNY: Mrs Peachum, you leave me speechless.

PEACHUM: Fall in. We assemble in one hour outside Buckingham Palace. Quick march.

*The beggars fall in.*

FILCH *dashes in:* Cops! I didn't even get to the police station. The police are here already.

PEACHUM: Hide, gentlemen! *To Mrs Peachum:* Call the band together. Shake a leg. And if you hear me say 'harmless', do you understand, *harmless* . . .

MRS PEACHUM: Harmless? I don't understand a thing.

PEACHUM: Naturally you don't understand. Well, if I say *harmless* . . . *Knocking at the door.* Thank God, that's the answer, *harmless*, then you play some kind of music. Get a move on!

*Mrs Peachum goes out with the beggars. The beggars, except for the girl with the sign 'A Victim of Military Tyranny', hide with their things upstage right behind the clothes rack. Enter Brown and constables.*

BROWN: Here we are. And now, Mr Beggar's Friend, drastic action will be taken. Put the derbies on him, Smith. Ah, here are some of those delightful signs. *To the girl:* 'A Victim of Military Tyranny' – is that you?

PEACHUM: Good morning, Brown, good morning. Sleep well?

BROWN: Huh?

PEACHUM: Morning, Brown.

BROWN: Is he saying that to me? Does he know one of you? I don't believe I have the pleasure of your acquaintance.

PEACHUM: Really? Morning, Brown.

BROWN: Knock his hat off. *Smith does so.*

PEACHUM: Look here, Brown, since you're passing by, *passing*, I say, Brown, I may as well ask you to put a certain Macheath under lock and key, it's high time.

BROWN: The man's mad. Don't laugh, Smith. Tell me, Smith, how is it possible that such a notorious criminal should be running around loose in London?

PEACHUM: Because he's your pal, Brown.

BROWN: Who?

PEACHUM: Mac the Knife. Not me. I'm no criminal. I'm a poor man, Brown. You can't abuse me, Brown, you've got the worst hour in your life ahead of you. Care for some coffee? *To the whores:* Girls, give the chief of police a sip, that's no way to behave. Let's all be friends. We are all law-abiding people. The law was made for one thing alone, for the exploitation of those who don't understand it, or are prevented by naked misery from obeying it. And anyone who wants a crumb of this exploitation for himself must obey the law strictly.

BROWN: I see, then you believe our judges are corruptible?

PEACHUM: Not at all, sir, not at all. Our judges are absolutely incorruptible: it's more than money can do to make them give a fair verdict.

*A second drum roll.*

The troops are marching off to line the route. The poorest of the poor will move off in half an hour.

BROWN: That's right, Mr Peachum. In half an hour the poorest of the poor will be marched off to winter quarters in the Old Bailey. *To the constables:* All right, boys, round them all up, all the patriots you find here. *To the beggars:* Have you fellows ever heard of Tiger Brown? Tonight, Peachum, I've hit on the solution, and I believe I may say, saved a friend from mortal peril. I'll simply smoke out your whole nest. And lock up the lot of you for – hm, for what? For begging on the street. You seem to have intimated your intention of embarrassing me and the Queen with these beggars. I shall simply arrest the beggars. Think about it.

PEACHUM: Excellent, but . . . what beggars?

BROWN: These cripples here. Smith, we're taking these patriots along with us.

PEACHUM: I can save you from a hasty step; you can thank the Lord, Brown, that you came to me. You see, Brown, you can arrest these few, they're harmless, *harmless* . . .

*Music starts up, playing a few measures of the 'Song of the Insufficiency of Human Endeavour'.*

BROWN: What's that?

PEACHUM: Music. They're playing as well as they can. The Song of Insufficiency. You don't know it? Think about it.

*Song lighting: golden glow. The organ is lit up. Three lamps are lowered from above on a pole and the signs say:*

SONG OF THE INSUFFICIENCY OF HUMAN ENDEAVOUR

Mankind lives by its head
Its head won't see it through
Inspect your own. What lives off that?
At most a louse or two.
    For this bleak existence
    Man is never sharp enough.
    Hence his weak resistance
    To its tricks and bluff.

Aye, make yourself a plan
They need you at the top!
Then make yourself a second plan
Then let the whole thing drop.
    For this bleak existence
    Man is never bad enough
    Though his sheer persistence
    Can be lovely stuff.

Aye, race for happiness
But don't you race too fast.
When all start chasing happiness
Happiness comes in last.
    For this bleak existence
    Man is never undemanding enough.
    All his loud insistence
    Is a load of guff.

PEACHUM: Your plan, Brown, was brilliant but hardly realistic. All you can arrest in this place is a few young fellows celebrating their Queen's Coronation by arranging a little fancy dress party. When the real paupers come along – there aren't any here – there will be thousands of them. That's the point: you've forgotten what an immense number of poor people there are. When you see them standing outside the Abbey, it won't be a festive sight. You see, they don't look good. Do you know what grogblossom is, Brown? Yes, but how about a hundred and twenty noses all flushed with grogblossom? Our young Queen's path should be strewn with blossom, not with grogblossom. And all those cripples at the church door. That's something one wishes to avoid, Brown. You'll probably say the police can handle us poor folk. You don't believe that yourself. How will it look if six hundred poor cripples have to be clubbed down at the Coronation? It will look bad. It will look disgusting. Nauseating. I feel faint at the thought of it, Brown. A small chair, if you please.

BROWN *to Smith:* That's a threat. See here, you, that's blackmail. We can't touch the man, in the interests of public order we simply can't touch him. I've never seen the like of it.

PEACHUM: You're seeing it now. Let me tell you something. You can behave as you please to the Queen of England. But you can't tread on the toes of the poorest man in England, or you'll be brought down, Mr Brown.

BROWN: So you're asking me to arrest Mac the Knife? Arrest him? That's easy to say. You have to find a man before you can arrest him.

PEACHUM: If you say that, I can't contradict you. So I'll find your man for you; we'll see if there's any morality left. Jenny, where is Mr Macheath at this moment?

JENNY: 21 Oxford Street, at Suky Tawdry's.

BROWN: Smith, go at once to Suky Tawdry's place at 21 Oxford Street, arrest Macheath and take him to the Old Bailey. In the meantime, I must put on my gala uniform. On this day of all days I must wear my gala uniform.

PEACHUM: Brown, if he's not on the gallows by six o'clock . . .

BROWN: Oh, Mac, it was not to be. *Goes out with constables.*

PEACHUM *calling after him:* Think about it, eh, Brown?
*Third drum roll.*
Third drum roll. Change of objective. You will head for the dungeons of the Old Bailey.
*The beggars go out.*

*Peachum sings the fourth stanza of the 'Song of Human In-sufficiency':*

Man could be good instead
So slug him on the head
If you can slug him good and hard
He may stay good and dead.
> For this bleak existence
> Man's not good enough just yet.
> You'll need no assistance.
> Slug him on the head.


*Curtain. Jenny steps before the curtain with a hurdy-gurdy and sings the*


### SOLOMON SONG

You saw sagacious Solomon
You know what came of him.
To him complexities seemed plain.
He cursed the hour that gave birth to him
And saw that everything was vain.
How great and wise was Solomon!
But now that time is getting late
The world can see what followed on.
It's wisdom that had brought him to this state –
How fortunate the man with none!


You saw the lovely Cleopatra
You know what she became.
Two emperors slaved to serve her lust.
She whored herself to death and fame
Then rotted down and turned to dust.
How beautiful was Babylon!
But now that time is getting late
The world can see what followed on.
It's beauty that had brought her to this state –
How fortunate the girl with none!

You saw the gallant Caesar next
You know what he became.
They deified him in his life
Then had him murdered just the same.
And as they raised the fatal knife
How loud he cried 'You too, my son!'
But now that time is getting late
The world can see what followed on.
It's courage that had brought him to this state –
How fortunate the man with none!

You know the ever-curious Brecht
Whose songs you liked to hum.
He asked, too often for your peace
Where rich men get their riches from.
So then you drove him overseas.
How curious was my mother's son!
But now that time is getting late
The world can see what followed on.
Inquisitiveness brought him to this state –
How fortunate the man with none!

And now look at this man Macheath
The sands are running out.
If only he'd known where to stop
And stuck to crimes he knew all about
He surely would have reached the top.
But one fine day his heart was won.
So now that time is getting late
The world can see what followed on.
His sexual urges brought him to this state –
How fortunate the man with none!

# 8

## Property in dispute.

*A young girl's room in the Old Bailey.*

*Lucy.*

SMITH *enters:* Miss, Mrs Polly Macheath wishes to speak with
you.
LUCY: Mrs Macheath? Show her in.
*Enter Polly.*
POLLY: Good morning, madam. Madam, good morning.
LUCY: What is it, please?
POLLY: Do you recognise me?
LUCY: Of course I know you.
POLLY: I've come to beg your pardon for the way I behaved
yesterday.
LUCY: Very interesting.
POLLY: I have no excuse to offer for my behaviour, madam,
but my misfortunes.
LUCY: I see.
POLLY: Madam, you must forgive me. I was stung by Mr
Macheath's behaviour. He really should not have put us in
such a situation, and you can tell him so when you see him.
LUCY: I . . . I . . . shan't be seeing him.
POLLY: Of course you will see him.
LUCY: I shall not see him.
POLLY: Forgive me.
LUCY: But he's very fond of you.
POLLY: Oh no, you're the only one he loves. I'm sure of that.
LUCY: Very kind of you.
POLLY: But, madam, a man is always afraid of a woman who
loves him too much. And then he's bound to neglect and
avoid her. I could see at a glance that he is more devoted to
you than I could ever have guessed.
LUCY: Do you mean that sincerely?

POLLY: Of course, certainly, very sincerely, madam. Do believe me.

LUCY: Dear Miss Polly, both of us have loved him too much.

POLLY: Perhaps. *Pause*. And now, madam, I want to tell you how it all came about. Ten days ago I met Mr Macheath for the first time at the Cuttlefish Hotel. My mother was there too. Five days later, about the day before yesterday, we were married. Yesterday I found out that he was wanted by the police for a variety of crimes. And today I don't know what's going to happen. So you see, madam, twelve days ago I couldn't have imagined ever losing my heart to a man. *Pause*.

LUCY: I understand, Miss Peachum.

POLLY: Mrs Macheath.

LUCY: Mrs Macheath.

POLLY: To tell the truth, I've been thinking about this man a good deal in the last few hours. It's not so simple. Because you see, Miss, I really can't help envying you for the way he behaved to you the other day. When I left him, only because my mother made me, he didn't show the slightest sign of regret. Maybe he has no heart and nothing but a stone in his breast. What do you think, Lucy?

LUCY: Well, my dear Miss, I really don't know if Mr Macheath is entirely to blame. You should have stuck to your own class of people, dear Miss.

POLLY: Mrs Macheath.

LUCY: Mrs Macheath.

POLLY: That's quite true – or at least, as my father always advised me, I should have kept everything on a strict business footing.

LUCY: Definitely.

POLLY *weeping*: But he's my only possession in all the world.

LUCY: My dear, such a misfortune can befall the most intelligent woman. But after all, you are his wife on paper. That should be a comfort to you. Poor child, I can't bear to see you so depressed. Won't you have a little something?

POLLY: What?

LUCY: Something to eat.

POLLY: Oh yes, please, a little something to eat. *Lucy goes out. Polly aside:* The hypocritical strumpet.

LUCY *comes back with coffee and cake:* Here. This ought to do it.

POLLY: You really have gone to too much trouble, madam. *Pause. She eats.* What a lovely picture of him you've got. When did he bring it?

LUCY: Bring it?

POLLY *innocently:* I mean when did he bring it up here to you?

LUCY: He didn't bring it.

POLLY: Did he give it to you right here in this room?

LUCY: He never was in this room.

POLLY: I see. But there wouldn't have been any harm in that. The paths of fate are so dreadfully crisscrossed.

LUCY: Must you keep talking such nonsense? You only came here to spy.

POLLY: Then you know where he is?

LUCY: Me? Don't you know?

POLLY: Tell me this minute where he is.

LUCY: I have no idea.

POLLY: So you don't know where he is. Word of honour?

LUCY: No, I don't know. Hm, and you don't either?

POLLY: No. This is terrible. *Polly laughs and Lucy weeps.* Now he has two commitments. And he's gone.

LUCY: I can't stand it any more. Oh, Polly, it's so dreadful.

POLLY *gaily:* I'm so happy to have found such a good friend at the end of this tragedy. That's something. Would you care for a little more to eat? Some more cake?

LUCY: Just a bit! Oh, Polly, don't be so good to me. Really, I don't deserve it. Oh, Polly, men aren't worth it.

POLLY: Of course men aren't worth it, but what else can we do?

LUCY: No! Now I'm going to make a clean breast of it. Will you be very cross with me, Polly?

POLLY: About what?

LUCY: It's not real!

POLLY: What?

LUCY: This here! *She indicates her belly.* And all for that crook!

POLLY *laughs:* Oh, that's magnificent! Is it a cushion? Oh, you really are a hypocritical strumpet! Look — you want

Mackie? I'll make you a present of him. If you find him you can keep him. *Voices and steps are heard in the corridor.* What's that?

LUCY *at the window:* Mackie! They've caught him once more.

POLLY *collapses:* This is the end.

*Enter Mrs Peachum.*

MRS PEACHUM: Ha, Polly, so this is where I find you. You must change your things, your husband is being hanged. I've brought your widow's weeds. *Polly changes into the widow's dress.* You'll be a lovely widow. But you'll have to cheer up a little.


# 9

Friday morning. 5 am. Mac the Knife, who has been with the whores again, has again been betrayed by whores. He is about to be hanged.

*Death cell.*

*The bells of Westminster ring. Constables bring Macheath shackled into the cell.*

SMITH: Bring him in here. Those are the bells of Westminster. Stand up straight, I'm not asking you why you look so worn out. I'd say you were ashamed. *To the constables:* When the bells of Westminster ring for the third time, that will be at six, he's got to have been hanged. Make everything ready.

A CONSTABLE: For the last quarter of an hour all the streets around Newgate have been so jammed with people of all classes you can't get through.

SMITH: Strange! Then they already know?

CONSTABLE: If this goes on, the whole of London will know in another quarter of an hour. All the people who would otherwise have gone to the Coronation will come here. And the Queen will be riding through empty streets.

SMITH: All the more reason for us to move fast. If we're
through by six, that will give people time to get back to the
Coronation by seven. So now, get going.

MAC: Hey, Smith, what time is it?

SMITH: Haven't you got eyes? Five oh-four.

MAC: Five oh-four.

*Just as Smith is locking the cell door from outside, Brown enters.*

BROWN, *his back to the cell, to Smith:* Is he in there?

SMITH: You want to see him?

BROWN: No, no, no, for God's sake. I'll leave it all to you.
*Goes out.*

MAC *suddenly bursts into a soft unbroken flow of speech:* All right,
Smith, I won't say a word, not a word about bribery, never
fear. I know all about it. If you let yourself be bribed, you'd
have to leave the country for a start. You certainly would.
You'd need enough to live on for the rest of your life. A
thousand pounds, eh? Don't say anything! In twenty
minutes I'll tell you whether you can have your thousand
pounds by noon. I'm not saying a word about feelings. Go
outside and think it over carefully. Life is short and money
is scarce. And I don't even know yet if I can raise any. But
if anyone wants to see me, let them in.

SMITH *slowly:* That's a lot of nonsense, Mr Macheath. *Goes out.*

MAC *sings softly and very fast the 'Call from the Grave':*
Hark to the voice that's calling you to weep.
Macheath lies here, not under open sky
Not under treetops, no, but good and deep.
Fate struck him down in outraged majesty.
God grant his dying words may reach a friend.
The thickest walls encompass him about.
Is none of you concerned to know his fate?
Once he is gone the bottles can come out
But do stand by him while it's not too late.
D'you want his punishment to have no end?

*Matthew and Jake appear in the corridor. They are on their way
to see Macheath. Smith stops them.*

SMITH: Well, son. You look like a soused herring.

MATTHEW: Now the captain's gone it's my job to put our
girls in pod, so they can throw themselves on the mercy of

the court. It's a job for a horse. I've got to see the Captain. *Both continue towards Mac.*

MAC: Five twenty-five. You took your time.

JAKE: Yes, but, you see, we had to . . .

MAC: You see, you see. I'm being hanged, man! But I've no time to waste arguing with you. Five twenty-eight. All right: How much can you people draw from your savings account right away?

MATTHEW: From our . . . at five o'clock in the morning?

JAKE: Has it really come to this?

MAC: Can you manage four hundred pounds?

JAKE: But what about us? That's all there is.

MAC: Who's being hanged, you or me?

MATTHEW *excitedly:* Who was lying around with Suky Tawdry instead of clearing out? Who was lying around with Suky Tawdry, us or you?

MAC: Shut your trap. I'll soon be lying somewhere other than with that slut. Five-thirty.

JAKE: Matt, if that's how it is, we'll just have to do it.

SMITH: Mr Brown wishes to know what you'd like for your . . . repast.

MAC: Don't bother me. *To Matthew:* Well, will you or won't you? *To Smith:* Asparagus.

MATTHEW: Don't you shout at me. I won't have it.

MAC: I'm not shouting at you. It's only that . . . well, Matthew, are you going to let me be hanged?

MATTHEW: Of course I'm not going to let you be hanged. Who said I was? But that's the lot. Four hundred pounds is all there is. No reason why I shouldn't say that, is there?

MAC: Five thirty-eight.

JAKE: We'll have to run, Matthew, or it'll be no good.

MATTHEW: If we can only get through. There's such a crowd. Human scum! *Both go out.*

MAC: If you're not here by five to six, you'll never see me again. *Shouts:* You'll never see me again . . .

SMITH: They've gone. Well, how about it? *Makes a gesture of counting money.*

MAC: Four hundred. *Smith goes out shrugging his shoulders. Mac, calling after him:* I've got to speak to Brown.

SMITH *comes back with constables:* Got the soap?

CONSTABLE: Yes, but not the right kind.

SMITH: You can set the thing up in ten minutes.

CONSTABLE: But the trap doesn't work.

SMITH: It's got to work. The bells have gone a second time.

CONSTABLE: What a shambles!

MAC *sings:*

Come here and see the shitty state he's in.
This really is what people mean by bust.
You who set up the dirty cash you win
As just about the only god you'll trust
Don't stand and watch him slipping round the bend!
Go to the Queen and say that her subjects need her
Go in a group and tell her of his trouble
Like pigs all following behind their leader.
Say that his teeth are wearing down to rubble.
D'you want his punishment to have no end?

SMITH: I can't possibly let you in. You're only number sixteen. Wait your turn.

POLLY: What do you mean, number sixteen? Don't be a bureaucrat. I'm his wife. I've got to see him.

SMITH: Not more than five minutes, then.

POLLY: Five minutes! That's perfectly ridiculous. Five minutes! How's a lady to say all she's got to say? It's not so simple. This is goodbye forever. There's an exceptional amount of things for man and wife to talk about at such a moment . . . where is he?

SMITH: What, can't you see him?

POLLY: Oh yes, of course. Thank you.

MAC: Polly!

POLLY: Yes, Mackie, here I am.

MAC: Oh yes, of course!

POLLY: How are you? Are you quite worn out? It's hard.

MAC: But what are you going to do now? What will become of you?

POLLY: Don't worry, the business is doing very well. That's the least part of it. Are you very nervous, Mackie? . . . By the way, what was your father? There's so much you still haven't told me. I just don't understand. Your health has always been excellent.

MAC: Polly, can't you help me to get out?

POLLY: Oh yes, of course.

MAC: With money, of course. I've arranged with the warder . . .

POLLY *slowly:* The money has gone off to Manchester.

MAC: And you have got none on you?

POLLY: No, I have got nothing on me. But you know, Mackie, I could talk to somebody, for instance . . . I might even ask the Queen in person. *She breaks down.* Oh, Mackie!

SMITH *pulling Polly away:* Well, have you raised those thousand pounds?

POLLY: All the best, Mackie, look after yourself, and don't forget me! *Goes out.*

*Smith and a constable bring in a table with a dish of asparagus on it.*

SMITH: Is the asparagus tender?

CONSTABLE: Yes. *Goes out.*

BROWN *appears and goes up to Smith:* Smith, what does he want me for? It's good you didn't take the table in earlier. We'll take it right in with us, to show him how we feel about him. *They enter the cell with the table. Smith goes out. Pause.* Hello, Mac. Here's your asparagus. Won't you have some?

MAC: Don't you bother, Mr Brown. There are others to show me the last honours.

BROWN: Oh, Mackie!

MAC: Would you have the goodness to produce your accounts? You don't mind if I eat in the meantime, after all it is my last meal. *He eats.*

BROWN: I hope you enjoy it. Oh, Mac, you're turning the knife in the wound.

MAC: The accounts, sir, if you please, the accounts. No sentimentality.

BROWN *with a sigh takes a small notebook from his pocket:* I've got them right here, Mac. The accounts for the past six months.

MAC *bitingly:* Oh, so all you came for was to get your money before it's too late.

BROWN: You know that isn't so . . .

MAC: Don't worry, sir, nobody's going to cheat you. What do

I owe you? But I want a detailed bill, if you don't mind. Life has made me distrustful . . . in your position you should be able to understand that.

BROWN: Mac, when you talk that way I just can't think.

*A loud pounding is heard rear.*

SMITH *off:* All right, that'll hold.

MAC: The accounts, Brown.

BROWN: Very well, if you insist. Well, first of all the rewards for murderers arrested thanks to you or your men. The Treasury paid you a total of . . .

MAC: Three instances at forty pounds a piece, that makes a hundred and twenty pounds. One quarter for you comes to thirty pounds, so that's what we owe you.

BROWN: Yes . . . yes . . . but really, Mac, I don't think we ought to spend our last . . .

MAC: Kindly stop snivelling. Thirty pounds. And for the job in Dover eight pounds.

BROWN: Why only eight pounds, there was . . .

MAC: Do you believe me or don't you believe me? Your share in the transactions of the last six months comes to thirty-eight pounds.

BROWN *wailing:* For a whole lifetime . . . I could read . . .

BOTH: Your every thought in your eyes.

MAC: Three years in India – John was all present and Jim was all there – five years in London, and this is the thanks I get. *Indicating how he will look when hanged.*

Here hangs Macheath who never wronged a flea
A faithless friend has brought him to this pass.
And as he dangles from the gallowstree
His neck finds out how heavy is his arse.

BROWN: If that's the way you feel about it, Mac . . . The man who impugns my honour, impugns me. *Runs furiously out of the cage.*

MAC: Your honour . . .

BROWN: Yes, my honour. Time to begin, Smith! Let them in! *To Mac:* Excuse me, would you?

SMITH *quickly to Macheath:* I can still get you out of here, in another minute I won't be able to. Have you got the money?

MAC: Yes, as soon as the boys get back.

SMITH: There's no sign of them. The deal is off.

*People are admitted. Peachum, Mrs Peachum, Polly, Lucy, the whores, the parson, Matthew and Jake.*

JENNY: They weren't anxious to let us in. But I said to them: If you don't get those pisspots you call heads out of my way, you'll hear from Low-Dive Jenny.

PEACHUM: I am his father-in-law. I beg your pardon, which of the present company is Mr Macheath?

MAC *introduces himself:* I'm Macheath.

PEACHUM *walks past the cage, and like all who follow him stations himself to the right of it:* Fate, Mr Macheath, has decreed that though I don't know you, you should be my son-in-law. The occasion of this first meeting between us is a very sad one. Mr Macheath, you once had white kid gloves, a cane with an ivory handle, and a scar on your neck, and you frequented the Cuttlefish Hotel. All that is left is your scar, no doubt the least valuable of your distinguishing marks. Today you frequent nothing but prison cells, and within the foreseeable future no place at all . . .

*Polly passes the cage in tears and stations herself to the right.*

MAC: What a pretty dress you're wearing.

*Matthew and Jake pass the cage and station themselves on the right.*

MATTHEW: We couldn't get through because of the terrible crush. We ran so hard I was afraid Jake was going to have a stroke. If you don't believe us . . .

MAC: What do my men say? Have they got good places?

MATTHEW: You see, Captain, we thought you'd understand. You see, a Coronation doesn't happen every day. They've got to make some money while there's a chance. They send you their best wishes.

JAKE: Their very best wishes.

MRS PEACHUM *steps up to the cage, stations herself on the right:* Mr Macheath, who would have expected this a week ago when we were dancing at a little hop at the Cuttlefish Hotel.

MAC: A little hop.

MRS PEACHUM: But the ways of destiny are cruel here below.

BROWN *at the rear to the parson:* And to think that I stood shoulder to shoulder with this man in Azerbaidjan under a hail of bullets.

JENNY *approaches the cage:* We Drury Lane girls are frantic. Nobody's gone to the Coronation. Everybody wants to see you. *Stations herself on the right.*

MAC: To see me.

SMITH: All right. Let's go. Six o'clock. *Lets him out of the cage.*

MAC: We mustn't keep anybody waiting. Ladies and gentlemen. You see before you a declining representative of a declining social group. We lower middle-class artisans who toil with our humble jemmies on small shopkeepers' cash registers are being swallowed up by big corporations backed by the banks. What's a jemmy compared with a share certificate? What's breaking into a bank compared with founding a bank? What's murdering a man compared with employing a man? Fellow citizens, I hereby take my leave of you. I thank you for coming. Some of you were very close to me. That Jenny should have turned me in amazes me greatly. It is proof positive that the world never changes. A concatenation of several unfortunate circumstances has brought about my fall. So be it – I fall.

*Song lighting: golden glow. The organ is lit up. Three lamps are lowered on a pole, and the signs say:*

### BALLAD IN WHICH MACHEATH BEGS ALL MEN FOR FORGIVENESS

You fellow men who live on after us
Pray do not think you have to judge us harshly
And when you see us hoisted up and trussed
Don't laugh like fools behind your big moustaches
Or curse at us. It's true that we came crashing
But do not judge our downfall like the courts.
Not all of us can discipline our thoughts –
Dear fellows, your extravagance needs slashing.
Dear fellows, we've shown how a crash begins.
Pray then to God that He forgive my sins.

The rain washes away and purifies.
Let it wash down the flesh we catered for
And we who saw so much, and wanted more –
The crows will come and peck away our eyes.
Perhaps ambition used too sharp a goad
It drove us to these heights from which we swing
Hacked at by greedy starlings on the wing
Like horses' droppings on a country road.
O brothers, learn from us how it begins
And pray to God that He forgive our sins.

The girls who flaunt their breasts as bait there
To catch some sucker who will love them
The youths who slyly stand and wait there
To grab their sinful earnings off them
The crooks, the tarts, the tarts' protectors
The models and the mannequins
The psychopaths, the unfrocked rectors
I pray that they forgive my sins.

Not so those filthy police employees
Who day by day would bait my anger
Devise new troubles to annoy me
And chuck me crusts to stop my hunger.
I'd call on God to come and choke them
And yet my need for respite wins:
I realise that it might provoke them
So pray that they forgive my sins.

**Someone must take a huge iron crowbar
And stave their ugly faces in
All I ask is to know it's over
Praying that they forgive my sins.**

SMITH: If you don't mind, Mr Macheath.

MRS PEACHUM: Polly and Lucy, stand by your husband in his last hour.

MAC: Ladies, whatever there may have been between us . . .

SMITH *leads him away:* Get a move on!

*Procession to the Gallows.*
*All go out through doors left. These doors are on projection screens.*
*Then all re-enter from the other side of the stage with dark lan-*
*terns. When Macheath is standing at the top of the gallows steps*
*Peachum speaks.*

Dear audience, we now are coming to
The point where we must hang him by the neck
Because it is the Christian thing to do
Proving that men must pay for what they take.

But as we want to keep our fingers clean
And you're the people we can't risk offending
We thought we'd better do without this scene
And substitute instead a different ending.

Since this is opera, not life, you'll see
Justice give way before humanity.
So now, to stop our story in its course
Enter the royal official on his horse.

### THIRD THREEPENNY FINALE
### APPEARANCE OF THE DEUS EX MACHINA

CHORUS:
Hark, who's here?
A royal official on horseback's here!
*Enter Brown on horseback as deus ex machina.*

BROWN: I bring a special order from our beloved Queen to
have Captain Macheath set at liberty forthwith – *All cheer.* –
as it's the coronation, and raised to the hereditary peerage.
*Cheers.* The castle of Marmarel, likewise a pension of ten
thousand pounds, to be his in usufruct until his death. To
any bridal couples present Her Majesty bids me to convey
her gracious good wishes.

MAC:
Reprieved! Reprieved! I was sure of it.
When you're most despairing
The clouds may be clearing

POLLY: Reprieved, my dearest Macheath is reprieved. I am so happy.

MRS PEACHUM: So it all turned out nicely in the end. How nice and easy everything would be if you could always reckon with saviours on horseback.

PEACHUM: Now please remain all standing in your places, and join in the hymn of the poorest of the poor, whose most arduous lot you have put on stage here today. In real life the fates they meet can only be grim. Saviours on horseback are seldom met with in practice. And the man who's kicked about must kick back. Which all means that injustice should be spared from persecution.

*All come forward, singing to the organ:*

Injustice should be spared from persecution:
Soon it will freeze to death, for it is cold.
Think of the blizzards and the black confusion
Which in this vale of tears we must behold.

*The bells of Westminster are heard ringing for the third time.*

The Mother

*Collaborators:* H. EISLER, G. WEISENBORN, S. DUDOW

*Translator:* STEVE GOOCH

*Characters*
PELAGEA VLASOVA
PAVEL VLASOV
ANTON
ANDREI
IVAN
MASCHA
POLICEMAN
COMMISSIONER
FACTORY PORTER
SMILGIN
KARPOV
NIKOLAI VESOVCHIKOV
SIGORSKI
PRISON WARDEN
LUSHIN
BUTCHER
VASIL YEFIMOVITCH
BUTCHER'S WIFE
WORKERS, NEIGHBOURS, STRIKEBREAKERS, WOMEN

# I

## Vlasovas of all countries.

*Pelagea Vlasova's room in Tver.*

VLASOVA: I'm almost ashamed to offer my son this soup. But I can't put any more fat in it, not even half a spoonful. Because only last week they took a kopeck per hour off his wages, and I can't bring that back, whatever I do. I know, in a long hard job like his he needs more substantial food. It's bad I can't serve my only son up better soup; he's young and virtually still growing. He's quite different from what his father was. He's always reading books, and the food never was good enough for him. Now the soup's got even worse. So he just gets more and more discontented.

*She carries a tray with soup on it over to her son. When she gets back, she watches as the son, without looking up from his book, lifts the lid from the bowl, sniffs at the soup, then replaces the lid and pushes the bowl away.*

Now he's turning his nose up at the soup again. I can't provide him with any better. And soon he'll realise I'm no help to him any more, just a burden. Why should I eat with him, live in his room, clothe myself on his money? He'll go away, you'll see. What can I, Pelagea Vlasova, a worker's widow and a worker's mother, do? Every kopeck I turn over three times. I try it this way, I try it that way. One day I'm scrimping on wood, the next on clothes. But it's not enough. I don't see any answer.

*The son, Pavel Vlasov, has taken his cap and the tray and gone.*

CHORUS
*sung to Vlasova by the Revolutionary Workers*

Brush down that coat
Brush it twice over!
When you've finished brushing it
You're left with just a clean rag.

Cook too with care
Give it all you're able!
When your last kopeck's gone
Then your soup is just water.

Work at it, work at it more
Save up, make your money last
Budget, budget much better!

When your last kopeck's gone
There's nothing you can do.

Whatever you do
It won't be enough, though
Your position is bad
It'll get worse
You can't go on this way
And yet what is the answer?

Like the crow that no longer
Is able to feed its young
And defenceless against the winter blizzard
It can't see what to do and whines
You too can see no answer
And whine.

Whatever you do
It won't be enough, though
Your position is bad
It'll get worse
You can't go on this way
And yet what is the answer?

You work for no reward, no effort is too great
To replace the irreplaceable
Catching up with what can't be caught up with
When your last kopeck's gone, there is no work that's
    enough
Whether you get the meat that's missing from your
    kitchen
Will not be decided in the kitchen.

> Whatever you do
> It won't be enough, though
> Your position is bad
> It'll get worse
> You can't go on this way
> And yet what is the answer?

2

## Pelagea Vlasova is disturbed to see her son in the company of revolutionary workers.

*Pelagea Vlasova's room.*
*Three workers and a young girl-worker arrive early in the morning with a duplicating machine.*

ANTON: When you joined our movement two weeks ago, Pavel, you said we could come to your place if we had any special job to do. Your place is safest because we've never worked here before.
PAVEL: What do you want to do?
ANDREI: We've got to print today's leaflets. The latest wage cuts have really stirred the men up. For three days now we've been handing out leaflets at the factory. Today's the crucial day. Tonight the workers' assembly will decide

whether we let them take a kopeck from us or whether we strike.

IVAN: We've brought the duplicator and some paper.

PAVEL Sit down. My mother'll make us some tea.

*They go over to the table.*

IVAN *to Andrei:* You wait outside and keep an eye open for the police.

*Andrei goes out.*

ANTON: Where's Sidor?

MASCHA: My brother's not coming. On his way home last night he saw someone following him who looked like a policeman. So he thought he'd better go straight to the factory today.

PAVEL: Keep your voices down. It's best if my mother doesn't hear us. I haven't told her anything about all this up till now, she's no longer young enough and couldn't help us anyway.

ANTON: Here's the stencil.

*They start working. One of them has hung a thick cloth in front of the window.*

VLASOVA: I don't like seeing my son Pavel in these people's company. They'll end up taking him away from me completely. They're leading him on and getting him involved in something or the other. I'm not serving tea to people like that. *She goes up to the table.* Pavel, I can't make you any tea. There's not enough left. It won't make proper tea.

PAVEL: Then make us weak tea, Mother.

VLASOVA, *having gone back and sat down:* If I don't do as he says now, they'll realise I can't stand them. It doesn't suit me at all, them hanging round here, speaking soft so I can't hear anything. *She goes back to the table.* Pavel, it'd be very awkward for me, if the landlord noticed people getting together here at five o'clock in the morning and printing things. We can't pay the rent as it is.

IVAN: Believe me, Mrs Vlasova, we're concerned more about your rent than anything else. Basically we're concerned about nothing else, even if it doesn't look like it.

VLASOVA: I don't know so much.

*She goes back.*

ANTON: Your mother doesn't like us being here, Pavel?

IVAN: It's very difficult for your mother to understand that we've got to do what we're doing here, so that she can buy tea and pay the rent.

VLASOVA: Talk about thick-skinned! They just pretend not to have noticed anything. What are they up to with Pavel? He went to the factory and was glad to have a job. He didn't earn much, and this last year it's got less and less. If they take one more kopeck off him again now I'd sooner not eat myself. It worries me, though, the way he reads those books; and it bothers me, him running off to meetings of an evening, where things only get stirred up, instead of resting properly. All that'll do is lose him his job.

*Mascha sings Vlasova the 'Song of the Answer'.*

### SONG OF THE ANSWER

If you've not got any soup
How can you stick up for yourself?
That's when you must turn the whole state
Upside down from top to bottom
Till at last you've got your own soup.
And then you will be your own guest.

If there's not any work to be found for you
Then you must stick up for yourself!
That's when you must turn the whole state
Upside down from top to bottom
Till you find you are your own employer.
And then there will be work on hand for you
When they laugh at you and say you're weak
You just can't afford to waste time.
That's when you must make quite sure that
All the weak march together.
And then you'll be a mighty force.
Whom no-one will laugh at again.

ANDREI, *comes in:* Police!

IVAN: Hide the paper!

*Andrei takes the duplicator from Pavel and hangs it out of the window. Anton sits on the paper.*

VLASOVA: You see, Pavel, now the police are coming. Pavel, what are you up to, what's on those leaflets?

MASCHA *leads her over to the window and sits her on the divan:* You just sit there quietly, Mrs Vlasova.

*A Policeman and a Commissioner come in.*

POLICEMAN: Stay where you are! Anyone who moves will be shot! That's his mother, sir, and that's the man himself.

COMMISSIONER: Pavel Vlasov, I've a warrant to search these premises. What sort of smutty bunch is this you've dug up?

POLICEMAN: Sidor Khalatov's sister's here too – the man we arrested this morning. They're the ones all right.

MASCHA: What's happened to my brother?

COMMISSIONER: Your brother sends his best wishes. He's at our place now, revolutionising the bedbugs and enjoying a huge turnout. Only trouble is, he hasn't got any leaflets. *The workers look at each other.*
We might just have a cell or two free still, next to his. You could't help me out with a few leaflets by any chance? Dear Mrs Vlasova, it's very much to my regret it should be your house in particular I have to come looking for leaflets in. *Goes over to the divan.* You see, Mrs Vlasova, now I'm forced for example, to open up your divan. You don't need that, do you? *He slits it open.*

PAVEL: No rouble notes in there, are there. That's because we're workers. We don't earn much.

COMMISSIONER: What about this mirror on the wall? Does it have to be smashed by the rude hand of a policeman? *He smashes it in.* You're a decent woman, Mrs Vlasova, I know that. And there was nothing in the divan either, that might have been construed as indecent. But what about this chest of drawers? A fine old piece. *He tips it over.* Well, well, look. Nothing behind that either, Mrs Vlasova, Mrs Vlasova! Honest people aren't cunning. Why should they be? And there's the dripping-pot, look, with its little spoon, the touching little dripping-pot. *He takes it from the shelf and drops it.* Now it's fallen on the floor, and now it turns out there's dripping in it.

PAVEL: Not very much. There's not much dripping in it, Commissioner. And there's not much bread in the bread-bin either, and not much tea in the caddy.

COMMISSIONER, *to the Policeman:* So it was a political dripping-pot after all. Mrs Vlasova, do you have to get mixed up with us bloodhounds at your age? Your curtains are washed so clean. You don't come across that often. It's a pleasure to look at them. *He rips them down.*

IVAN, *to Anton who has jumped up out of anxiety for the duplicator:* Don't move, they'll shoot you.

PAVEL, *loudly, to distract the Commissioner:* What's the point of chucking a pot of dripping on the floor?

ANDREI, *to the Policeman:* Pick that dripping-pot up!

POLICEMAN: That's Andrei Nakhodka, from Little Russia.

COMMISSIONER, *steps up to the table:* Andrei Maximovitch Nakhodka, you've been in police custody before for political activities, haven't you son?

ANDREI: Yes, in Rostov and Saratov. Only there the police called me 'sir'.

COMMISSIONER, *pulls a leaflet from his pocket:* Are you acquainted with the scum handing out these highly treasonable leaflets in the Suchlinov Works?

PAVEL: We're seeing scum here for the first time.

COMMISSIONER: You, Pavel Vlasov, are going to be taken down a peg or two. Sit down in a proper manner when I'm talking to you!

VLASOVA: Don't shout like that. You're a young man still. You've never known hardship. You're an official. You get a lot of money regularly for cutting open divans and looking to see there's no dripping in people's pots.

COMMISSIONER: You cry too soon, Mrs Vlasova. You'll be needing your tears later. You'd do better to keep an eye on your son. He's going the wrong way. *To the workers:* The day will come when even your cunning won't help you any more. *The Commissioner and the Policeman go. The workers clear up.*

ANTON: Mrs Vlasova, we must ask you to forgive us. We

didn't realise we were already under suspicion. Now your home's been smashed to pieces.

MASCHA: Are you very shaken, Mrs Vlasova?

VLASOVA: Yes. I can see Pavel's going the wrong way.

MASCHA: So you think it's right they can smash your home to pieces because your son's fighting for his kopeck?

VLASOVA: They're not doing right, but he's not doing right either.

IVAN, *back at the table:* What are we going to do now about handing out the leaflets?

ANTON: If we don't give the leaflets out today, everything we've said before is just hot air. The leaflets have got to be given out.

ANDREI: How many are there?

PAVEL: About five hundred.

IVAN: And who's giving them out?

ANTON: It's Pavel's turn today.

*Vlasova beckons Ivan over to her.*

VLASOVA: Who's supposed to be giving out the leaflets?

IVAN: Pavel. It's necessary.

VLASOVA: It's necessary! It starts with reading books and coming home late. Then there's these goings-on here in the house with machines like that, which you have to hang out the window. A cloth has to be hung up at the window. And all discussion has to be held in low voices. It's necessary! Then suddenly the police are in the house, and the policemen treat you like a criminal. *She stands.* Pavel, I forbid you to give out those leaflets.

ANDREI: It's necessary, Mrs Vlasova.

PAVEL, *to Mascha:* Tell her the leaflets have got to be given out for Sidor's sake, so he'll be cleared.

*The workers go over to Vlasova. Pavel stays by the table.*

MASCHA: Mrs Vlasova, it's necessary for my brother's sake too.

IVAN: Otherwise Siberia is all Sidor can look forward to.

ANDREI: If no more leaflets are given out today, they'll know for sure it must have been Sidor who gave them out yesterday.

ANTON: For that reason alone it's necessary to give out leaflets again today.

VLASOVA: I can see it's necessary to stop that young man you got into this being destroyed. But what'll happen to Pavel if he gets arrested?

ANTON: It's not that dangerous.

VLASOVA: I see, it's not that dangerous. A person's led astray and gets pulled in. To save him this and that is necessary. It's not dangerous, but it's necessary. We're under suspicion but we've got to give out leaflets. It's necessary, so it's not dangerous. And so it goes on. And at the end of it all a man stands by the gallows; put your head in the noose, it's not dangerous. Give me the leaflets. I'll go and hand them out, not Pavel.

ANTON: But how are you going to go about it?

VLASOVA: Don't you worry about that. I can bring it off as well as you can. My friend Maria Korsunova sells snacks at the factory in the lunch-hour. I'll do it for her today, and I'll wrap the food up in your leaflets. *She goes and fetches her shopping-bag.*

MASCHA: Pavel, your mother's offered to hand out the leaflets for us herself.

PAVEL: Think over what's for it and against it, I ask you, though not to have me voice an opinion on my mother's offer.

ANTON: Andrei?

ANDREI: I think she can do it. She's known amongst the workers and she won't be suspected by the police.

ANTON: Ivan?

IVAN: I think so too.

ANTON: Even if she's caught, less can happen to her. She doesn't belong to the movement and she'll have done it solely for her son's sake. Comrade Vlasov, in view of the urgency of the situation and the extreme danger to Comrade Sidor, we're in favour of accepting your mother's offer.

IVAN: We're convinced she runs the least risk.

PAVEL: It's all right by me.

VLASOVA, *to herself:* I'm definitely helping out in a bad cause here, but I've got to keep Pavel out of it.

ANTON: Mrs Vlasova, we'll hand this packet of leaflets over to you, then.

ANDREI: So now you're fighting for us, Pelagea Vlasova.

VLASOVA: Fighting? I'm not a young woman any more and I'm no fighter. I'm happy just to scrape my few kopecks together. That's enough of a fight for me.

ANDREI: D'you know what's in the leaflets, Mrs Vlasova?

VLASOVA: No, I can't read.


3


# The swamp kopeck.

*Factory yard.*

VLASOVA, *with a large basket, in front of the factory gates:* It all depends what kind of man the porter is. Whether he's lazy or particular. All I've got to do is persuade him to issue me with a pass. Then I can wrap the food in the leaflets. If they catch me I'll just say: someone planted them on me. I can't read. *She observes the factory porter.* He's fat and lazy. I'll see what he does when I offer him a pickled onion. His kind like their food and never have a penny.
*She goes up to the gates and drops a parcel in front of the porter.*
Here, you, I've dropped one of my parcels.
*The porter looks the other way.*
Well fancy that. I completely forgot I only need to put the basket down and then I've got my hands free. And there I was, nearly troubling you. *To the audience:* The hard-boiled type, this one. You've got to come the old flannel with him, then he'll do anything, just for peace and quiet's sake.
*She goes up to the entrance and speaks quickly.* That's just typical of Maria Korsunova. I said to her only the day before yesterday: whatever you do, don't get wet feet. But d'you think she listened to me? No. She goes out digging potatoes again and gets wet feet. Next morning she's feeding the goats. Wet feet! What about that, eh? Next thing, of course, she's on her back. Only instead of staying put in bed, she's off out again in the evening. It rains of course, so what does she get? Wet feet.

PORTER: You can't come in here without a pass.

VLASOVA: That's what I told her. You know, we're as thick as thieves us two, but talk about obstinate, you've never seen the like. Vlasova, I'm ill, you've got to go to the factory and sell my food. You see, Maria, I said, now you've got a sore throat. But why have you got a sore throat? You just throw those wet feet in my face once more, she says – and all this in a voice more'n a croak – and I'll chuck this cup at that big head of yours! Talk about obstinate!
*The porter sighs and lets her through.*
Quite right, I'm only holding you up.
*It's the lunch-hour. The workers sit on crates, etc. and eat. Vlasova offers her wares. Ivan Vesovchikov helps her wrap them up.*

VLASOVA: Pickled onions, tobacco, tea, fresh pies!

IVAN: And the wrapping-paper's the best part.

VLASOVA: Pickled onions, tobacco, tea, fresh pies!

IVAN: And the wrapping-paper's free.

A WORKER: Got a pickled onion?

VLASOVA: Yes, pickled onions here.

IVAN: And don't throw the wrapping-paper away.

VLASOVA: Pickled onions, tobacco, tea, hot pies!

A WORKER: Here, anything interesting in the wrapping-paper today? I can't read.

ANOTHER WORKER: How should I know what your wrapping-paper says?

1ST WORKER: Come on, mate, you've got the same thing in your hand.

2ND WORKER: You're right. There's something on it.

1ST WORKER: What, though?

SMILGIN, *an old worker:* I'm against leaflets like this being given out while negotiation's still going on.

2ND WORKER: They're quite right. Once we let ourseves in for negotiation, we're up shit creek.

VLASOVA, *across the yard:* Pickled onions, tobacco, tea, fresh pies!

3RD WORKER: They got the police on their backs, control on the factory gate's been sharpened up, and still another leaflet turns up. They know what they're doing these blokes, and they won't be stopped. There's something in what they're after.

1ST WORKER: Yeah, I got to say myself, when I see something like this, I'm all for it.

PAVEL: Here comes Karpov at long last.

ANTON: I wonder how far he's got.

KARPOV, *comes in:* Are all the shop stewards here?

*In one corner of the factory-yard the shop-stewards of the factory gather together. Amongst them Smilgin, Anton and Pavel.*

Brothers, we have negotiated!

ANTON: How far d'you get?

KARPOV: Brothers, it is not without some success we return to you.

ANTON: D'you get the kopeck?

KARPOV: Brothers, we put our calculations to Mr Suchlinov. The deduction of a kopeck per hour from the wages of 800 workers comes to 24,000 roubles a year. These 24,000 roubles would, from now on, have flowed into the pocket of Mr Suchlinov. This had to be avoided at all costs. Now, after a struggle lasting four hours, we've got there. We avoided it. Those 24,000 roubles will not flow into Mr Suchlinov's pocket.

ANTON: So you got the kopeck?

KARPOV: Brothers, it has always been our contention that the factory's sanitary conditions are intolerable.

PAVEL: D'you get the kopeck, though?

KARPOV: The swamp outside the East Gate of the factory has always been a basic menace.

ANTON: Ah I see. You want to get round it with the swamp!

KARPOV: Remember the clouds of flies that make it impossible for us to spend any time in the fresh air every summer; the high sickness rate from swamp-fever; the constant threat to our children. Brothers, for 24,000 roubles the swamp can be dried out. And that Mr Suchlinov is prepared to do. Enlargement of the factory would then be set in motion on the reclaimed land. That'll provide more jobs. As you well know, what's good for the factory is also good for you. Brothers, the factory is not doing as well as we may perhaps believe. We cannot conceal from you what Mr Suchlinov has communicated to us: our sister-factory in Tver is being closed down, and as from tomorrow 700 colleagues will be out on the street. We are in favour of the lesser evil. Every man of unclouded vision must realise with sorrow that we stand on the brink of one of the greatest economic crises our country has ever known.

ANTON: So capitalism's sick, and you're the doctor. Are you saying you're in favour of accepting the wage cut?

KARPOV: We could find no other solution in the course of our negotiations.

ANTON: In that case we demand that negotiation with the management be broken off. You couldn't stop the wage cut, and we reject the swamp kopeck.

KARPOV: I must warn you not to break off negotiation with the management.

SMILGIN: You have to realise this means a strike.

ANTON: In our view only a strike can save our kopeck.

IVAN: The question before this meeting today is quite simply this: should Mr Suchlinov's swamp be dried out, or should our kopeck be saved? We must go ahead with our strike, and by the first of May, which is only a week off, we must try to effect the shut-down of all other factories where wages are to be cut.

KARPOV: I'm warning you!

*The factory siren. The workers stand up to go back to work. They sing the 'Song of the Patch and the Coat' back over their shoulders to Karpov and Smilgin.*

SONG OF THE PATCH AND THE COAT

Every time that our coat's in tatters
Then you come running and say: this won't do at all
It must be put right this minute, we'll use all our powers!
Full of fervour your run to the bosses
While we stand here freezing, waiting.
Until you come back and show in triumph
What it is you've brought us from your conquest:
Just a little patch.

Fine, you've got a patch
But where's the rest
The coat itself?

Every time we cry out in hunger
Then you come running and say: this won't do at all
It must be put right this minute, we'll use all our powers!
Full of fervour you run to the bosses
While we stand here hungry, waiting.
Until you come back and show in triumph
What it is you've brought us from your conquest:
A slice of bread.

Fine, you've got the slice
But where's the rest
The loaf itself?

We need a bit more than patches
We need the whole coat itself.
We need a bit more than slices
We need the whole loaf itself.
We don't just need a mere job to do
We now need the whole factory.
And the coalmines and the ore
And power in the state.

So, that is what we're asking
But what is
Offered us instead?

*The workers, except for Karpov and Smilgin go off.*
KARPOV: All right then, strike! *He goes off.*
*Vlsaova comes back and sits down, counting her takings.*
SMILGIN, *with a leflet in his hand:* So it's you handing these out.
 Do you realise these pieces of paper mean a strike?
VLASOVA: A strike? How come?
SMILGIN: These leaflets call on the employees of 'the
 Suchlinov plant to strike.
VLASOVA: I don't understand any of that.

SMILGIN: Why are you giving them out then?

VLASOVA: We've got our reasons all right. Why are they arresting our people?

SMILGIN: Have you got any idea what's on these things?

VLASOVA: No, I can't read.

SMILGIN: This is how our people get stirred up. A strike's a nasty business. Tomorrow morning they won't be going to work. But what'll happen tomorrow evening? And what'll happen next week? It makes no difference to the firm whether we go on working or not. But for us it's life itself. *The factory policeman comes running up with the porter.* Anton Antonovitch, are you looking for something?

PORTER: Yes, leaflets have been handed out again, calling for a strike. I don't know how they've been getting in. What's that you've got there?

*Smilgin tries to hide the leaflet in his pocket.*

POLICEMAN: What's that you're sticking in your pocket? *He pulls it out.* A leaflet!

PORTER: Do you read those leaflets, Smilgin?

SMILGIN: Anton Antonovitch, my friend, surely we're allowed to read what we want.

POLICEMAN: Oh Yes? *He grabs him by the collar and drags him along with him.* I'll show you what it means to read leaflets calling for a strike in your factory!

SMILGIN: I'm against the strike. Karpov can bear me out.

POLICEMAN: Tell me where you got that leaflet then.

SMILGIN, *after a pause:* It was lying on the ground.

POLICEMAN, *hits him:* I'll give you leaflets!

*The factory policeman and the porter go off with Smilgin.*

VLASOVA: All the man did, though, was buy a pickled onion!

4

# Pelagea Vlasova is given her first lesson in economics.

*Pelageo Vlasova's room.*

VLASOVA: Pavel, on your behalf I gave out the leaflets you people gave me today to avert suspicion from the young man you'd got into all this. When I'd finished giving them out, I had to look on while another man, who'd done nothing but read that leaflet was arrested in front of my eyes. What have you made me do?

ANTON: Mrs Vlasova, we thank you for your skilful work.

VLASOVA: So you call that skilful do you? But what about Smilgin, who I've put in prison with my skilfulness?

ANDREI: You didn't put him in prison. To our mind it was the police who put him in prison.

IVAN: He was let free again, because they had to admit he was one of the few who spoke against the strike. Now, though, he's for the strike. Mrs Vlasova, you've been instrumental in uniting the workers at the Suchlinov plant. As you must have heard, the strike has been almost unanimously agreed on.

VLASOVA: I didn't want to cause a strike. I wanted to help a man. Why do people get arrested for reading leaflets? What did it say in that leaflet?

MASCHA: When you handed it out you were giving good help to a good cause.

VLASOVA: What did it say in that leaflet?

PAVEL: What do you think it said?

VLASOVA: Something wrong.

ANTON: Mrs Vlasova, we realise we owe you an explanation.

PAVEL: Sit down with us, Mother, we want to explain it to you.

*They lay a cloth over the divan. Ivan hangs a new mirror on the wall. Mascha puts a new dripping pot on the table. Then they fetch themselves chairs and sit down around Vlasova.*

IVAN: You see, in the leaflet it said we workers shouldn't put up with Mr Suchlinov cutting the wages he pays us and when he pleases.

VLASOVA: Nonsense, what are you going to do to stop him? Why shouldn't Mr Suchlinov be able to cut the wages he pays you as and when he pleases? Does his factory belong to him or doesn't it?

PAVEL: It belongs to him.

VLASOVA: Right then. This table, for example, belongs to me. Now I'll ask you a question: can I do what I like with this table?

ANDREI: Yes, Mrs Vlasova. You can do what you like with it.

VLASOVA: Right then. Can I, for example, smash it to pieces if I like?

ANTON: Yes, you can smash it to pieces if you like.

VLASOVA: Aha! In that case Mr Suchlinov, whose factory belongs to him just as my table does to me, can do what he likes with it.

PAVEL: No.

VLASOVA: Why not?

PAVEL: Because he needs us workers for his factory.

VLASOVA: But what if he says he doesn't need you anymore?

IVAN: Look, Mrs Vlasova, look at it this way: some days he needs us some days he doesn't.

ANTON: Right.

IVAN: When he needs us, we have to be there. When he doesn't need us we're still there. Where else can we go? And he knows that. He doesn't always need us, but we always need him. He counts on that. Mr Suchlinov has got his machines standing there, all right. But those are our tools. We haven't got any others. We haven't got any other looms or lathes for the very reason it's Mr Suchlinov's machines we use. His factory belongs to him, but when he shuts it, he takes our tools away.

VLASOVA: Because your tools belong to him the way my table does to me.

ANTON: Yes, but do you think it's right our tools belong

to him?

VLASOVA, *loudly:* No! But whether I think it's right or whether I don't, they still belong to him, don't they? Somebody could just as well not think it right my table belongs to me.

ANDREI: Then we say, there's a difference between owning a table and owning a factory.

MASCHA: Of course a table can belong to you, a chair too. That doesn't hurt anybody, does it. Even if you put it on the roof, what harm can it do? If you own a factory, though, you can hurt many hundreds of people.

IVAN: Because you have their tools in your possession, and that way you can use people.

VLASOVA: Yes all right, he can use us. Don't treat me as if I hadn't noticed that over the last forty years. There's only one thing I haven't noticed, though, and that is that there's anything you can do about it.

ANTON: Mrs Vlasova, we've now reached the point in talking about Mr Suchlinov's property where we've established that his factory is property of a totally different kind from, say, your table. He can use his property to use us.

IVAN: And his property has yet another unusual property: unless he uses us with it, it's absolutely worthless to him. Only as long as it's our tool is it worth anything to him. When it's no longer our means of production, it's a heap of old iron. So he's also dependent on us with his property.

VLASOVA: All right. But how are you going to prove to him that he's dependent on you?

ANDREI: Look: if he, Pavel Vlasov, goes up to Mr Suchlinov and says: Mr Suchlinov, without me your factory is a heap of old iron, so you can't knock my wages down as and when you please, Mr Suchlinov will laugh and throw Vlasov out. But when all the Vlasovs in Tver, eight hundred Vlasovs, stand there and say the same thing, Mr Suchlinov won't be laughing any more.

VLASOVA: And that's what your strike is?

PAVEL: Yes, that's what our strike is.

VLASOVA: And that's what it said in that leaflet?

PAVEL: Yes, that's what it said in that leaflet.

VLASOVA: A strike's a nasty business. What am I supposed to cook with? What's going to happen about the rent? You won't be goig to work tomorrow morning, but what about next week? All right, though, we'll get round that somehow too. But if it only said all that about the strike, why'd the police arrest people? What's the police got to do with it?

PAVEL: Well, mother, that's what we're asking you: what have the police got to do with it?

VLASOVA: If we carry out our strike with Mr Suchlinov, it's got nothing to do with the police. You must've gone about it in the wrong way. Misunderstandings occurred, I expect. People thought you were up to something violent. What you should have done is show the whole town your quarrel with the management is a just and peaceful one. That'd make a big impression.

IVAN: That's exactly what we intend to do, Mrs Vlasova. On the first of May, the international day of workers' struggle, when all the factories in Tver will be demonstrating for the liberation of the working class, we will carry banners calling on all factories in Tver to support our fight for the kopeck.

VLASOVA: If you march peacefully through the streets and only carry your banners, no one can object to that.

ANDREI: We're assuming Mr Suchlinov won't stand for it.

VLASOVA: Well, he's got to stand for it.

IVAN: The police will probably break the demonstration up.

VLASOVA: What's the police got to do with this Suchlinov? I mean, the police watch over us, yes, but they watch over Mr Suchlinov just as much.

PAVEL: So you think the police'll take no action against a peaceful demonstration, do you mother?

VLASOVA: Yes I do. There's nothing violent in it after all. We'd never agree on anything violent. You know I believe in a God in heaven. I don't want anything to do with violence. I've got to know it over the past forty years, and I've never been able to do anything against it. But when I die, I should like, at least not to have done anything violent.

5

# Report on the 1st May, 1905.

*Street.*

PAVEL: As we, the workers from the Suchlinov plant, crossed over the Wool Market, we met the column from the other factories. There were already many thousands of us. We carried banners saying: 'Workers, support our fight against the wage cut! Workers, unite!'

IVAN: We marched in a quiet and orderly fashion. Songs like 'Arise, ye prisoners of starvation' and 'Comrades, the bugles are sounding' were sung. Our factory marched immediately behind the great red flag.

ANDREI: Beside me, close behind her son, marched Pelagea Vlasova. When we'd gone round early that morning to pick him up, she suddenly came out of the kitchen, dressed to go out. And when we asked where she was going, she answered.

VLASOVA: With you.

ANTON: Many like her went with us. The harsh winter, the wage cuts in the factories and our agitation had led many to us. Before we arrived at the Boulevard of Our Saviour we saw only a few policemen and no soldiers, but on the corner of the Boulevard of Our Saviour and the Tverskaya there suddenly stood a double chain of soldiers. When they saw our flag and our banners, a voice suddenly called out to us 'Attention! Disperse immediately! We have orders to shoot!' And: 'Drop your flag.' Our column came to a halt.

PAVEL: But because the ones marching at the back were still moving forward, the ones at the front couldn't stop, and so they opened fire. As the first people turned, what followed was nothing but confusion. Many couldn't believe that what they saw had actually happened. Then the soldiers started to move towards the crowd.

VLASOVA: I went along to demonstrate for the workers'

cause. The people marching there were all quite orderly people who'd worked their whole lives. Of course there were desperate ones amongst them too, people driven by unemployment to extremes, and hungry people too weak to defend themselves.

ANDREI: We were still standing quite near the front, and we still didn't break up when they opened fire.

PAVEL: We had our flag. Smilgin was carrying it, and we had no intention whatsoever of giving it away, for it seemed to us then, without consulting each other in any way, that it was important it should be us in particular they hit and threw down and our flag in particular, the red flag, they took away. The reason we wanted that, though, was so that all workers would see who we were and who we were for, namely the workers.

ANDREI: Those who were against us had to behave like wild animals. That was what they received their livelihood from the Suchlinovs for.

MASCHA: In the end everyone would see it, and our flag, the red flag, had to be held especially high, so that everyone could see it, not least the soldiers, but everyone else too.

IVAN: And for those who didn't see it, to them it would have to be told today, tomorrow or in the years to come, as long as it took for it to be seen again. For we felt we knew, and many came to know for sure at that moment, that it would be seen again and again from now on until everything we were marching against had changed completely. Our flag, which is the most dangerous for all exploiters and rulers, the most relentless!

ANTON: But for us workers, supreme!

EVERYONE: That's why you will always see it
Over and over
Gladly or sadly
Depending where you stand in this fight
Which can end in no other way
Than victory once and for all
For the sore oppressed of every nation.

VLASOVA: But on that day it was Smilgin, the worker, who carried it.

SMILGIN: My name is Smilgin. I've belonged to the movement twenty years. I was one of the first to spread revolutionary consciousness in the factory. We fought for our wages and for better working conditions. During which, in my colleagues' interest, I often had dealings with the management. To begin with full of antagonism, but then, I must admit, I thought it might be easier the other way. If we widened our influence, I thought, we would get a say in things. That was wrong, of course. I'm standing here now, behind me there are already many thousands, but once again power blocks our path. Should we give up the flag?

ANTON: Don't give it up, Smilgin. Bargaining won't work, we said. And Pelagea Vlasova told him:

VLASOVA: You mustn't give it up. Nothing can happen to you. The police can't object to a peaceful demonstration.

MASCHA: At that moment an officer called out to us: 'Hand over your flag!'

IVAN: And Smilgin looked back and saw our banners behind his flag: and on those banners, our demands. And behind the banners stood the strikers from the Suchlinov plant. And we watched what he, one of us, standing beside us, would do with the flag.

PAVEL: Twenty years in the movement, worker, revolutionary, on the first of May 1905, 11 o'clock in the morning on the corner of the Boulevard of Our Saviour, at the decisive moment. He said:

SMILGIN: I will not hand it over! There will be no negotiation!

ANDREI: Good, Smilgin, we said. That's right. Now everything's straight.

IVAN: Yes, he said and pitched forward on his face, for they'd shot him down.

ANDREI: And then they ran up, four, five men, to pick up the flag. But the flag lay beside him. So our Pelagea Vlasova bent down the quiet, even-tempered one, the comrade, and picked up the flag.

VLASOVA: Give me this flag, Smilgin, I said. Give it here. I'll carry it. All this is going to be changed!

6

# The teacher Vesovchikov's flat in Rostov.

**a. After the arrest of her son, Pelagea Vlasova is taken by Ivan Vesovchikov to his brother, Nikolai, the teacher.**

IVAN: Nikolai Ivanovitch, I've brought you our friend Pavel's mother, Pelagea Vlasova. Her son was arrested because of what happened at the demonstration on the first of May. Since then she's been served notice to leave her old flat, and we promised her son we'd see her safe. Your flat isn't under suspicion. No one can claim you have anything at all to do with the revolutionary movement.

VESOVCHIKOV: Certainly, that is only too true. I'm a teacher. I'd lose my job if I started pursuing the kind of wild fancies you do.

IVAN: Anyway, I hope you'll keep Mrs Vlasova on here all the same. She's got nowhere else to go. You'd be doing your brother a great favour.

VESOVCHIKOV: I've got no reason to do you a favour. I disapprove of everything you do in the extreme, it's all nonsense. I've proved that to you often enough. But that doesn't apply to you, Mrs Vlasova. I can well appreciate your plight. Besides I'm in need of a housekeeper anyway. As you can see, this place is terribly untidy.

IVAN: You'll have to give her some money for her work of course. She has to send her son a bit now and then.

VESOVCHIKOV: I could only offer you a very small allowance, naturally.

IVAN: He knows as much about politics as that chair, but he's not inhuman.

VESOVCHIKOV: You're an idiot, Ivan. Mrs Vlasova, there's a sofa in the kitchen. You can sleep on there. I see you've brought your own linen. The kitchen's this way, Mrs Vlasova.

*Pelagea Vlasova takes her bundle into the kitchen and starts installing herself there.*

IVAN: I thank you, Nikolai Ivanovitch, and ask you to watch over her. She mustn't have anything to do with politics again just yet. She got involved in the first of May disturbances and ought to take it easy for a while. She's very concerned about what will happen to her son. I'll hold you responsible for her.

VESOVCHIKOV: I shan't draw her into politics, the way you people do.

### b. The teacher Vesovchikov catches his housekeeper at her agitation work.

*Neighbours sit in the kitchen around Pelagea Vlasova.*

WOMAN: We heard communism was a crime, though.

VLASOVA: That's not true. Communism's good for people like us. What can be said against it? *she sings.*

#### IN PRAISE OF COMMUNISM

It's quite straightforward, you'll understand it. It's not hard.
Because you're not an exploiter, you'll quickly grasp it.
It's for your good, so find out all about it.
They're fools who describe it as foolish, and foul who describe it as foulness.
It's against all that's foul and against all that's foolish.
The exploiters will tell you that it's criminal
But we know better:
It puts an end to all that's criminal.
It isn't madness, but puts
And end to all madness.
It doesn't mean chaos
It just means order.
It's just the simple thing
That's hard, so hard to do.

WOMAN: Why don't all workers see that, though?

SIGORSKI, *quotes:* 'Because they are kept in ignorance of their being exploited, of this being a crime, and of it being possible to put an end to this crime.'

*They fall silent. Vesovchikov has come into the next room.*

VESOVCHIKOV: I come home tired from the public house, my head still full of debates during which I once again got very angry with that idiot Sachar, who kept on contradicting me, although I was, of course, in the right, and now I'm looking forward to the peace and quiet of my own four walls. I think I'll just bathe my feet and read the paper while doing so.

VLASOVA, *comes in:* Oh, you're back early, Nikolai Ivanovitch?

VESOVCHIKOV: Yes, and I'd like you to prepare me a hot footbath, please. I'll take it in the kitchen.

VLASOVA: It's good that you've come, Nikolai Ivanovitch, very good, because you've got to go out again straight away. The lady next door told me just this minute that your friend Sachar Smerdyakov was here an hour ago. He couldn't leave a message, though, as he had to speak to you urgently in person.

VESOVCHIKOV: Mrs Vlasova, I've been with my friend Sachar Smerdyakov the whole evening.

VLASOVA: Really? But the kitchen's a mess, Nikolai Ivanovitch. The washing's hanging up.

*Murmurs from the kitchen.*

VESOVCHIKOV: Since when has my washing talked while it's drying, and – *He points to the samovar she's holding* – since when have my shirts drunk tea?

VLASOVA: Nikolai Ivanovitch, I must confess to you, I've invited some friends for tea, to sit and talk.

VESOVCHIKOV: I see. What kind of people are they?

VLASOVA: I don't know if you'll feel at ease with them, Nikolai Ivanovitch. They're not particularly well-off as people.

VESOVCHIKOV: Aha, so you're talking politics again! Is that unemployed chap, Sigorski, with them?

VLASOVA: Yes. And his wife and his brother with his son and his uncle and his aunt. They're very intelligent people. I'm sure even you would follow their arguments with interest.

VESOVCHIKOV: Mrs Vlasova, have I not already made it clear to you that I don't want anything political in this house? Now I come home tired from my local and find my kitchen full of politics. I'm surprised, Mrs Vlasova, I'm very surprised.

VLASOVA: Nikolai Ivanovitch, I'm sorry I've had to let you down. I was telling the people about the first of May. They didn't know enought about it.

VESOVCHIKOV: What do you know of politics, Mrs Vlasova? Only this evening I was saying to my friend Sachar, a very intelligent man: 'Sachar Smerdyakov, there is nothing on earth more difficult and more impenetrable than politics.'

VLASOVA: You must be very tired and tense, Nikolai Ivanovitch. But if you had a little time to spare – we were all agreed this evening that you might be able to explain a lot to us, even concerning the first of May, which is a very impenetrable subject.

VESOVCHIKOV: I may say I have little desire to argue the toss with the redundant Mr Sigorski. At best I might try to educate them in the fundamentals of politics. But really, Mrs Vlasova, I have grave misgivings, finding you in the company of such dubious individuals. Bring the samovar in and some bread and a few pickled onions.

*They go into the kitchen.*


### c. Pelagea Vlasova learns to read.


VESOVCHIKOV, *in front of a blackboard:* So you want to learn to read. I don't understand of course why you people should need it in your position. Some of you are also a little old for it. However, I shall try, as a favour to Mrs Vlasova. Do you all have something to write with? Right, I shall now write three simple words up: sap, nest, fish. I repeat: sap, nest, fish. *He writes.*

SIGORSKI: Why words like that?

VLASOVA, *sitting at the table with the others:* Excuse me, Nikolai Ivanovitch, does it absolutely have to be sap, nest, fish? We're old people. We've got to learn the words we need quickly, you know.

VESOVCHIKOV, *smiles:* But you see, *what* you learn to read by is completely irrelevant.

VLASOVA: What do you mean? How'd you spell 'worker' for instance? That's what interests our Pavel Sigorski.

SIGORSKI: 'Sap' never comes up at all.

VLASOVA: He's a metal-worker.

VESOVCHIKOV: The letters come up in it, though.

WORKER: But the letters come up in the word 'class-struggle' too!

VESOVCHIKOV: Yes, but you've got to start off with what's simplest, not tackle the most difficult straight away. 'Sap' is simple.

SIGORSKI: 'Class-struggle' is a lot simpler.

VESOVCHIKOV: But there's no such thing as class-struggle. We ought to get that straight from the start.

SIGORSKI, *stands up:* In that case, if you think there's no class-struggle, there's nothing I can learn from you.

VLASOVA: You're here to learn reading and writing, and you can do that here. Reading is class-struggle.

VESOVCHIKOV: All this is nonsense in my opinion. What's that supposed to mean anyway: reading is class-struggle? Why are you talking like this in the first place? *He writes.* Right then, here we have: worker. Copy it.

VLASOVA: Reading is class-struggle. What I meant by that was, if the soldiers in Tver had been able to read our banners, perhaps they wouldn't have shot at us. They were all peasant boys.

VESOVCHIKOV: Look here, I'm a teacher myself, and I've been teaching reading and writing eighteen years, but I'll tell you something. Deep inside me I know it's all nonsense. Books are nonsense. Men are only made worse by them. A simple peasant is a better human being for that reason alone, that he hasn't been spoiled by civilisation.

VLASOVA: So how d'you spell 'class-struggle'? Pavel Sigorski, you have to hold your hand firmly or it'll shake and your writing won't be clear.

VESOVCHIKOV, *writes:* Class-struggle. *To Sigorski:* You must write in a straight line and not go over the margin. He who trangresses the margin also trangresses the law. Generation after generation after all has heaped knowledge upon knowledge and written book after book. Science has advanced further than ever before. And what use has it been? Confusion too is greater than ever before. The whole lot ought to be thrown in the sea at its deepest point. Every book and machine in the Black Sea. Down with knowledge! Have you finished yet? I sometimes have lessons in which I sink into total melancholy. What, I ask then, what have such truly great thoughts, which encompass not only the Now, but also the Ever and Eternal, Human Nature, what have they to do with class-struggle?

SIGORSKI, *muttering:* Thoughts like that are no use to us. As long as your kind are sinking in melancholy, you're exploiting us.

VLASOVA: Quiet, Pavel Sigorski! Please, how d'you spell 'exploitation'?

VESOVCHIKOV: 'Exploitation'! That only exists in books too. As if I'd ever exploited anyone! *He writes.*

SIGORSKI: He only says that cos he doesn't see any of the profits.

VLASOVA, *to Sigorski:* The 'o' in 'exploitation' is just like the 'o' in 'worker'.

VESOVCHIKOV: Knowledge doesn't help, you know. It's kindness that helps.

VLASOVA: You give us your knowledge then, if you don't need it.

IN PRAISE OF LEARNING
*sung by the Revolutionary workers to those who are learning*

Learn what is easiest, for all
Those whose day has come at last
It is not too late!
Learn up your ABC, it is not enough but

Learn it! Don't let it overawe you
Start now! You must omit nothing!
It's you who'll have to give the orders.

Learn on, man put away!
Learn on, man put in prison!
Learn on, woman in kitchen!
Learn on, old age pensioner!
It's you who'll have to give the orders
Go off and find a school, if you're homeless!
Go get yourself knowledge, you who freeze!
Starving, you reach for the book: it is your best
    weapon.
It's you who'll have to give the orders.

Don't be afraid to ask questions, comrade!
Don't be talked into things
See for yourself!
What you don't know yourself
You don't know.
Study the bill for
It's you who must pay it.
Point with your finger at every item
Ask how it comes to be there.
It's you who'll have to give the orders.

VLASOVA, *stands up:* That's enough for today. We can't take
    all that much in at once any more. Otherwise our Pavel
    Sigorski won't get any sleep again tonight. Thank you,
    Nikolai Ivanovitch. We can only say you help us a lot by
    teaching us reading and writing.
VESOVCHIKOV: I don't believe it. By the way, I don't say
    your opinions don't make sense. I shall come back to that
    in our next lesson.

**d. Ivan Vesovchikov doesn't recognise his brother anymore.**

IVAN: The comrades here in Rostov have spoken to me about your work, Pelagea Vlasova – about your mistakes too. They've asked me to pass something on to you: your party card.

VLASOVA: Thank you. *She receives it.*

IVAN: Has Pavel written to you?

VLASOVA: No. I'm very worried about him. The worst thing is, I never know at any moment what he's doing or what they're doing to him. I don't even know for example if they're giving him enough food or if he's not getting cold perhaps. Do they get blankets there in fact?

IVAN: There were blankets in Odessa.

VLASOVA: I'm very proud of him. I'm lucky. I have a son who's needed. *She recites.*

IN PRAISE OF THE REVOLUTIONARY

Many are too much.
When they've gone, it's for the better
But when he's not there we miss him.

When oppression increases
Many get discouraged
But his courage grows.

He's ready to organise, fight
For a wage rise, to strike for a tea break and
Fight for power in the state.

He asks of property:
Where d'you come from?
He asks of factions
Whom do you serve?

Where things always get hushed up
He'll ask awkward questions

And where the oppressors rule and there's those who
　　blame fate for it
That's when he'll name the guilty.

Where he sits at table
Dissatisfaction also sits at table.
Food becomes bad
And it's seen that the room is tiny.

Wherever they chase him, with him
Goes rebellion, and where he is banished
Discontent stays behind.

VESOVCHIKOV, *comes in:* Good day, Ivan.

IVAN: Good day, Nikolai.

VESOVCHIKOV: I'm glad to see you're still a free man.

IVAN: I just wanted to look in on Pelagea Vlasova once again
and bring her a few of our papers. *Vesovchikov grabs the
papers.* The arrests have been very bad for our movement.
Sidor and Pavel, for example, are the only ones who know
many of the addresses of the peasants who want to read
our newspaper.

VLASOVA: I understand. We've talked a lot too about the
need to speak to the peasants.

VESOVCHIKOV: You would be needing to speak a lot of
people too. 120 million peasants, you couldn't do it.
Revolution of any kind isn't possible in this country with
people like that. The Russian will never make a revolution.
It's more a thing for the West. The Germans now, they're
revolutionaries, they'll make a revolution.

IVAN: We've heard from several provinces that the peasants
are already destroying estate farms and appropriating
estate land. They've confiscated grain and other provisions
from the owners and they're distributing them to the
starving. The peasants are on the move.

VESOVCHIKOV: Yes, but what does that mean? *To Pelagea
Vlasova:* Just read what the progressive writers of the last
century wrote about the psychology of the Russian peasant.

VLASOVA: I'd like to. I was able to read the report on the

third party conference just recently, thanks to Nikolai Ivanovitch's classes in reading and writing.

VESOVCHIKOV: That's just another of your Lenin's mad ideas, trying to convince the proletariat it can take over the leadership of the revolution. It's doctrines like that which will destroy the last particle of the possibility of a revolution taking place. They simply make the progressive bourgeoisie afraid of making a revolution.

IVAN: What do you think, Pelagea Vlasova?

VLASOVA: Leading is very difficult. Even Sigorski the metal-worker makes life difficult for me with his pig-headedness, and you can't prove anything at all to educated people.

VESOVCHIKOV: Couldn't you write your newspaper in a slightly more entertaining way? No one's going to read that.

VLASOVA: We don't read it for entertainment, Nikolai Ivanovitch. *Ivan laughs.*

VESOVCHIKOV: What's the matter?

IVAN: What've you done with your pretty picture of the Tsar? The room looks quite bare without it.

VESOVCHIKOV: I thought I'd take it down for a while. It gets boring having it in front of you all the time. By the way, why is there nothing in your newspapers about conditions in schools?

IVAN: I just thought – you can't have put that picture away just because it was boring, surely?

VLASOVA: Don't say that! Nikolai Ivanovitch is always looking for something new.

IVAN: I see.

VESOVCHIKOV: At all events, I don't like to see myself being treated like an idiot. I asked you something in connection with your newspaper.

IVAN: Nikolai, I can't remember anything ever changing in your flat. The frame alone costs 12 roubles.

VESOVCHIKOV: In that case I can hang the frame back up again, can't I. You've always taken me for a fool, which is why you're a fool yourself.

IVAN: Nikolai, I'm surprised. Your inflammatory talk and your scornful attitude towards our Tsar amaze me. You seem to have become an agitator. You've developed such

a determined stare too. It's downright dangerous just to
look at you.

VLASOVA: Stop annoying your brother! He's a very sensible
person. I made him think again about the Tsar's Bloody
Sunday. And since a lot of children learn things from him,
it's very important what he says about things. Besides, he
taught us reading and writing.

IVAN: I hope, as you taught them to read and write, you
learnt something yourself.

VESOVCHIKOV: No. I learned absolutely nothing. These
little people still understand very little about Marxism.
I don't want to offend you, Mrs Vlasova. It's a very
complicated subject of course, and for an untrained mind
totally incomprehensible. The extraordinary thing about
it is that it's the people who'll never understand it who
gulp it down like hot cakes. Marxism in itself is not a bad
thing. It even has much in its favour, though there are
large holes in it of course, and Marx on many key issues
sees the whole thing in completely the wrong light. There
are all kinds of things I could say on the subject. Of course
economics are important, but it's not only economics that
are important. They are *also* important. What about
sociology? I imagine biology could be just as important
too. Where, I ask is human nature in this doctrine? Man
will always remain true to his nature.

VLASOVA, *to Ivan:* But he's changed quite a bit, hasn't he.
*Ivan takes his leave.*

IVAN: Mrs Vlasova, I don't recognise my brother anymore.


7


Pelagea Vlasova visits her son in prison.


*Prison.*

VLASOVA: The warden'll be keeping a close watch, but I've

still got to find out the addresses of the peasants who used
to ask for our newspaper. I only hope I can keep all the
names in my head.

*The warden brings Pavel in.*

Pavel!

PAVEL: How are you, Mum?

WARDEN: You have to sit so there's space between you.
There and there. Political conversation is not allowed.

PAVEL: In that case, tell me about home, Mother.

VLASOVA: Yes, Pavel.

PAVEL: Have you got a place to live?

VLASOVA: At Vesovchikov's, the teacher.

PAVEL: They look after you all right?

VLASOVA: Yes. But how are you?

PAVEL: I was worried whether they'd be able to support you
sufficiently.

VLASOVA: Your beard's got thick.

PAVEL: Yes. Makes me look older, doesn't it.

VLASOVA: I went to Smilgin's funeral, you know. The police
let fly again and arrested a few people. We were all there.

WARDEN: That's politics, Mrs Vlasova!

VLASOVA: Oh? Really? It's hard to know what you *can*
talk about.

WARDEN: In that case your visits are a waste of time. You've
got nothing to talk about, but you still come running in
here disturbing us. Remember: I'm held responsible.

PAVEL: Are you helping out around the house?

VLASOVA: That too. Vesovchikov and me are thinking of
going out to the country next week.

PAVEL: The teacher?

VLASOVA: No.

PAVEL: You thinking of having a rest?

VLASOVA: Yes. *Quiet.* We need the addresses. *Loud.* Oh
Pavel, we all miss you so much.

PAVEL, *quiet:* I swallowed the addresses when I got arrested. I
just know one or two by heart.

VLASOVA: Oh Pavel, I'd never have thought I'd see my days
out like this.

PAVEL, *quiet:* Lushin in Pirogovo.

VLASOVA, *quiet:* And in Krapivna? *Loud.* Really, you worry me so much!

PAVEL, *quiet:* Sulinovski.

VLASOVA: I pray for you too. *Quiet.* Sulinovski in Krapivna. *Loud.* I spend my evenings sitting on my own, by the lamp.

PAVEL, *quiet:* Terek in Tobraya.

VLASOVA: And Vesovchikov the teacher complains if I have noisy company.

PAVEL, *quiet:* And the rest of the addresses you can get from them.

WARDEN: Time's up.

VLASOVA: One more minute please, sir. I'm so confused. Ah Pavel, what's left for us old folk but to creep away so people don't have to see us any more. We're no good for anything any more. *Quiet.* Lushin in Pirogovo. *Loud.* People let us know our days are over. We've got nothing to look forward to. Everything we know belongs to the past. *Quiet.* Sulinovski in Tobraya. *Pavel shakes his head.* In Krapivna. *Loud.* And our experiences don't count for anything any more. Our advice does more harm than good, because between us and our sons is an unbridgeable gap. *Quiet.* Terek in Tobraya. *Loud.* We go one way and you go the other. *Quiet.* Terek in Tobraya. We've got nothing in common. The times to come are yours.

WARDEN: Visiting-time, though is over!

PAVEL, *bows:* Farewell, Mother.

VLASOVA, *bows too:* Farewell, Pavel.


SONG
*sung by the actor playing Pavel*

They've got all their law-books and their regulations
They've got all their prisons and fortresses
(All their welfare institutions don't really count!)
They've got all their prison guards and judges
Who are overpaid and far too keen to oblige them
Well, why's that then?
Do they really think they'll wear us down with all that?

Before they vanish, and that will be soon
They will surely notice that all that cannot help
    them any more.

They've got their newspapers and printing-presses
With which to attack us and silence our voices
(All their statesmen we don't need to count!)
They've got their parsons and their professors
Who are overpaid and far too keen to oblige them
Well, why's that then?
Is it because the truth's so frightening?
    Before they vanish, and that will be soon
    They will surely notice that all that cannot help
        them any more.

They've got their tanks and their cannon
Their machine-guns and their hand-grenades
(Their rubber truncheons don't really count!)
Their policemen and their soldiers
Who are underpaid but far too keen to oblige them.
Well, why's that then?
Is it because their enemy's so powerful?
They think they must find some support soon
To halt their imminent fall
One fine day though, and that will be soon
They'll come to see that that's no good to them
    at all.
They can shout out then all they want 'Stop now!'
Neither money nor cannon will answer their call!

8

# In the summer of 1905 the country was shaken by peasant uprisings and agricultural strikes.

### a. Country road.

*Pelagea Vlasova, who is approaching accompanied by two workers, is greeted by a shower of thrown stones. Her companions run off.*

VLASOVA, *with a large lump on her forehead, to the stone-throwers:* Why are you throwing stones at us?

LUSHIN: Because you're strike-breakers.

VLASOVA: Oh, I see, we're strike-breakers, are we? That's why we're in such a hurry! Where's the strike, then?

LUSHIN: On the Smirnov estate.

VLASOVA: And you're the strikers? I can tell that from this lump. Only I'm not a strike-breaker. I've come from Rostov and I want to speak to a labourer on the estate. His name's Yegor Lushin.

LUSHIN: I'm Lushin.

VLASOVA: Pelagea Vlasova.

LUSHIN: Are you the woman people round here call 'The Mother'?

VLASOVA: Yes. I've brought our papers for you. We didn't know you were on strike, but I can see you're carrying on a hard fight. *She hands the papers over to Lushin.*

LUSHIN: I'm sorry we gave you that lump. Our strike's not going well. Strike-breakers came with you from town and tomorrow we're expecting more. We've got nothing to eat, but for them the estate butcher's already slaughtering pigs and calves. There look. Can you see the estate kitchen chimney smoking for the strike-breakers?

VLASOVA: It's really a shame.

LUSHIN: The estate butcher's, the estate baker's and the estate dairy, of course, aren't on strike.

VLASOVA: Why not? Have you talked to them?

LUSHIN: There's no point. Why should they strike? They only cut us labourer's wages this time.

VLASOVA: Give me back the papers. *She divides the bundle of newspapers into two parts and gives him only half.*

LUSHIN: What about those? Why aren't you giving us all of them?

VLASOVA: These are going to the estate butcher's, the estate baker's and the estate dairy. There's workers there too, don't forget. We've got to talk to them. Where there's a worker, there's a way.

LUSHIN: Save yourself the trouble! *He goes.*

VLASOVA: That's how we carve each other up, worker against worker, and the exploiters laugh at us.


## b. Estate kitchen.

*Two strike-breakers sit eating and talk to the estate butcher.*

1ST STRIKEBREAKER, *chewing, to the other:* The man who lets his country down in its hour of danger is a bastard. And the worker who strikes is letting his country down.

BUTCHER, *chopping meat:* How d'you mean, his country?

2ND STRIKEBREAKER: They're Russians and this is Russia. And Russia belongs to the Russians.

BUTCHER: You don't say.

2ND STRIKEBREAKER: Dead right. If man can't feel that – this meat's not quite done – there's no explaining it to him. You can smash his head in, though.

BUTCHER: Right!

1ST STRIKEBREAKER: This table's the fatherland. This meat's the fatherland.

BUTCHER: Only it's not quite done.

2ND STRIKEBREAKER: This seat I'm sitting in's the fatherland. And you, look – *to the butcher* – you're a piece of the fatherland too.

BUTCHER: Only I'm not quite done either.

1ST STRIKEBREAKER: It's every man's duty to defend his fatherland.

BUTCHER: Yeh, if it *is* his!

2ND STRIKEBREAKER: That's just your low-minded materialism.

BUTCHER: Arsehole!

*The butcher's wife brings in Pelagea Vlasova, who is exaggerating the wound in her head.*

WIFE: You sit down here. I'll make you a cold compress and then you must have something to eat to help you get over your shock. *To the others.* They threw a stone at her.

1ST STRIKEBREAKER: Yeh, that's the woman. She came down on the train with us.

2ND STRIKEBREAKER: The strikers did that to her. We were worried sick for her.

WIFE: Is it getting any better?

*Vlasova nods.*

2ND STRIKEBREAKER: Thank God.

WIFE: They fight like animals, just for a little bit of work. Look at that lump! *She goes to fetch water.*

VLASOVA, *to the audience:* How much more sympathy a lump arouses from people expecting lumps than from people handing them out!

1ST STRIKEBREAKER, *points with his fork to Vlasova:* This Russian woman was pelted with stones by Russian workers. Are you a mother?

VLASOVA: Yes.

1ST STRIKEBREAKER: A Russian mother pelted with stones!

BUTCHER: Yeh, and Russian ones too! *To the audience:* And I'm supposed to serve this trash my best soup. *To Vlasova:* Why'd they throw those things at you, then?

VLASOVA, *cooling her lump with a damp cloth:* They saw me walking along together with the strikebreakers.

2ND STRIKEBREAKER: The bastards!

VLASOVA: How come they're bastards? I was only thinking to myself just now, perhaps they're not bastards at all.

WIFE: Why'd they throw stones at you, then?

VLASOVA: Because they thought I was a bastard.

WIFE: How could they think you were a bastard?

VLASOVA: Because they thought I was a strike-breaker.

BUTCHER, *smiles:* So you think it's all right to throw stones at strike-breakers?

VLASOVA: Yes, of course.

BUTCHER, *beaming, to his wife:* Give her something to eat! Give her something to eat this minute! Give her two helpings! *He steps up to Vlasova.* My name's Vasil Yefimovitch. *Calling to his wife.* And bring the staff in! They can learn something here.

*The staff appear in the doorway.*

BUTCHER: This woman had stones thrown at her by strikers. She's got a lump on her head. Look, there it is. So I ask her: 'Why've you got that lump? She says: 'Because they thought I was a strike-breaker.' I ask her: 'Should people throw stones at strike-breakers then?' And what does she say?

VLASOVA: Yes.

BUTCHER: My friends, when I heard that, I said: 'Give her something to eat. Give her two helpings!' *To Vlasova:* Why aren't you eating, then? Is it too hot for you? *To wife:* Do you have to serve the food up boiling hot? D'you want her to burn her mouth?

VLASOVA, *pushes the plate away:* No, Vasil Yefimovitch, the food isn't too hot.

BUTCHER: Why aren't you eating then?

VLASOVA: Because this was cooked for the strike-breakers.

BUTCHER: Who's it cooked for?

VLASOVA: The strike-breakers.

BUTCHER: I see! That's interesing. So I'm a bastard too? You see that? I'm a bastard. And why am I a bastard? Because I'm supporting the strike-breakers. *To Vlasova:* Is that right? *He sits down next to her.* Isn't striking wrong, though? You'd say it depends what people are striking for. *Vlasova nods.* You'd say people's wages were being cut. But why shouldn't their wages be cut? Look around. Everything you see here belongs to Mr Smirnov, who lives in Odessa. Why shouldn't he cut our wages? *As the strike-breakers agree with him heartily.* It's his money, isn't it? So you don't think he should let the wage be two roubles one day and two kopecks the next? So you don't think he should? What happened last year, then? Even my wages got cut then.

And what did I do – *To his wife* – on your advice? Nothing!
And what's going to happen in September? I'll get cut
again! And what am I making myself guilty of now? Of
treason against the people who are also getting cut and
who aren't putting up with it. So what am I? *To Vlasova:* So
you won't eat my food. That's all I've been waiting for: one
decent person to say to my face that she as a decent person
won't eat my food. Now the cup's full. It's been full a long
time in fact. It just needed one drop. – *He points to Vlasova* –
to make it overflow. Anger and discontent aren't enough.
A thing like this has got to have practical consequences. *To
the strike-breakers:* Tell your Mister Smirnov he'll have to
have his food sent out from Odessa. Best of all, he can
cook it for himself, the pig.

WIFE: Don't get so excited.

BUTCHER: It wasn't for nothing I used to cook in factory
canteens. I left because crap management didn't suit me.
*As his wife tries to calm him down.* I thought, I'll go to the
country, it's decent there. And what do I find? Another
crap-hole, where I'm supposed to stuff strike-breakers full.

WIFE: We can always move on again.

BUTCHER: Dead right, we're leaving. *Grandly.* Bring in the
pot of lentils. And you, fetch all the bacon. Whatever's
hanging about. What's it been cooked for, after all?

WIFE: You'll only make yourself miserable. You'll ruin
us yet.

BUTCHER, *to the strike-breakers:* Out of it, you saviours of the
fatherland! We're striking. The kitchen-staff is on strike.
Out! *He drives the strike-breakers out.* As a butcher I'm used
to being the one to laugh last, and not the pig. *With his arm
round his wife's shoulder, he steps up to Vlasova.* Now go out and
tell the men who threw stones at you their soup's waiting
for them.


IN PRAISE OF VLASOVA
*recited by the estate builder and his people*

This is our comrade Vlasova, a good fighter
Hard-working, cunning and reliable.

Reliable in struggle, cunning against our enemy and
hard-working
In her agitation. Her work is small
Carried out with a will and indispensable.
She's not alone, wherever she fights.
Others like her fight cunningly, reliably and with a will
In Twer, Glasgow, Lyons and Chicago
Shanghai and Calcutta
Vlasovas of all countries, good little moles
Unknown soldiers of the revolution
Indispensable.

9

## 1912. Pavel returns from exile in Siberia.

*Teacher Vesovchikov's flat.*
*Vlasova, Vasil Yefinovitch and a young worker carry a printing-press
into the teacher Vesovchikov's flat.*

VESOVCHIKOV: Pelagea Vlasova, you can't set up a printing-
press here in my home. You're abusing my sympathy for
the movement. You know that theoretically I share the
same ground as you, but this is going much too far.

VLASOVA: Do I understand you right, Nikolia Ivanovitch?
You're for our leaflets – I remind you that you drew up the
last one for the Workers Commune yourself – but you're
against their being printed?
*They set up the machine.*

VESOVCHIKOV: No. But printing them here, that's what
I'm against.

VLASOVA, *hurt:* We'll bear that in mind, Nikolai Ivanovitch.
*They work on.*

VESOVCHIKOV: And then what?

WORKER: Once Mrs Vlasova's got a thing in her head,
there's nothing you can do. We've already had considerable

difficulty with her in the past in that respect. No one'll notice anything anyway.

VLASOVA: The reason we've got to print more papers now is because they keep confiscating them from us.

*Vesovchikov goes into the next room and reads. They start printing. The machine makes a lot of noise. Vesovchikov rushes in.*

It's a bit loud, isn't it.

VESOVCHIKOV: The lamp's falling off the wall in my room! I'm afraid your printing illegal publications here is quite impossible, if it's going to make such a noise.

VLASOVA: Nikolai Ivanovitch, we noticed ourselves that the machine was a bit loud.

YEFIMOVITCH: If we had something to put underneath it, you wouldn't be able to hear a thing in the flats next door. Have you got something to put underneath it, Nikolai Ivanovitch?

VESOVCHIKOV: No, nothing at all.

VLASOVA: Not so loud! The lady next door showed me a piece of felt she brought to make coats for her children. I'll go and ask her for it. Don't do any more printing till I come back. *She goes next door.*

YEFIMOVITCH, *to Vesovchikov:* Nikolai Ivanovitch, we're sorry if she's upset you.

WORKER: In fact we brought her here so she'd have a rest from politics. We'd never have set up an illegal press here ourselves, would we, Vasil Yefimovitch? But she wouldn't have it any other way, you see.

VESOVCHIKOV: I'm very cross. For example, I also disapprove most strongly of your continuing to take money from her. Recently I came home and was forced to look on as she stood there with her old purse fishing out her few kopecks membership dues.

YEFIMOVITCH: Yes, but we don't get anything for nothing. The revolution is directed against poverty. But even then it costs money. The Mother's very strict about collecting dues. That's another half a loaf we've got to go without, she says, for the sake of the cause. Our firm's got to go places, she says when she's collecting them in.

*A knock. They hide the machine. Vesovchikov opens the door.*

PAVEL'S VOICE, *outside:* Does Pelagea Vlasova live here? My name's Pavel Vlasov.

VESOVCHIKOV: Her son!

PAVEL, *comes in:* Good day.

EVERYONE: Good day.

PAVEL: Where's my mother, then?

VESOVCHIKOV: Next door.

YEFIMOVITCH: She'll be back in a minute. Your mother told us you were ...

PAVEL: Away for a while!

YEFIMOVITCH, *laughs:* Yes.

*They hear Vlasova coming back.*

VESOVCHIKOV: Sit over here. Let's make it a real surprise for your mother.

*They make Pavel sit on a chair opposite the door and arrange themselves around him. Vlasova comes in.*

VLASOVA: Pavel! *She embraces him.* He gets thinner and thinner! Instead of fatter, he gets thinner! I didn't think they'd be able to hold you for long. How did you get away from them? How long can you stay here?

PAVEL: I've got to move on this evening.

VLASOVA: You can still take your coat off, though, can't you? *Pavel takes his coat off.*

VESOVCHIKOV: I heard your aim was to fight for freedom, but in the process you set up in your party the very worst kind of slavery. Some freedom! Nothing but orders and compulsion!

VLASOVA: Look here, Nikolai Ivanovitch, this is the way it is: we're not as much against those orders as you are. We've got a more urgent need for them. We're taking on more – and don't take this the wrong way – than you. It's the same with freedom as it is with your money, Nikolai Ivanovitch. Since I've only been giving you a little pocket-money, you're able to buy yourself a lot more. By spending less money for a while, you can then spend more money. You can't argue with that.

VESOVCHIKOV: I shall give up arguing with you. You're a terrible tyrant.

VLASOVA: Yes, well, we have to be, don't we.

YEFIMOVITCH: Did you get the felt? *To Pavel:* We've got to have the paper ready by eight o'clock.

PAVEL: Get printing then.

VLASOVA, *beaming:* Start printing right away, so we'll have a little more time later. What about this then: that Marfa Alexandrovna turned my request down flat in my face. Her reason: the felt was meant for coats for her children. I say: 'Marfa Alexandrovna, I saw your children coming out of school only recently. In coats.' 'Coats,' she says, 'those aren't coats, they're patched up rags. The other children at school laugh at them.' 'Marfa Alexandrovna,' I say, 'poor people have bad coats. Give me the felt, until tomorrow morning at least. I assure you it'll be of more use to your children to give it to me than a fancy coat would be.' She was so unreasonable though! She actually didn't give it to me! Not for two kopecks of good sense! *She takes a couple of pieces of felt from under her apron and lays them under the machine.*

VESOVCHIKOV: What's that, then?

VLASOVA: The felt, of course!
*They all laugh.*

YEFIMOVITCH: Why d'you keep complaining about this Marfa Alexandrovna woman so much, then?

VLASOVA: Because she forced me to steal the stuff. We've got to have it after all. And it's very good for her children that papers like this get printed. That's the honest truth!

YEFIMOVITCH: Pelagea Vlasova, in the name of the revolution we thank you for the felt!
*Laughter.*

VLASOVA: I'll take it back round tomorrow. *To Pavel, who has sat down:* D'you want some bread?

YEFIMOVITCH, *by the machine:* Who's going to take the finished pages out, if he does?
*Vlasova stands by the machine. Pavel gets himself some bread.*

VLASOVA: Look in the bin.

PAVEL: Don't worry about me. I even found a piece of bread in Siberia once.

VLASOVA: D'you hear that? He's accusing me. I don't look after him. At least I can slice that loaf for you.

VESOVCHIKOV: And who's going to take the finished pages

out here?

PAVEL, *cuts himself a piece of bread from the loaf while the others print:* The pages will be taken out by the mother of the revolutionary Pavel Vlasov, the revolutionary Pelagea Vlasova. Does she look after him? No chance! Does she make him a cup of tea? Does she run his bath for him? Does she slaughter a calf? No chance! Fleeing from Siberia to Finland amid the icy blasts of the North Wind, the salvoes of the gendarmes in his ears, he finds no refuge where he can lay his head down, except in an illegal printing-shop. And his mother, instead of stroking his hair, takes the finished pages out!

VLASOVA: If you want to help us, come here. Andrei'll make room for you.

*Pavel takes over the place opposite his mother at the printing machine. They recite:*

VLASOVA: Things weren't bad for you, were they?

PAVEL: Everything was fine, except for the typhus.

VLASOVA: You've always eaten properly at least?

PAVEL: Except for when I had nothing, yes.

VLASOVA: Look after yourself. Will you be away long?

PAVEL: If you work well here, no.

VLASOVA: Will you be working there too?

PAVEL: Definitely. And it's as important there as here.

*There is a knock. Sigorski comes in.*

SIGORSKI: Pavel, you've got to leave at once. Here's the ticket. Comrade Issay will be waiting for you at the station with the passport.

PAVEL: I thought it'd be a few hours at least. *He takes his coat.*

VLASOVA, *goes to get her coat:* I'll go down with you.

SIGORSKI: No, it'd be dangerous for Pavel. They know you, but they don't know him.

*She helps him back into his coat.*

PAVEL: Goodbye, Mother.

VLASOVA: Next time let's hope I can slice the bread for you.

PAVEL: Let's hope so. Goodbye, Comrades.

*Pavel and Sigorski go.*

VESOVCHIKOV: God will help him, Pelagea Vlasova.

VLASOVA: I don't know so much.
*She turns back to the printing-machine. They print on. Vlasova recites:*

### IN PRAISE OF THE THIRD CAUSE

Over and over you hear
How mothers have sons who forsake them, but then I
Held on to my son. How'd I keep my son? Through
The third cause.
For he and I were two, but the third
Common cause that we followed bound us so close
Together.
I have often myself heard
Sons speak with their parents.
How much better we got on when we talked
About the cause we shared, the third cause which bound
    us as one
Shared by so many, the great common cause that binds
    them.
How close to each other we were, standing close to our
Great cause! How good to each other we were
Close to our great cause!


10

## Attempting to cross the Finnish border, Pavel Vlasov is arrested and shot.

*Vesovchikov's flat.*
*Vlasova sits in the kitchen, a letter in her hand.*

### CHORUS
*sung by the Revolutionary Workers to Vlasova*

Comrade Vlasova, your son
Has been shot. But as
He made his way there, towards the wall of execution
He walked towards a wall made by his own fellow
    workers.

The very rifles that aimed at his heart and the bullets
   that followed
Had been made by his fellow workers. Only they had all
   departed
Or had all been driven, driven away, yet still for him
   were present
And with him in the work of their hands. Not even
Those who shot at him were different from him, nor
   would they always be unteachable either.
Granted, he still went out bound fast in irons, in irons
Forged by his comrades, and now used to shackle a
   comrade,
And though he understood, he could not see why.
And he saw how, from the roadway, the works packed
   together,
Chimney on chimney, and as it was morning now –
For they take them all out as a rule in the morning –
They were all bare, but he alone could see them filled
With that mighty army, that army which grew and grew
And grows on still.
But it was men just like him who were leading him out to
   the wall
And though he understood, he could not see why.


*Living-room. Three women come in, bringing a bible and a pot of food.*
THE LANDLADY, *in the door:* We'll forget all our differences
   with Mrs Vlasova, shall we, and sit down with her as
   Christians and offer her our sympathy.
*They come in.*
Dear Mrs Vlasova, you are not alone in these trying times.
The whole house feels for you.
*Two of the women are overcome with emotion and sit down. They
sob loudly.*
VLASOVA, *after a pause:* Have some tea. It'll refresh you.
*She brings them tea.*
Are you feeling easier now?
THE LANDLADY: You're so composed, Mrs Vlasova.
HER NEICE FROM THE COUNTRY: You're quite right, though.
   We're all in God's hands.

THE POOR WOMAN: And God knows what He's doing.
*Vlasova is silent.*
We thought we'd take it on ourselves to look after you a
bit. I expect you've not been feeding yourself properly
these past few days. Here's a pot of food. All you have to
do is warm it up. *She hands over the pot.*

VLASOVA: Thank you very much, Lydia Antonovna. It's very
kind of you to have thought of it. And it's very kind of you
all to come.

THE LANDLADY: Dear Vlasova, I've brought you a bible too,
in case you should want something to read. You may keep
it as long as you wish. *She gives Vlasova the bible.*

VLASOVA: Thank you for the kind thought, Vera Stepanovna.
It's a beautiful book. Would you be very offended,
though, if I gave it you back? When the teacher
Vesovchikov went on holday, he allowed me to use his
books. *She gives the bible back.*

THE LANDLADY: I just thought you probably wouldn't want
to be reading your political newspapers at this time.

THE NIECE: Do you really read them every day?

VLASOVA: Yes.

THE LANDLADY: Mrs Vlasova, my bible has often been a
great comfort to me.
*Silence.*

THE POOR WOMAN: Don't you have any photographs of him?

VLASOVA: No. I had some. But then we destroyed them all,
so the police wouldn't get hold of them.

THE POOR WOMAN: It's nice to have something for memory's
sake though.

NIECE: They say he was such a good-looking young man too!

VLASOVA: I remember now, I have got a photograph. It's a
wanted notice. He cut it out of a paper for me.
*The women look at the wanted notice.*

THE LANDLADY: Mrs Vlasova, it's down here in black and
white. Your son was a criminal. He had no faith, and you
yourself have never made any secret of it – I'd even say
you've taken every opportunity to let us know what you
think of our faith.

VLASOVA: That's right, Vera Stepanovna. Nothing.

THE LANDLADY: And even now you've not come to any other conclusion?

VLASOVA: No, Vera Stepanovna.

THE LANDLADY: So you're still of the opinion that man can do everything by reason alone?

THE POOR WOMAN: I told you I was sure Mrs Vlasova wouldn't have changed her mind, Vera Stepanovna.

THE LANDLADY: But I heard you weeping only the other night – through the wall, you know.

VLASOVA: I'm sorry.

THE LANDLADY: There's no need to be sorry. That wasn't the way I meant it, of course. But tell me, was that weeping rational?

VLASOVA: No.

THE LANDLADY: There, you see, that's how far reason gets you.

VLASOVA: My weeping wasn't rational. But when I stopped, my stopping was rational. What Pavel did was good.

THE LANDLADY: Why was he shot then?

THE POOR WOMAN: Everyone was against him, weren't they?

VLASOVA: Yes, but by being against him, they were against themselves.

THE LANDLADY: Mrs Vlasova, mankind needs God. Against Fate we are powerless.

VLASOVA: We say: man is his own fate.

NIECE: Dear Mrs Vlasova, we in the country . . .

THE LANDLADY, *points to her:* My niece – she's just on a visit here.

NIECE: We in the country see these things differently. You folk here don't have seed lying in the fields, just the loaf in the cupboard. You only see the milk, you don't see the cow. You don't have a sleepless night when there's storms in the sky. And what's hail to you?

VLASOVA: I see, and in situations like that you pray to God?

NIECE: Yes.

VLASOVA: And in spring you go on processions and pilgrimages.

NIECE: Right.

VLASOVA: And then the storms come and then it hails. And the cow gets sick anyway. Haven't the farmers in your region got some kind of insurance against a bad harvest or cattle diseases yet? Insurance can help when praying hasn't helped at all. So you don't need to pray to God any more when there are storms in the sky, but you do have to be insured. It'll help you, you see. If he's that unimportant, that's bad for God. But then the hope is that once this God has disappeared from your fields, he might disappear from your heads too. In my youth everyone still believed firmly he sat somewhere in heaven, looking like an old man. Then came aeroplanes, and it said in the newspapers that even in the heavens everything was now measurable. No one talked any more about a God sitting in heaven. Instead of that you then often heard the view he was like a sort of gas, nowhere and yet everywhere. But when you then read about all the different things gases were composed of, God wasn't amongst them, so he couldn't even remain a gas because people knew them all. So he just got thinner and thinner till he vanished into thin air, so to speak. From time to time you read these days that all he is really is a spiritual symbol, but that's very suspect, isn't it.

THE POOR WOMAN: So you think because people don't notice him any more, he's no longer so important.

THE LANDLADY: Mrs Vlasova, don't forget why God took your Pavel away from you.

VLASOVA: It was the Tsar who took him from me, and I haven't forgotten why either.

THE LANDLADY: God took him, not the Tsar.

VLASOVA, *to the poor woman:* Lydia Antonovna, I hear that God, who took my Pavel from me, is currently planning to take your room away from you next Saturday. Is that true? God gave you notice?

THE LANDLADY: I gave her notice because she's failed to pay her rent three times now.

VLASOVA: So when God ordained you shouldn't get your three weeks' rent, Vera Stepanovna, what did you do? *Vera Stepanovna is silent.*

You threw Lydia Antonovna out on the street. And you, Lydia Antonovna, what did you do when God ordained you should be thrown out on the street? I'd advise you to ask the landlady to lend you her bible. Then when you're sitting out in the street in the cold, you can leaf through it and read from it to your children that man must fear God.

THE LANDLADY: If you'd read to your son from the bible more, he'd still be living today.

VLASOVA: But very badly, he'd be living very badly. Why are you people so afraid of death? My son wasn't all that afraid of death. *She recites:*

> He was very alarmed though, at the misery
> In our cities, apparent to every eye.
> It's the hunger appals us, the degradation
> Of those who feel it and those who cause it.
> Don't be afraid of death so much as an inadequate life.

*Pause.*

What good does it do you to fear God, Lydia Antonovna? You'd be better off fearing Vera Stepanovna. Just as it wasn't the unfathomable law of God that snatched my son Pavel away, but the fathomable law of the Tsar, so Vera Stepanovna has thrown you out in the street because a man who lives in a villa and has nothing godlike about him at all has chased you away from your place of work. Why talk about God? That there are many mansions in 'our Father's house' they tell you; but there are too few flats in Rostov and why, that they don't tell you.

THE POOR WOMAN: Give me the bible a moment, Vera Stepanovna. In the bible it says quite clearly: Love Thy Neighbour. So why are you throwing me out on the street? Give me the bible, I'll find the page for you. It stands to reason they shot Pavel Vlasov. He was for the workers and a worker himself. *She grabs the bible.* Give me the book, I'll show you the page . . .

THE LANDLADY: You won't get the bible from me for that purpose, not for that purpose.

THE POOR WOMAN: For what purpose, then? For no good one, I bet!

THE LANDLADY: That is the Word of God!

THE POOR WOMAN: That's just the point. Your God is of no use to me, if I can't see any sign of him! *She tries to tear the bible away from the landlady.*

THE LANDLADY: Now I'll find a passage for you, namely the one about laying hands on other people's property.

THE POOR WOMAN: I want the book.

THE LANDLADY, *holding on hard to the bible:* It's my property.

THE POOR WOMAN: Yes, like the whole house, you mean? *The bible is torn to shreds.*

THE NIECE, *picks up the pieces of the bible:* Now it's torn.

VLASOVA, *who has put the pot of food in a safe place:* Better a torn-up bible than spilt food.

THE POOR WOMAN: If I didn't believe there was a God in heaven who requires everything, good and bad, I'd join Pelagea Vlasova's party today. *She goes.*

THE LANDLADY: Pelagea Vlasova, you see what you've done to Lydia Antonovna. It was because he spoke the way you are now your son was shot, and you deserve no better. Come.

*She goes with her relative.*

VLASOVA: You unhappy people! *She sits down, exhausted.* Pavel!


11

The death of her son and the years of the Stolypin reaction have brought Vlasova's revolutionary activity to a standstill. On her sickbed she receives news of the outbreak of World War.

*Vesovchikov's flat.*

VESOVCHIKOV, *to the Doctor:* She hasn't been well since her son died. I don't mean her housework, but a quite particular job she always used to do, she doesn't do any more.

THE DOCTOR: She's completely exhausted and on no account should she get up. She's an old woman after all. *He goes. Vesovchikov goes into the kitchen and sits by Vlasova's bed.*

VLASOVA: What's in the papers?

VESOVCHIKOV: The war's here.

VLASOVA: War? What are we doing?

VESOVCHIKOV: The Tsar's declared a state of siege. Of all the socialist parties only the Bolsheviks have spoken out against the war. Our five members in the Duma have already been arrested and packed off to Siberia for high treason.

VLASOVA: That's bad. – If the Tsar's mobilising, then we workers've got to mobilise too. – I've got to get up.

VESOVCHIKOV: On no account may you get up. You're ill. What can we do against the Tsar and all the potentates of Europe? I'll go down and buy the late extra edition. Now they'll annihilate the Party totally. *He goes.*

CHORUS
*sung by the Revolutionary Workers to Vlasova*

Get up, for the Party is in danger!
You are ill, but the Party's dying
You are weak, but you must help us!
Get up, for the Party is in danger!

You who have doubted in us
Doubt us no longer
Our time has come now.
You who have sometimes cursed the Party
Curse no more the Party which
They are destroying.

Get up, for the Party is in danger!
Up quickly!
You are ill, but we still need your help.
Don't die, you've got to help us.
Don't stay away, we're going into battle.
Get up, for the Party is in danger! Get up!

*During this chorus Pelagea Vlasova has got up with some difficulty, dressed herself, picked up her bag and unsteadily, but walking faster and faster, has crossed the room and gone out of the door.*

12

## Against the stream.

*Street corner.*
*Several workers carry Vlasova, who has been bloodily beaten, into a corner between two houses.*

1ST WORKER: What's wrong with her?

2ND WORKER: We saw this old woman in the middle of the crowd cheering the troops off to war. Suddenly she shouted out: 'Down with the war, long live the revolution!' Then the police came up and beat her over the head with their truncheons. We dragged her here between these houses quick. Wash her face off for her then!

THE WORKERS: Come on, old girl, you'd better run now, or they'll catch you again!

VLASOVA: Where's my bag?

THE WORKERS: It's here.

VLASOVA: Wait! I've got some pamphlets here in my bag. There's something in them about the position of us workers in the war: the truth.

THE WORKERS: Go home, old girl, leave the truth in your handbag. It's dangerous. If they're found on us, we'll only get locked up. Haven't you had enough yourself?

VLASOVA: No, no, you ought to know about it! It's not knowing that keeps us under.

THE WORKERS: And the police.

VLASOVA: They don't know either.

THE WORKERS: But our leaders tell us we've got to help beat the Germans first and defend our country.

VLASOVA, *recites:*

What kind of leaders are those?
Side by side you fight with your class enemy
Worker against worker.
Your organisations, painfully built up
By denying yourself pennies, will be smashed to pieces.
Everything you've learned is forgotten
And the solidarity of all workers in all countries is
  forgotten.

THE WORKERS: None of that applies any more. We went on
strike against the war in several factories. Our strikes were
smashed. The revolution won't come now. Go home, old
girl, see the world the way it is. What you want will never
be. Never, never!

VLASOVA: Well, at least read what we've got to say about the
situation, won't you? *She offers them the pamphlets.* You don't
even want to read them?

THE WORKERS: We can see you mean well, but we don't
want to take your pamphlets any more. We don't want to
get ourselves into trouble any more.

VLASOVA: Ye-es, but remember: the whole world – *Shouting
so that the terrified workers have to hold her mouth shut* – lives in a
monstrous darkness, and until now you alone were the
only ones who could still be reached by reason. Think
before you give up!


13


## 1916. Tirelessly, the Bolsheviks fight against the imperialist war.


*Patriotic copper collection centre.*
*Seven women carrying copper utensils stand lined up in front of a door*
*decorated with a flag and the inscription: 'Patriotic copper collection*
*centre.' Among them is Vlasova with a small beaker. An official in*
*civilian clothes comes and opens the door.*

OFFICIAL: It has just been announced that our brave troops, with exemplary and heroic courage and for the fourth time, have seized the fortress of Przemysl from the enemy. 100,000 dead, 2,000 prisoners. Army High Command have decreed that throughout Russia all schools be closed and bells rung. Long live our Holy Russia! Hurrah! Hurrah! Hurrah! The copper delivery counter will be open in five minutes. *He goes inside.*

VLASOVA: Hooray!

A WOMAN: That's really nice, our war going so well.

VLASOVA: I've only got this tiny little beaker, though. It'll only make five six cartridges at the most. How many of those are going to hit anybody? Two out of six perhaps, and out of those two, one at most will be fatal. That kettle of yours must be twenty cartridges at least, and that jug that lady up front's got's a grenade even. A grenade can pick off five to six men in one go, just like that. *Counts the utensils.* One, two, three, four, five, six, seven – hang on, that's lady's got two, hasn't she, so that's eight. Eight. Well, that's another small offensive mounted, isn't it. *She laughs gently.* I nearly didn't bring my little beaker here, you know. I meet these two soldiers on my way here –someone ought to report them really – they say to me: 'That's right, you old bag, give your copper in so the war'll never stop.' What about that, eh? Isn't that terrible? 'You ought to be shot,' I said. 'On the spot. If I was giving in my little beaker only so they could stop your dirty mouths with it, it wouldn't have been given in vain. It'd just about go to two cartridges. Because why am I, Pelagea Vlasova, giving in my copper beaker? I'm giving it in so the war won't end!

WOMAN: What are you saying? The war won't end if we hand in our copper? That's exactly why we are handing it in, so it will end.

VLASOVA: No, we're handing it in, so it won't end.

A LADY DRESSED IN BLACK: No, if they've got copper and can make grenades out there, they'll win a lot quicker, won't they? Then the war'll stop!

VLASOVA: Ah no, if they've got grenades it stands to reason

it won't stop, because then they can just keep going. As long as they've got ammunition they'll carry on. They're giving it in on the other side too, you know.

WOMAN, *points to a sign:* 'Give in your copper and shorten the war.' Can't you read?

VLASOVA: Give in your copper and lengthen the war! It's for spies, that stuff!

LADY IN BLACK: But why do you want the war to go on longer?

VLASOVA: 'Cos my son'll be a sergeant in six months' time. Another two offensives and my son'll make sergeant. And then he'll get twice the pay, won't he. And besides, we've got to get Armenia yet, haven't we, and Galicia, and we really need Turkey.

LADY IN BLACK: What do we need?

VLASOVA: Turkey, And the money we borrowed from France, that's got to be paid back too, hasn't it. In that sense it's a war of liberation.

WOMAN: Naturally. Of course it's a war of liberation. But that's no reason why it should last into eternity, is it?

VLASOVA: Yes, of course. Another six months at least.

LADY IN BLACK: And you think it'll last that long if they get more copper?

VLASOVA: Yes, of course. The soldiers aren't fighting for nothing after all. You've got someone out there too, have you?

LADY IN BLACK: Yes, my son.

VLASOVA: You see? You've got your son out there already, and now you're giving your copper too. That way it'll go on another six months for sure.

LADY IN BLACK: Now I don't know where I am at all. One minute the word is the war'll get shorter, the next it'll get longer. Which am I supposed to believe? I've lost my husband already, and now my son's at Przemysl. I'm going home. *She goes.*

*The bells start ringing.*

WOMAN: Victory bells!

VLASOVA: Yes, we're winning! We give our little beakers away, our kettles and our copper jugs, but we're winning!

We've got nothing left to eat, but we're winning! You're either for the Tsar and his victory or you're against him. We're winning, but we've also got to win! Or there'll be a revolution. That's certain. And then what'll happen to our beloved Tsar? We've got to stand by him in times like these. Look at the Germans. They're already eating the leaves off the trees for their Kaiser!

WOMAN: What are you talking about exactly? Only a minute ago a woman here took her kettle and ran away, and all because of you.

A WOMAN WORKER: You shouldn't have gone and told her that, you up the front there, about wanting the war to go on longer. No one else wants that, do they?

VLASOVA: What? What about the Tsar? And the generals? D'you think they're afraid of war with the Germans? What they say is: Keep on at the enemy! Victory or death! And that's right. Can't you hear the bells? You only hear them at victories and funerals. Why are you against the war anyway? Who are you in any case? We here are a cut above the rest, if I'm not mistaken. You're a working woman, aren't you? Are you a working woman or not? Go on, admit it! You chuck yourself in here with the rest of us! Don't forget there's still a difference between people like you and us!

A GIRL IN SERVICE: You shouldn't say that to her. She's giving up her things for the fatherland too.

VLASOVA, *to the working woman:* Rubbish. You can't be standing there whole-heartedly, can you. What use is the war to you? It's pure hypocrisy, you standing there isn't it. We can get along quite well without you and your kind. This is our war! No one objects if you workers want to join in, but that doesn't mean you've been with us that long. You go back to you factory and see you get a better wage and don't come pushing in here where you don't belong. *To the girl in service:* You can take her old lumber from her, if she absolutely has to hand it in.

*The working woman goes away, angry.*

THIRD WOMAN: Who is that anyway, shooting her mouth off down there?

FOURTH WOMAN: I've been listening to her drive people away for the last half-hour now!

SECOND WOMAN: D'you what she is? She's a Bolshevik!

WOMEN: What? D'you think she is? – She's a Bolshevik! And a very clever one at that! – Don't get involved with her, take no notice of her. – Beware of Bolshevism, it has a thousand faces! – As soon as a policeman comes along, she'll be led off!

VLASOVA, *leaves the queue:* Yes, I'm a Bolshevik! But you're murderesses, standing there! No animal would give up its young the way you have yours: without sense and understanding, for a bad cause. You deserve to have the wombs torn out of you, they should dry up and you become sterile where you stand. Your sons don't need to come back. To mothers like you? Shooting for a bad cause, they should be shot for a bad cause. But you are the murderesses.

FIRST WOMAN, *turns round:* I'll show you what you deserve, you Bolshevik!

OFFICIAL: The copper delivery counter is open.

*The woman advances on Vlasova with her jug in her hand and hits her in the face. Another turns round too and spits in front of her. Then the three women go in.*

GIRL IN SERVICE: Don't take it to heart. Tell me what I'm to do, though. I know you Bolsheviks are against the war, but I'm in service. I can't go back to my master and mistress with these copper jugs, can I. I don't want to hand them in, but if I don't, I shan't have been of use to anybody and I'll be dismissed. So what should I do?

VLASOVA: You can't do anything on your own. Hand the copper kettles in in your master's name. In the name of your master people like you will shoot with it. But against that, people like you will decide at whom! Come this evening to – *She whispers the address in her ear.* A worker from the Putilov plant will be speaking there, and we can explain to you what you should do. Only don't tell anyone the address who shouldn't know it.

14

1917. Amid the ranks of striking workers and mutinying soldiers marches Pelagea Vlasova, 'The Mother'.

*Street.*

IVAN: As we crossed the Lubin Prospekt we were already many thousand. Something like fifty factories were on strike, and the strikers joined our ranks to demonstrate against the war and Tsarist domination.

VESOVCHIKOV: In the winter of 1916–7, 250,000 men struck in the factories.

GIRL IN SERVICE: We carried banners with the inscription 'Down with the War! Long live the Revolution!' and red flags. A sixty-year-old woman carries our flag. We said to her: 'The flag isn't too heavy for you, is it? Give us the flag.' She, however, said:

VLASOVA: No. I'll give you it when I'm tired, then you can carry it. For I, Pelagea Vlasova, a worker's widow and a worker's mother, still have a lot of things to do. When I saw with sorrow many years ago how my son no longer ate his fill, at first all I did was whine. So nothing changed. Then I helped him in his fight for the kopeck. In those days we used to take part in small strikes for better wages. Now we're taking part in a huge strike in the ammunition factories and fighting for power in the state.

GIRL IN SERVICE: A lot of people say that what we want will never happen. We ought to be satisfied with what we have. The power of the ruling class is secure. We would always be beaten down, again and again. Even a lot of workers say: 'It'll never happen.'

VLASOVA, *recites:*

While you're alive, don't say never!
Security isn't certain
And things won't stay as they are.
When the ruling class has finished speaking
Those they ruled will have their answer.
Who dares to answer never?
On whom is the blame if their oppression stays? On us!
On whom does it fall to destroy it? On us!
So if you are beaten down, you just rise again!
If you think you've lost, fight on!
Once you have seen where you stand, there is nothing
    can hold you back again.
For those defeated today will be the victors tomorrow
And from 'never' comes our 'today'.

Further titles in the
World Dramatists series
of paperback play collections
are described on the following pages

# Jean Anouilh

## Five Plays

Antigone, Becket, The Lark, Leocadia,
The Waltz of the Toreadors

INTRODUCTION BY Ned Chaillet

# John Arden

## Plays : One

Serjeant Musgrave's Dance,
The Workhouse Donkey,
Armstrong's Last Goodnight

INTRODUCTION BY John Arden

# Brendan Behan

## The Complete Plays

The Quare Fellow, The Hostage,
Richard's Cork Leg, Moving Out,
A Garden Party, The Big House

INTRODUCTION BY Alan Simpson

# Edward Bond

INTRODUCTIONS BY Edward Bond

## Plays : One

Saved, Early Morning, The Pope's Wedding

## Plays : Two

Lear, The Sea, Narrow Road to the Deep North,
Black Mass, Passion

# Georg Büchner

## The Complete Plays

Danton's Death, Leonce and Lena, Woyzeck
with The Hessian Courier, Lenz,
On Cranial Nerves and Selected Letters

INTRODUCTION BY Michael Patterson

# Caryl Churchill

## Plays : One

Owners, Traps, Vinegar Tom,
Light Shining in Buckinghamshire, Cloud Nine

INTRODUCTION BY Caryl Churchill

# Noël Coward

## Plays : One

Hay Fever, The Vortex, Fallen Angels,
Easy Virtue

INTRODUCTION BY Mander and Mitchenson

## Plays : Two

Privates Lives, Bitter-Sweet, The Marquise,
Post-Mortem

INTRODUCTION BY Sheridan Morley

## Plays : Three

Design for Living, Cavalcade, Conversation Piece,
To-night at 8.30 (Hands Across the Sea,
Still Life, Fumed Oak)

INTRODUCTION BY Sheridan Morley

## Plays : Four

Blithe Spirit, Present Laughter,
This Happy Breed,
To-night at 8.30 (Ways and Means,
The Astonished Heart, 'Red Peppers')

INTRODUCTION BY Mander and Mitchenson

## Plays : Five

Relative Values, Look After Lulu!,
Waiting in the Wings, Suite in Three Keys

INTRODUCTION BY Mander and Mitchenson

# David Edgar

## Plays : One

Destiny, Mary Barnes,
The Jail Diary of Albie Sachs, Saigon Rose,
O Fair Jerusalem

INTRODUCTION BY David Edgar

# Michael Frayn

## Plays : One

Alphabetical Order, Donkeys' Years, Clouds,
Make and Break, Noises Off

INTRODUCTION BY Michael Frayn

# John Galsworthy

## Five Plays

Strife, Justice, The Eldest Son, The Skin Game,
Loyalties

INTRODUCTION BY Benedict Nightingale

# Simon Gray

## Plays : One

Butley, Otherwise Engaged, The Rear Column,
Quartermaine's Terms, The Common Pursuit

INTRODUCTION BY Simon Gray

# Henrik Ibsen

TRANSLATED AND INTRODUCED BY Michael Meyer

## Plays : One

Ghosts, The Wild Duck, The Master Builder

## Plays : Two

A Doll's House, An Enemy of the People,
Hedda Gabler

## Plays : Three

Rosmersholm, The Lady from the Sea,
Little Eyolf

## Plays : Four

The Pillars of Society, John Gabriel Borkman,
When We Dead Awaken

## Plays : Five

Brand, Emperor and Galilean

# Molière

## Five Plays

The School for Wives, Tartuffe,
The Misanthrope, The Miser,
The Hypochondriac

TRANSLATED BY Alan Drury and Richard Wilbur
INTRODUCTION BY Donald Roy

# Peter Nichols

## Plays : One

Forget-me-not Lane, Hearts and Flowers,
Neither Up Nor Down, Chez Nous,
The Common, Privates on Parade

INTRODUCTION BY Peter Nichols

# Clifford Odets

## Six Plays

Waiting for Lefty, Awake and Sing!,
Till the Day I Die, Paradise Lost, Golden Boy,
Rocket to the Moon

INTRODUCTION BY Harold Clurman

# Joe Orton

## The Complete Plays

Entertaining Mr Sloane, Loot,
What the Butler Saw, The Ruffian on the Stair,
The Erpingham Camp, Funeral Games,
The Good and Faithful Servant

INTRODUCTION BY John Lahr

# Arthur Wing Pinero

## Three Plays

The Magistrate, The Second Mrs Tanqueray,
Trelawny of the 'Wells'

INTRODUCTION BY Stephen Wyatt

# Harold Pinter

INTRODUCTIONS BY Harold Pinter

## Plays : One

The Birthday Party, The Room,
The Dumb Waiter, A Slight Ache,
The Hothouse, A Night Out

## Plays : Two

The Caretaker, The Dwarfs, The Collection,
The Lover, Night School, Trouble in the Works,
The Black and White, Request Stop, Last to Go,
Special Offer

## Plays : Three

The Homecoming, Tea Party, The Basement,
Landscape, Silence, That's Your Trouble,
That's All, Applicant, Interview,
Dialogue for Three, Night

## Plays : Four

Old Times, No Man's Land, Betrayal,
Monologue, Family Voices

# Luigi Pirandello
## Three Plays

The Rules of the Game,
Six Characters in Search of an Author, Henry IV

TRANSLATED BY Robert Rietty and Noel Creegan,
John Linstrum, Julian Mitchell
INTRODUCTION BY John Linstrum

# Terence Rattigan

INTRODUCTIONS BY Anthony Curtis

## Plays : One

French Without Tears, The Winslow Boy,
The Browning Version, Harlequinade

## Plays : Two

The Deep Blue Sea, Separate Tables,
In Praise of Love, Before Dawn

# Sophocles
## The Theban Plays

Oedipus the King, Oedipus at Colonus, Antigone

TRANSLATED AND INTRODUCED BY Don Taylor

# August Strindberg

TRANSLATED AND INTRODUCED BY Michael Meyer

## Plays : One

The Father, Miss Julie and The Ghost Sonata

## Plays : Two

A Dream Play, The Dance of Death,
The Stronger

# J. M. Synge

## The Complete Plays

The Playboy of the Western World,
The Tinker's Wedding,
In the Shadow of the Glen, Riders to the Sea,
The Well of the Saints, Deirdre of the Sorrows

INTRODUCTION BY T. R. Henn

# Oscar Wilde

## Three Plays

The Importance of Being Earnest,
Lady Windermere's Fan, An Ideal Husband

INTRODUCTION BY H. Montgomery Hyde